Praise for Robert Isaak's
The Globalization Gap

"In this day and age where Globalization is all the rage and attracts adulation and scorn in roughly equal measures, Isaak's book is a welcome "must-read." It casts light on the false promises of development and on the underlying ideology that surrounds the issue: globalization is far from being a positive-sum game. It embodies geopolitical tensions, financial volatility, spillover effects of economic crises, regulatory challenge, and spreading poverty."

—Michel Henry Bouchet
General Manager DEFI/Developing Finance-Paris Head/
Global Finance Chair-Ceram School of Management-Sophia Antipolis

"An impassioned report on the dangerous side of globalization, the book is a much needed counter to the widespread propensity of economists to spring automatically to its defense. Recognizing that globalization cannot be wished away, the author turns to the proper question: how can we ensure that its potential contribution to welfare is not lost?"

—William Baumol
co-author of Downsizing in America: Reality, Causes and Consequences

"Robert Isaak is unique among critics of Globalization in that he accepts it as inevitable but goes determinedly to propose innovations that can make it work better economically and socially for the rich and the poor."

—Seymour Topping
San Paolo Professor Emeritus of International Journalism
Columbia University
Former Managing Editor, The New York Times

"This book maps out with wit and insight the elements creating the growing gap that corporate globalization entails. It dissects the actors of the divide and offers a worthy alternative."

—Virginia Sánchez Navarro,
founder of the NGO Seeds for Self Reliance.

"Too many books on Globalization? Not, if you want to know everything about one crucial consequence of Globalization. Read this book: you come away enlightened,convinced by cogent arguments, ready to join the battle."

"Robert Isaak's new book presents fresh ideas on globalization that will enrich a polarized debate between the pessimists and the hyper-optimists. His work brings back Ortega y Gasset's classic ideas of the late 1930's when the "masses" brought down globalization and with it the worst recession and the bloodiest war. I am sure that Isaak's book will guide the readers to look forward after learning from past ideas and experiences."

"An extremely powerful and convincing analysis of widening gaps between the rich and the poor emanating from globalization and a lucid and informative presentation of critical issues to make globalization work for all."

THE GLOBALIZATION GAP

FT Prentice Hall

FINANCIAL TIMES

In an increasingly competitive world, it is quality
of thinking that gives an edge—an idea that opens new
doors, a technique that solves a problem, or an insight
that simply helps make sense of it all.

We work with leading authors in the various arenas
of business and finance to bring cutting-edge thinking
and best-learning practices to a global market.

It is our goal to create world-class print publications
and electronic products that give readers
knowledge and understanding that can then be
applied, whether studying or at work.

To find out more about our business
products, you can visit us at www.ft-ph.com.

Pearson
Education

THE
GLOBALIZATION GAP

How the Rich Get Richer
and the Poor
Get Left *Further* Behind

Robert A. Isaak

FT Prentice Hall
FINANCIAL TIMES

An Imprint of PEARSON EDUCATION
Upper Saddle River, NJ • New York • London • San Francisco • Toronto • Sydney
Tokyo • Singapore • Hong Kong • Cape Town • Madrid
Paris • Milan • Munich • Amsterdam

www.ft-ph.com

Library of Congress Cataloging-in-Publication Number: 2004046505

Editorial/production supervision: *Kerry Reardon*
Cover design director: *Jerry Votta*
Art director: *Gail Cocker-Bogusz*
Manufacturing buyer: *Dan Uhrig*
V.P., Editor-in-chief: *Tim Moore*
Editorial assistant: *Richard Winkler*
Marketing director: *John Pierce*
Marketing manager: *Martin Litkowski*
Development editor: *Russ Hall*
Full-service production managers: *Anne R. Garcia and Sarah Kearns*

© 2005 Robert A. Isaak
Published by Pearson Education, Inc.
Publishing as Financial Times Prentice Hall
Upper Saddle River, NJ 07458

Financial Times Prentice Hall offers excellent discounts on this book when ordered in quantity for bulk purchases or special sales. For more information, please contact: U.S. Corporate and Government Sales, 1-800-382-3419, corpsales@pearsontechgroup.com. For sales outside of the U.S., please contact: International Sales, 1-317-581-3793, international@pearsontechgroup.com

Printed in the United States of America

First printing

ISBN 0-13-142896-9

Pearson Education LTD.
Pearson Education Australia PTY, Limited
Pearson Education South Asia, Pte. Ltd.
Pearson Education Asia Ltd.
Pearson Education Canada, Ltd.
Pearson Educación de Mexico, S.A. de C.V.
Pearson Education–Japan
Pearson Malaysia S.D.N. B.H.D.

FINANCIAL TIMES PRENTICE HALL BOOKS

For more information, please go to www.ft-ph.com

Business and Society

Douglas K. Smith
On Value and Values: Thinking Differently About We in an Age of Me

Current Events

Alan Elsner
Gates of Injustice: The Crisis in America's Prisons

John R. Talbott
Where America Went Wrong: And How to Regain Her Democratic Ideals

Economics

David Dranove
What's Your Life Worth? Health Care Rationing...Who Lives? Who Dies? Who Decides?

Entrepreneurship

Dr. Candida Brush, Dr. Nancy M. Carter, Dr. Elizabeth Gatewood, Dr. Patricia G. Greene, and Dr. Myra M. Hart
Clearing the Hurdles: Women Building High Growth Businesses

Oren Fuerst and Uri Geiger
From Concept to Wall Street: A Complete Guide to Entrepreneurship and Venture Capital

David Gladstone and Laura Gladstone
Venture Capital Handbook: An Entrepreneur's Guide to Raising Venture Capital, Revised and Updated

Thomas K. McKnight
Will It Fly? How to Know if Your New Business Idea Has Wings... Before You Take the Leap

Stephen Spinelli, Jr., Robert M. Rosenberg, and Sue Birley
Franchising: Pathway to Wealth Creation

Executive Skills

Cyndi Maxey and Jill Bremer
It's Your Move: Dealing Yourself the Best Cards in Life and Work

John Putzier
Weirdos in the Workplace

Finance

Aswath Damodaran
The Dark Side of Valuation: Valuing Old Tech, New Tech, and New Economy Companies

Kenneth R. Ferris and Barbara S. Pécherot Petitt
Valuation: Avoiding the Winner's Curse

For the Pace Univerity community,
which has sustained me, and its motto of Opportunitas.

Contents

About the Author

Robert A. Isaak is the Henry George Professor of International Management at Pace University, New York, where he teaches international management, comparative management, and creativity and entrepreneurship across cultures. The author of nine books, including *Green Logic*, *Managing World Economic Change*, and *Modern Inflation* (with Wilhelm Hankel), Dr. Isaak received his BA at Stanford University and his PhD at New York University. In addition to consulting for firms such as Siemens, Technicon, Prudential Intercultural, and Global Intercultural, he has taught at the University of Heidelberg, Groupe École Superieure de Commerce de Grenoble, CERAM European Graduate School of Management in Sophia Antipolis, Franklin College in Lugano, the Johns Hopkins School of Advanced International Studies in Bologna, and New York University.

Also by Robert A. Isaak

- *Managing World Economic Change*

- *Green Logic: Ecopreneurship, Theory and Ethics*

- *American Political Thinking*

- *Modern Inflation* (with Wilhelm Hankel)

- *European Politics*

- *The Real American Politics* (with Ralph Hummel)

- *Individuals and World Politics*

- *American Democracy and World Power*

- *Politics for Human Beings* (with Ralph Hummel)

Preface

The rich have always lived differently than the poor. What is new is that globalization speeds up the economy, magnifying the chasm between them. Both at home and abroad, the extremes of wealth and deprivation have become so great that the stability of the global system is threatened. Indeed, the very existence of individual freedom and dignity promised by the Western democratic tradition is at risk. Globalization has not only boosted the technological capacity to increase productivity, development, and progress but has accelerated the spread of poverty, disease, and the disintegration of traditional cultures. Those at the top of the global heap have great buffers of wealth to help them cope with the radical transformations, but the poor do not.

There is a general failure to respond to the relentless downward spiral of poverty for millions of people. Rich individuals and corporate and government "drivers" of change are in part responsible for the excessive poverty that results from reckless efforts to push for rapid economic growth and competition at all costs.

Socioeconomic inequality on a global scale became the focus of my attention due to my research on the factors behind the emergence of "economic miracles" in some nations; on the prerequisites for "ecopreneurship," or sustainable job creation; and on attempts to mimic Silicon Valley in other cultures. My interest in the puzzle of uneven development intensified with the extreme contradictions I experienced on a trip to India, where layers of culturally intricate poverty are woven beside small islands of luxury and modernity.

If what is happening is not totally random, how have the rich helped to fashion a world order that maximizes their advantages, creating greater social and economic distance from the poor? The wealth generated by globalization is supposed to spill over and trickle down to where it is needed. But so far, things are not working out that way, apart from newly industrialized countries in Southeast Asia and perhaps, as the big exceptions, parts of China and India—exceptions exactly *because* they *are* big. (In a free market world, the size of the market is what counts.)

Even in industrialized countries, the differences between rich and poor are growing without restraint. In this group, the United States is the most important country, because what happens in this superpower has, by necessity, a huge impact on other nations. Therefore, this book also examines the American situation, where there has been a disconcerting downward spiral hidden by the distraction of the boom of the 1990s and by the shiny residual pockets of growth and glamour which are applified by the media. In the post-boom era, poverty has been growing in the United States. Median income has been falling. Pensions are threatened. Social Security is underfunded. Health care costs are shooting up. Manufacturing jobs have fled the country. Unemployment and underemployment are widespread. The latest economic fashion is "jobless recovery" as the salaries of the corporate elite continue to skyrocket. The outsourcing of jobs has gone from a trickle to a flood. Those without up-to-date skills and training are retired early, often without benefits. The same trends are unfolding in different variations throughout Europe and Japan.

The model of capitalist democracy has been thrown into question because of growing inequalities between the well-off and the disadvantaged. The promise of the Western tradition is *opportunity* resulting from economic growth. But domination of globalization by Anglo-Saxon ideas has not delivered the goods in many areas of the world. Partly as a result of this disappointment, the legitimacy of the institutions governed by these ideas is melting down. Annual meetings of the International Monetary Fund, the World Bank, the World Trade Organization, and multinational corporations confront massive demonstrations, as well as critical exposés by the media.

This book is about the failure to live up to the promise of opportunity as the rich get richer while poverty proliferates at home and in the least developed nations. It ends by attempting to sketch a blueprint for sharing opportunity, a tentative plan for creating sustainable, innovative communities in poor regions. This would be but one step among many we all must take toward reversing the systemic crisis.

—*Robert A. Isaak*

INTRODUCTION

1 The Revolt of the Rich

Revolts from true birth, stumbling on abuse,
Virtue itself turns vice, being misapplied;
And vice sometime's by action dignified

—WILLIAM SHAKESPEARE,
Romeo and Juliet

A *conservative revolt increases economic growth, speeds up the global economy, and exaggerates the gap between the rich and poor.*

In the early twentieth century, the "mass man" emerged. He had a commonplace mind. He was a person who was satisfied with material convenience and rested comfortably inert, rather than striving for excellence or accepting authority outside of himself.[1] The late twentieth century was marked by what can be called the "revolt of the rich" against any conception of the mass man—whether bourgeois or socialist. This conservative reaction, led by British Prime Minister Margaret Thatcher and U.S. President Ronald Reagan in the 1980s, celebrated capitalist free markets as the abstract ideal, as the engine of individual mobility and freedom.

Wealthy conservatives used this Anglo-American vision of capitalism to push the world economy and political system toward less regulation and more power for private corporations and individuals. The "revolt" led to the triumph of this liberal, freedom-first capitalism with the end of the Cold War and the emergence of the dot-com boom of the late 1990s. The rich man replaced the mass man as the idol: The young, sovereign multibillionaire in the high-tech sector became the hottest role model. Individual and corporate competitiveness based on private property led the way. The result was a new, high-tech, globalized world of economic Darwinism—the survival of the quickest company to dominate the market. The historical gap between the rich and poor rapidly became a chasm. The speeding up of social and economic life was caused by revolutionary changes in finance, technology, and communication, culminating in a radical drop in the cost of information—what we now call *globalization*.

Globalization encourages the well-positioned to use tools of economics and politics to exploit market opportunities, boost technological productivity, and maximize short-term material interests in the extreme. The result is a rapid increase in inequality between the affluent and the poor.

But in the process, the wealthy inadvertently undermine their own stability. The gaps between rich and poor have become so extreme in the twenty-first century and the aggressive competitive policies of the wealthy so transparent that the legitimacy of the post–World War II rules of the global economy has been undermined. The continuous decline of respect for the rules of the Bretton Woods agreement, the International Monetary Fund, the World Bank, and the World Trade Organization come to mind. From the domineering excesses of Microsoft to the willingness of Italian Prime Minister Silvio Berlusconi to change laws in order to escape indictment and extend his media empire to the George W. Bush administration's efforts to reform the tax structure to the advantage of the richest 1% of the population, the revolt of the rich is anything but subtle. Rich, corporate individuals are here to call the tune, and the government should retreat into the background.

Democracy has been hollowed out by corporate plutocracy, media concentration, and the translation of "individualism" into materialistic wealth. The big stakeholders have overwhelmed the small ones faster than ever in the political process. Economic access became the consolation prize. This "privatized" revolution of globalization succeeded to such an extent that a global catastrophe may be in the making if the rich do not change their behavior and create opportunities for the poor to become more self-sufficient. The only ones who ultimately accept the legitimate power of the super-rich individual are other excessively wealthy people who perceive a common bond and, presumably, a network of interests for their own long-term security. Yet the affluent need to have the poor be marginally successful economically for much the same reason that the farmer needs to fatten up his cows before taking them to market. Absolute poverty leads to greater uncertainty and possible chaos. Just consider the shorter life expectancy of the average Russian since the Soviet Union was replaced by the crony capitalism of mafia business elites. Or consider the case of mushrooming poverty, unemployment, and social uncertainty in other "transitional" economies in Eastern Europe, such as Rumania, that serve as illustrations of the broken promises of the triumph of free market capitalism. Finally, consider the expansion of poverty in the United States in the twenty-first century, even as the salaries of chief executive officers (CEOs) of multinational companies continue to escalate.

* * *

Of course, rich individuals and institutions have always dominated, exploited, and "created" the poor. The pharaohs of Egypt used thousands of slaves to build their pyramids. The Taj Mahal in India was constructed by the thin fingers of the underclass. The wealthy and powerful Catholic Church dominated human affairs for centuries and still strives to spread its influence today. The czars of Russia proliferated thousands of peasants to do their bidding. The maharajas of India pushed the exploitation of human labor to the limit before the nation gained independence, much as American plantation owners did through slavery before the Civil War. Then, of course, came the wealth of the oil cartels—with a shift of control from multinational oil companies to wealthy individual leaders of oil-producing countries, such as Prince Alwaleed Bin Talal Alsaud (still the eleventh richest man in the world in 2002).[2]

What has changed since the late twentieth century is the sudden explosion of extremely rich individuals who were previously ordinary, middle-class citizens. Even more staggering is that in this era of the "knowledge economy," many young entrepreneurs dropped out of college only to become extraordinarily wealthy by creating, catching, or benefiting from what would become the dot-com venture capital wave (Bill Gates of Microsoft, Michael Dell of Dell Computer, and Richard Grasso, who headed the New York Stock Exchange). Those with access to private property and credit as well as educational and job opportunities could use the information technology (IT) revolution to maximize their economic advantages to the point that a surprising number of them became billionaires before they were 40 years old.

The IT revolution was funded by the Pentagon, which sought to create a fast system of communication that the Russians could not access—the Internet. The resulting spread of digital literacy throughout the American population was done "on the cheap" through the one-time speculative investment extravagances of the dot-com boom. That is, young Americans could "free-ride" on the public IT infrastructure, become computer literate quickly, and take full professional advantage of the unique dot-com venture capital-led boom of the late 1990s as a "learning-by-burning" training experience. By the time the European and Japanese populations joined in, the boom was half over, and venture capital was drying up. Nevertheless, billionaires emerged in these countries from the high-tech stimulated stock boom following the end of the Cold War, including Karl and Theo Albrecht and Johanna Quandt of Germany, Liliane Bettencourt and Serge Dassault of France, Gerald Gosvenor and David Sainsbury of the United Kingdom, Silvio Berlusconi and Luciano Benetton of Italy, Amancio Ortega and Rafael del Pino of Spain, Ernesto Bertarelli and Walter Haefner of Switzerland, Ingvar Kamprad and Hans Rausing of Sweden, Mikhail Khodorkovsky of Russia, and Nobutada Saji and Yasuo Takei of Japan. Meanwhile, over 99% of the people of Africa and South Asia had not used the Internet by the beginning of the twenty-first century.[3]

The aim of the emerging rich was their own individual sovereignty, that is, control over a private realm of their own making. Money was just an indicator of status. By 1998, the 225 richest individuals in the world (including 60 Americans) had a combined wealth of over $1 trillion—equal to the annual income of the poorest 47% of the world's population. The three richest people had assets exceeding the combined Gross Domestic Product of the 48 least developed countries![4]

Status was measured by the ability to set one's own rules, to call one's own shots, to create one's own world. Those survived best who came first to the market with innovation on a global scale large enough to outpace or out-compete all other competitors. Unions shriveled. Power shifted from governments to multinational corporations. Private capital flows replaced public aid flows. The status and power of corporate CEOs displaced the status of government ministers and policy makers. Average CEO pay in the United States rose 571% between 1990 and 2000, while average worker pay rose 37% in the same period.[5] Social welfare benefits were cut back while public services were privatized—including even prisons.

The objective of the revolt of the rich was to reduce government to the function of law and order at home in order to protect existing contracts (not owned by the poor), to increase defense spending, and to shift incentives toward total freedom for "the market." This political shift positioned the highly trained and well-connected with financial security for life, but the life chances of the overwhelming majority of people left over were delegated to the market's roller coaster.

For our purposes, *the rich* will be defined as those who clearly have more in assets and income than they require to cover the lifetime needs of their households and those of their extended families. We will use the American standard of a rich individual as a general point of departure here because by 2002, fully 227 of the richest 500 billionaires in the world were American citizens.[2]

The *super-rich* are those who have 1,000 times or more in assets and income than they require to satisfy their families' lifetime needs.

The poor are those without the income or assets to satisfy their own households' basic human needs, such as food, water, shelter, energy, education, and medical treatment.

Of course, what counts as "poverty" depends on the region and country where one lives. In the richest nation of the world, the United States, the official poverty threshold in 2002 for a family unit of four people with two related children under 18 years old was an annual household income of $18,244, not counting capital gains, non-cash benefits such as food stamps, and assets the family happened to own.[6] The United States, with a per capita income over $30,000, is in the World Bank's "high income" country category, a category that includes nations with $9,266 GNP (Gross National Product) per person or above. This compares with the "low income" nations having $799 GNP or less per person annually.[7]

In considering what counts as "middle class," the middle-class family in America has not done nearly as well as the top 1% over the past several decades. The average annual salary in the United States rose from $32,522 in 1970 to $35,864 in 1999. This is only about a 10% increase over those 29 years. Compare this with the income of the top 100 CEOs, which went from $1.3 million to $37.5 million; or, as economist Paul Krugman has noted, more than 1,000 times the wage of average workers. Indeed, in the United States, the 13,000 richest families have incomes almost equal to those of the 20 million poorest families and 300 times greater than average American middle-class families.[8] Given escalating health care and pension costs, the middle class in America is closer to the poor than to the top 10% economically (those with annual incomes over $81,000). Not to mention the distance of the middle class from the super-rich, who are located between the top 1% ($230,000) and the top 0.01% (over $790,000 in annual income) in the United States.[8]

What is happening is that economic benefits are accruing in the extreme at the very tip of the upper class, making the many near the bottom poorer and poorer in comparison. The speeding up of this economic polarization is not just the story of individuals but also the story of powerful, international companies that employ and compensate them.

Some of the ways that the rich distance themselves from the poor in this high-speed global game of bumper cars (companies) is that:

1. The biggest and fastest firms prevail.

2. A social reality is created that requires companies to use their goods and services to maximize their power positions.

3. This dominating social reality is targeted with logos or symbols and backed up with sophisticated financing and infrastructure.

4. This cultivated corporate social reality becomes a *global* reality, a potentially homogeneous blueprint or an almost inescapable channel of doing business.

Microsoft was the fastest big company to seize the global market for computer operating systems, creating a social reality of its own and one that its competitors could not match. Suddenly, customers had to turn in their Apple computers for IBM personal computers that used the Microsoft operating system to adapt to the machines their secretaries used. Intel aimed at the same kind of systematic, aggressive strategy with microchips for computers, using its constant innovative power to drive out lower-quality competition, then slashing prices to increase or maintain its global market share. By an astute marketing campaign (in a world where it costs $3 million a minute to advertise on television during the American Super Bowl football game), the "Intel Inside" logo became a fashion statement, consolidating its market domination.

Ted Turner and Rupert Murdoch used vast global media empires to establish the supremacy of their own networks, deliberately programming social reality for their own productions along the way.

Amazon.com and eBay plowed millions of dollars into their domination of cyberspace, putting local bookstore owners out of business and throwing other small-time competitors into poverty. Well-financed, competitive innovation machines were created that pushed other companies and countries to the wall. Protesters emerged from Seattle on the West Coast of the United States to Doha, Qatar, on the Persian Gulf, proclaiming corporate domination of the world through a homogenous globalization of culture and economics as embodied in the World Trade Organization.

At the national level, *New York Times* correspondent Thomas Friedman called this homogenous blueprint "the Golden Straight-jacket." The private sector is its primary engine of economic growth, stimulated by low inflation and the privatization of state-owned companies. It also demands efforts at achieving a balanced budget, minimal state bureaucracy, and a reduction of restrictions against foreign investment, trade, and capital flows.[9] In short, all nations that wanted to become competitive had to adapt to the stringent rules of this Anglo-American capitalist model of social reality. The countries that adapt get richer. The ones that don't become poorer.

What is new in the twenty-first century concerning the gap between the rich and the poor is that it is so thoroughly *systemic:* Globalization has made isolation from the fast-moving world economic system impossible. The emerging crises impact everyone from California to Madagascar. If the tariff barriers in rich countries just happen to be four times higher for poor countries than for industrialized countries, this is just too bad for Madagascar.[10] Never mind that Africa, partly as a result of these rules, ends up with less than 2% of world exports and imports.[11]

Wealthy states have the resources to adapt quickly, targeting emerging market niches with high-tech corporations and extensive financing. But even the rich do not have the time to focus on anything but the main chance of the moment—or they will risk losing the short-term competitive game. These few market-moving firms and investors help to increase the number of the poor through economic Darwinism, maximizing their own strength, technology, finance, information flows, and managerial skills to such an extent that increasing numbers of people are thereby marginalized. The many in the shadows fall into poverty through unemployment and find it increasingly difficult in a complex, technological world to be able to satisfy their own basic needs *by themselves*.

Disconnected from history by the speed of global competitiveness, the new rich tend to put too much faith in their technology, their organizational structures, and the taken-for-granted stability of their home countries. In a global village, without paying attention to the needs of the masses of poor people—who are having the most children—the wealthy face a looming socioeconomic disaster in terms of their own health and security. The emerging catastrophe could be nothing less than a collapse of the global system—the economic, political, and ecological world as we know it. Globalization—motored by new technology, communication, and the activities and policies of the corporate rich—has created a global speed trap in which neither the rich nor the poor can see a way out. This speeding up of social and economic life increasingly puts the jobless, the sick, and the old at risk.

What are some symptoms of this global speed trap? Productivity growth, while promising economic growth, concentrates jobs where skills are the greatest and costs are the lowest, driving masses of people into unemployment—the unskilled, the mis educated, and those who want to continue to be highly paid. Beyond the globalization of terrorism, the spread of disease from country to country can happen in a matter of hours; bankruptcy of countries can occur in a matter of days; environmental disasters in a matter of minutes— such as biological, chemical, and nuclear accidents or deliberate attacks, capable of spreading contagiously...The ethical and political legitimacy of the world system is breaking down.

If legitimacy means influence through credible "force and awe," who believes the United Nations can govern "the world" effectively at the moment? Pressures are building each day on borders as thousands of poor immigrants try to enter wealthy countries in search of opportunities to survive and develop. Meanwhile, counter-pressures mount within developed countries to restrict the entry of cheaper highly skilled labor and to put tariffs on incoming textiles, steel, and agricultural goods—areas critical to economic growth in many developing countries. This dilemma creates odd dances between the unequal partners.

Consider the example of the irregular efforts of the U.S. government to enforce immigration laws at the Mexican border in a way that seems deliberately to let in enough cheap labor to maintain national U.S. economic competitiveness. Technology has pushed productivity to such an extent that it has resulted in a surfeit of goods and services worldwide without enough demand to absorb them. The "supply-siders" won—those radical conservatives who assumed that if the supply of goods and services is increased, demand will automatically follow. Consider the telecom business: Millions were spent to lay fiberoptic cable around the world but only 3% of it is being used. Suddenly, there was so much supply and so little demand that the global economy was threatened in many nations with deflation.

As money and trade barriers were torn down in order to increase business, the key to success was to be big, efficient, and fast enough to take advantage of these opportunities. The question of how to distribute such opportunities fairly was largely ignored. No legitimate social barriers were left to constrain greed, particularly in the U.S. economy, where there was no greater power in the world to suggest or enforce limits. In fact, greed became a virtue. Translated by technology into the language of "speculative risk," status was measured by the extent your salary exceeded any possible future need, by the number of people who worked for you, by the ranking of your country or company in terms of global market share, and by economic size. Bigger and faster were always assumed to be better—regardless of the social or environmental consequences. This concentration of size, wealth, and speed after the fall of communism in 1989 led to inevitable resistance—particularly after the scandalous excesses of wealth and power emerged from the economic boom of the 1990s. Anglo-American capitalism became a threat to the non–Anglo-American world not merely as a money culture but as an insatiable, technological innovation machine that sought to get all markets of the world to adopt its way of life.

Naturally, this materialistic ideology evoked massive resistance on the part of cultures where economics, technology, and money were not the top priorities. Powerless, some groups resorted to terrorist violence. Others consolidated to defend their social democratic or religious traditions. Jose Bové became a national hero in France by sacking a McDonald's restaurant as a symbol of an imperial, fast-food threat. Other cultures were despondent and sank into a recessionary malaise. A coalition of countries against Anglo-American cultural and political domination became explicit with the 2003 war in Iraq. Somehow, the attempt to extend the ideas of "less government, more economic, political, and individual freedom" by force (led, of course, by government) did not export easily into non–Anglo-American cultures. In the same year, another coalition of resistance by 22 developing nations was led by Brazil in a confrontation with the developed country elite of World Trade Organization, the regime responsible for the multinational corporate "law and order" of competition.

In short, the globalist ambition of this revolution of the rich promised much more individual opportunity than it could deliver—particularly in terms of jobs. As a result, the legitimacy of the elites of the dominant government, corporate, and international organizations was undermined. Without legitimacy, that is, massive respect for the force and awe of governing institutions, the international system comes unglued. And the growing gap between the rich and the poor—so glaringly played out worldwide in the media—deepened the global crisis into one of permanent instability and uncertainty.

Yet the breakdown of the stability of the global system on which the rich (and all others) depend may not be inevitable. Short-term opportunistic perceptions and investments of the wealthy can be rerouted into longer-term opportunities for rich and poor alike. The affluent must not continue to hold back on their spending or to spend on conspicuous consumption in overdeveloped, gated communities or in collectors' stamps. Protective tariffs against Third World products need not remain as high. The diffusion of attention paid by the World Bank and the International Monetary Fund on too many targets at once, much less the focus on increasing the debt of those most vulnerable, is *not* inevitable. Nor is it necessary for the world's only superpower to keep issues of education, the environment, and the equality of opportunity on the back burner of policy priorities.

The global system has come to a critical juncture. No longer will the rich be able to buffer themselves easily from the poor. Those in the caboose of the train of humanity will spread their germs, their unemployment, and their financial and political problems to the middle-class and first-class cars. Globalization has made this inevitable. If a country such as Thailand or Russia goes bankrupt, stock markets in the United States, London, and Frankfurt tumble. If there is a SARS outbreak in Hong Kong, it arrives in Toronto and New York in a matter of hours. If a chain reaction of bioterrorism occurs in one country, it may erupt in other countries faster than the international community will be able to act to stop the cycle of violence.

The reactionary unilateralism of American foreign policy is a desperate attempt to head off the violent train wrecks that the global speed trap makes inevitable. The final argument always seems to be that there is no time for the slow mechanisms of multilateral diplomacy. The lone ranger must act to seize the stage and snuff out the bad guys before they develop weapons of mass destruction.

Is there a way out of this global spiral of diffusion and disintegration? The wealthy can act now to create opportunities for greater self-sufficiency for the poor. Their contributions can target investments to build environmentally sustainable, competitive, customized "pilot" communities. By doing this through a transparent, non-governmental organization, the rich may be able to bridge the chasm between themselves and the poor while avoiding the corruption of governments and the bureaucracies of international organizations. The affluent may be able to stabilize their own interests as well as the life chances of the less advantaged. Without a systematic, targeted effort on the part of philanthropists, the poorest countries in the world will not have the means to gain access to the education and technology required to compete in the world economy—the key to self-sufficiency. They must have primary education, books, computers to access information, and electricity to run computers. Without basic information, they cannot improve health care. Fancy clinics will help little without an awareness of simple hygiene, such as knowing to wash one's hands before eating or understanding how to go about obtaining clean water and air. In Asia—where half of the world's city dwellers live—1.5 billion residents of cities suffer from air pollution levels above the limits recommended by the World Health Organization, more than 1.5 million people die every year from pollution-related diseases, and 2.3 billion people in the world suffer from diseases related to water problems.[12]

Collective patterns of behavior of both the rich and the poor must be altered if the divergence between them is to be reduced. Somehow, the "winner-take-all" mentality of many of the new rich must be tilted toward sharing for sustainable development or the earth will become inhospitable for the well-to-do and the poor alike. The dominant model of democratic capitalism appears to be too short-term oriented and dependent on corporate interest groups to be successful on long-term environmental issues. For instance, President Luiz Inacio Lula da Silva, the so-called people's politician, caved in to the lobbyists of Brazil's giant state oil company, Petrobas, and supported running gas pipelines through the Amazon rain forest.[13] At the same time, in contrast, poor Indian farmers in Bolivia rose up in violent demonstrations against exporting gas from their country to the United States through a port in Chile, resentful that 21 years of free-market reforms have left them with less exports than before.[14] The month-long peasant uprising forced the newly elected president to resign and broadcast a warning to elites who would try to globalize too quickly.[15] A workable program for environmentally responsible economic growth is desperately needed for the sake of the rich as well as the poor. These examples suggest that such a social transformation may come about only through the trauma of some kind of widespread crisis.

Stabilizing the world system is not a question of lack of knowledge, technology, or financial means but one of political will and economic common sense for the long term. And as we have observed, the wealthy have a greater stake than the less fortunate in stabilizing the global system. Indeed, a large part of the problem is that the poor have little "ownership" in such stabilization and are, therefore, more open to appeals of extremists who would like to undermine the system.

If we passively accept the assumption that to understand the poor you must first be poor, global disintegration is inevitable. We must try to understand how the rich think, how the poor think, and what common ground they might have that could provide a set of values to help assure a stable world community. We are left with an uncomfortable set of questions, which globalization has made acute.

To attain full development themselves, the affluent must use some of the economic benefits they have received to help develop social solidarity with poorer communities—long-term investment that goes beyond short-term humanitarian aid. Can they afford to continue to ignore such bridging efforts at the increased risk of spreading terrorism, global pandemics, the devastation of tropical rain forests, financial meltdown in the world economy, and even nuclear weapons proliferation? The lack of opportunity perceived by the disadvantaged clearly has something to do with these phenomena. Any individual caught in a cycle of downward social mobility and diminishing expectations now can find access to the technology used for inexpensive bioterrorism, shoulder-launched missiles, or suicide bombing. Money alone will not dissuade potential terrorists. But legitimate economic opportunity and social inclusion might. The well-to-do influence the increase of poverty not just through economic neglect but also through psychological and social deprivation.

The wealthy have new global technological and financial capacities, making it increasingly less justifiable to deprive the disadvantaged of psychological and social support for learning and self-development. To persist in ignoring the poor and their problems will be perceived as arrogance on the part of the vulnerable. There are millions of unemployed, undereducated youth in poor countries who could aim to become either stable, middle-class citizens or desperate religious believers, drug dealers, soldiers of fortune, or terrorists. The path the rich should take morally and in terms of their own *individual* security in this global village seems to be straightforward.

If the difference in the living conditions between rich and poor is not narrowed but continues to widen, the world will become unstable at an increasing pace. Terrorism thrives not merely on poverty but also among disenchanted students in an era where no positive role models stand out who seem to provide hope for a healthier and more prosperous social environment. Globalization promises prosperity through instant worldwide communication, raising expectations that are bound to be disappointed, leading people to support radical policies. Disease spreads fastest where medical care is least available. Pollution will increase exponentially because people often begin to take it seriously only after a certain level of living standard has been achieved and they no longer have to worry about food, water, medicine, or jobs. These are not just issues of survival but of education—for all social classes. Wherever the rich may be, their social lives are apt to become hectic, isolated, and hard-hearted: Not yet culturally sophisticated enough for a complex global marketplace, they may be surprised at the hatred directed toward them by the emerging middle class in developing countries due to the suffering this former underclass has been through.

If the significant minority who are highly educated in developing countries such as India and China continues to expand while their wages stay down, quality jobs from developed countries will flow to these nations in numbers not yet imagined. This will leave an increasing number of educated workers in rich countries unemployed or underemployed. The need for poor workers to provide cheap labor and to do tasks that the rich prefer not to do themselves—from cleaning, cooking, and serving to child care and secretarial work—has been evident for centuries. Globalization has made the interdependence of rich and poor immediate and compelling. Thus, Ebookers PLC, a travel agency of London, is sending young Europeans to call-center jobs in India for about one fourth the wage they would get at home.[16] If the only way a young person in a wealthy country can find a satisfying future career is to cooperate with people in lesser developed countries, the parents of that child have a huge stake in building strong social, economic, and political ties with foreign nations offering such opportunities. After all, global opportunity differentiates candidates for success in careers, no matter what the country of origin. Once long-term and abstract, the movement of white-collar jobs to developing countries from developed countries due to globalization has made this job-drain threat a rapidly emerging reality.

Paradoxically, **in the long run, the rich will need the poor almost as much as the poor need the rich.** Who, for example, will buy the innovations the wealthy would sell? How will the masses of mankind tap into enough financial resources to be able to keep the global economy humming? Not enough people seem to be aware of this natural interdependence. We must widen our perspective and no longer link our own identity merely with the accidental material circumstances that surround us. The initial injustice in life—where you are born and into which family—is a chance event that has nothing to do with merit.

Should your life chances be determined by where you are born? Those born rich are positioned to have more educational, social, and economic opportunities with which to maximize their advantages. In the process, they unwittingly deprive the poor of any chance at equal opportunity. The revolt of the rich, like all revolutions, brings with it a certain pride and feeling of self-righteousness. But self-righteousness makes it difficult to move toward creating a sustainable world of more equitable sharing of jobs and resources. The more palpable global crises become, the greater will be the recognition that opportunities for hopeful life chances must be more justly distributed to include the least advantaged.

References

1. José Ortega y Gasset, *The Revolt of the Masses,* (New York: WW Norton, 1932: anonymous translation of 1930 Spanish original).
2. "The World's Richest People 2002," *Forbes*, December 10, 2002.

3. Charles Kenny, "Development's False Divide," *Foreign Policy*, Jan/Feb.2003, No. 134, pp. 76–78.

4. Barbara Crossette, "Kofi Annan's Amazing Facts," *The New York Times*, September 27, 1998.

5. Arianna Huffington, *Pigs at the Trough: How Corporate Greed and Political Corruption are Undermining America* (New York: Crown Publishers, 2003), p. 14.

6. Bernadette D. Proctor and Joseph Dalaker, *Poverty in the U.S.: 2002,* (Washington, DC: U.S. Census Bureau, U.S. Department of Commerce, September 2003), p. 4.

7. World Bank, "Attacking Poverty: Opportunity, Empowerment and Security," *World Bank Development Report: 2001* (Washington, DC: The World Bank, 2001), p. 271.

8. Paul Krugman, "The End of Middle-Class America," *The New York Times Magazine*, October 20, 2002, pp. 64–65.

9. Thomas Friedman, *The Lexus and the Olive Tree* (New York: Anchor Books, 2000), p. 105.

10. Kevin Watkins, "Eight Broken Promises: Why the WTO Isn't Working for the World's Poor," *Oxfam Briefing Paper* (Oxfam International, October 2001, p. 1.

11. Geoffrey E. Schneider, "Globalization and the Poorest of the Poor: Global Integration and the Development Process in Sub-Saharan Africa," *Journal of Economic Issues,* Vol. 37, No. 2, June 2003, p. 389.

12. "WHO Warns on Asian City Pollution," *The Wall Street Journal*, October 15, 2003.

13. Matt Moffett, "Brazil's President Sees New Growth in the Rain Forest," *The Wall Street Journal*, October 16, 2003.

14. Larry Rohter, "Bolivia's Poor Proclaim Abiding Distrust of Globalization," *The New York Times*, October 17, 2003.

15. Larry Rohter, "Bolivian Peasants' 'Ideology of Fury' Still Smolders," *The New York Times*, October 20, 2003.

16. Kevin Delany, "Outsourcing Job—and Workers—to India," *The Wall Street Journal*, October 13, 2003.

2 Time versus Opportunity

*Our culture leads to an unconcentrated
and diffused mode of life.*

—ERICH FROMM,
The Art of Loving (1963)

Globalization speeds up time, stimulating the rich to concentrate economic opportunities among themselves in order to maximize their own short-term interests. Wealthy nations neglect the fact that their infant manufacturing industries were protected by government policy until they were strong enough to compete in the world.

This is the age of diffuse uncertainty. Information, technology, finance, and energy are diffused so fast that there is no time to think. We feel pressured to act before having the time to systematically break down the uncertainty into risks we can understand in order make rational decisions. This applies not only to financial choices— for instance, taking the time to analyze the companies underneath the

This is the age of diffuse uncertainty. Information, technology, finance, and energy are diffused so fast that there is no time to think. We feel pressured to act before having the time to systematically break down the uncertainty into risks we can understand in order make rational decisions. This applies not only to financial choices—for instance, taking the time to analyze the companies underneath the letters of their stock market listings—but to personal and professional decisions, as well. No one can be said to be in control. Even the rich—as individuals, companies, or countries—are overwhelmed by information and radical change.

In the era of Charles Dickens, the "hard times" of the nineteenth century, there were rich, poor, and simpler economic rules. The use of machines expanded but had not yet overwhelmed mankind's capacity to cope with it.

Technology has sped up economic and social life with inventions that take off with lives of their own, such as e-mail or gene manipulation. Technical distractions and fast virtual processes serve to disconnect the rich from their memory of the past. There is little time to read history, to remember, or to understand others in earlier stages of economic development. Taking their own economic status for granted as a basis for narrowly focused economic activity, the well-to-do forget that their nations, too, once were economically dependent and were protected by the government until their companies and vital economic sectors could cope with global competition. This discounting of the past means that wealthy countries do not understand the significance of the demand for protection of infant industries or commodity production by the developing countries today. Fast-moving, competitive pressures cause the rich to concentrate on business opportunities and investments on the one hand and to ignore poor countries and their developmental needs on the other.

* * *

Old traditions and habits are blown away by the modernization of societies—their transformation to cope with free-market competitiveness. Secular democracy has spread globally, undermining the legitimacy of religious elites and disrupting traditional ways of living, for example, throughout Latin America. Individuals without education or tools are forced to make many more choices than in the past. They often do not understand the concepts of careers, investments, or lifestyles typical of the road to upward mobility and financial independence of the middle class striving to become wealthy. The poor are even overwhelmed by an infinite variety of consumer decisions, which can seduce them quickly into long-term debt. Globalization expands the range of choice and speeds up the decision process. Technology forces this diffusion of choice on people all over the world who are not prepared for it.

The wealthier one is, the more one seeks out and pays for expert professional advice in order to protect one's interests. The poorer one is, the more one is forced to become self-reliant before one is ready for it—without the education, family connections, or financial resources that help to identify the choices most apt to maximize one's life chances. The poor view *life chances* as sociologist Max Weber defined them: a competitive struggle for survival among individuals or types of people.[1] The middle class or rich, on the other hand, have the luxury of seeing life chances as sociologist Ralf Dahrendorf interpreted them: the odds of fulfilling the full range of human possibilities, given the individual's ties and options.[2]

The global sense of diffuse uncertainty affects all human beings today. This feeling of being overwhelmed with information and alternatives puts a premium on the value of *agency*—the ability to act in an educated, decisive way in order to improve one's circumstances. But informed self-confidence comes only with the time and health required to become educated and with the self-confidence that springs from opportunities to act out certain roles or to perform in good job situations. As Rousseau noted, "There is only one man who gets his own way—he who can get it single-handed: Therefore freedom, not power, is the greatest good. That man is truly free who desires what he is able to perform and does what he desires."[3]

Most people do not feel they have the knowledge or resources to be agents capable of steering their own futures. They are poor, passive pawns who anticipate that others will determine their fate. For example, poor blacks in the wealthiest country, the United States, who reside in urban ghettos in New York, Detroit, Chicago, or Los Angeles have the same probability of having their life chances end at age 45 as whites do at 65 nationwide. This premature death is usually caused by illness and stress rather than by violence.[4] The physical environment of poverty weathers the people like heavy storms damage old buildings, and the young find themselves aging very fast in the ghetto. In Chicago, more than 26% of young people between 20 and 24 years old were out of school and out of work in 2003, as were 45% of black men. These are critical years in building one's "human capital" and economic leverage for a lifetime.[5] Jobs or apprenticeship training with predictable incomes could help to transform the life chances of inner-city youth, but this is not a high priority of the wealthy elites running the country. Just sitting on the status quo is enough to create more poverty.

Thus, as the twenty-first century began, the average daily earnings of chief executive officers (CEOs) in the United States in a day was the same as the average worker earned in a year—this in the "richest" nation that would like to serve as a model for others. Meanwhile, in the poorest of countries, people living on less than $2 a day report worrying all the time. They worry about the lack of income-earning opportunities, their poor links to markets, the inability of state institutions to help them, the insecurities of health risks, unemployment risks, and agricultural risks (e.g., recurrent drought) that make life a fragile affair.[6] This negative, self-fulfilling prophecy of dependence on the part of the poorest countries is widespread. Meanwhile, perceptions are different on the other side of the social class divide. Studies show that rapid advances of technology have led many elites in rich countries to become so distracted from the past that they forget the lessons of history: They have forgotten the loss

*A point made by Bill Joy of Sun Microsystems at an OECD conference in Paris in 2000.[7]

of one third of Europe's population to an uncontrollable black plague, and the importance of AIDS has yet to sink in.[7]*

In Zambia, for example, which is experiencing one of the worst AIDS epidemics on earth, less than 1% of the 200,000 or so Zambians who need the antiretroviral treatment to halt the spread of the disease get the medicine. Neither they nor their government can afford it.[8]

In this century of diffuse uncertainty, the control habits of the "haves" to protect and maximize their interests work to assure the dependence of the "have-nots." If the wealthy countries do provide the poor with loans, they do it through institutions they can control, such as the World Bank, which demand interest payments that push the poor further into poverty and dependence. Not surprisingly, the retained earnings of the World Bank go up each year—from $19 billion in 2000 to $27 billion in 2003, with the net income growing from $1,489 billion in 2001 to $5,344 billion in 2003.[9] After all, the World Bank is headed by a former investment banker whose main professional function has always been to increase the profit of a bank. Rich institutions get richer, profiting from the poorest countries, which they are driving more deeply into debt and dependence through business practices designed more for established countries that can quickly adapt than for those without the means to cope with globalization. These practices assume a free world economy of competitors who start on an equal footing: Somehow, these transitional loans will bring the least advantaged countries up to this level playing field immediately so that interest can be repaid.

The rich nations controlling these international institutions have forgotten that as their countries began to industrialize, their governments protected their "infant industries" until the firms were strong enough to compete globally. Americans, for instance, often forget that their government had a protectionist trade policy in the late nineteenth century to help U.S. companies become competitive in the world. Moreover, except for wool, the United States, Britain, France, and Germany were almost self-sufficient in the raw materials they required for their industrialization—coal, iron ore, cotton, and wheat (for food). The poorest developing nations do not have such a basis for launching their industrialization.

The rich can create the poor intentionally or coincidentally. Some managers of multinational corporations are clearly cognizant of what they are doing—those who create sweat shops for children in order to manufacture their products cheaply in developing countries, for example, or the *maquiladoras* on the Mexican border, which import parts from the United States to be assembled for re-export to North America by young Mexican girls working under exploitative wages and living conditions. And such deliberate corporate strategies can take even more malevolent forms: In 1995, Shell Oil Corporation supplied the Nigerian government with arms when it sought to repress the Ogoni population, who were demanding that Shell stop polluting Ogoni land.[10] Living standards have nosedived since the discovery of oil in Nigeria forty years ago.

But other wealthy people do not always intend to make the poor dependent. Indeed, they often do not even perceive themselves to be "rich," habitually ignoring what seems to be remote from their everyday lives. Nevertheless, the result is the same for the poor. From the perspective of a man or a woman in Uganda, Malawi, or Ethiopia, not many in the world seem to care that you can expect to live for only 45 years. You just got a bad throw of the dice.

There have always been rich and poor in the world. There always will be. But what is new is the emergence of a global speed trap that pushes the rich into behavior patterns that create more poor and dependent people than existed ever before. In their "revolt," the rich have both deliberately and inadvertently foisted this speed trap on themselves and on the poor. They have sought to speed up the global economy by deregulating and privatizing it, tearing down barriers to technology, financial flows, information flows, and trade flows wherever possible for the sake of foreign investment, no matter what the cost in terms of traditional cultures and values. Technology digitizes communication, subverting local languages, and increases productivity, leading to greater underemployment in the traditional manufacturing sectors. Curiously, both rich and poor may be worse off in human terms, despite the increase in material

wealth generated. The time for human communication is cut shorter; the means more homogenous; the mode, cooler: Computer, fax,
and cell phone interactions replace face-to-face conversations and
the charm and nuances of body language. Charm, of course, requires
a certain amount of leisure and space for individual idiosyncrasies.

The revolt of the rich, arguing for less state regulation and support
for the private sector, has stimulated higher rates of economic growth
from the abstract "macro"—or abstract national—perspective in the
world. Hence, national income data is reported from international organizations in terms of Gross National Product per capita, dividing the
overall wealth created in a year by the number of people, as though they
each got the same share. For the well-to-do, the result of this economic
growth is a stimulating, rootless cosmopolitanism, a jet-set way of life.
But the competitive prerequisites for succeeding, given the speed of the
global economy, push beyond the capacities of the majority of human
beings and small businesses. And the higher up the class hierarchy,
the more inhuman the time pressure. Thus, the U.S. president has less
than 10 minutes to decide whether to respond to an incoming threat
(missiles or geese?). The global economy has become so complex that
even the rich spend more time than they would like trying to figure
out what is going on. They are time-starved, whereas the poor are
starved for everything but time.

**You get more of what you pay attention to. The rich pay at-
tention to promoting and protecting their prosperity. The poor
have to focus on survival.**

The affluent choose not to see the poor. They are too busy with
other activities. Like the Ito calculus used to track the trajectory of
rockets by breaking up the notion of continuous time into pieces, the
rich are tempted to chop up time at an increasing pace in order to
plan for their own future. The options increase for people with money,
but so does pressure on their time. Perception narrows, focused on
hard work to shore up short-term interests in an uncertain world.
In the first instance, it even appears as though the rich create the
poor through a kind of massive attention deficit disorder. That is, the
speed of the global economy forces them to shift so quickly from one
thing to another that they rarely find time to think about anything

but the problems in their own well-insulated world. From the perspective of the wealthy, saving time and money wherever possible are the keys to becoming rich, and this means saving time by narrowing one's focus to what is at hand. "Remember that time is money," Ben Franklin wrote in *Advice to a Young Tradesman*. Creating and preserving wealth, much less spending it, is a full-time preoccupation in the global economy of the twenty-first century. The well-to-do invest where the return is high or stable, meaning that they avoid investments in regions of the poorest people in the world: They distance themselves and their wealth from the poor as a result. The rich concentrate their attention in order to succeed in a world of distracting information. This concentration, in turn, can come to monopolize their time—and other things, as well.

Of course, there are different ways to become rich. Some people are rich because they own a lot of land. Others are born into extended, royal families. Some inherit money. Others create their own wealth through inventions, companies, or by seizing opportunities, whether legal or illegal. Given increased life spans and the rising expense of the newest medical therapies, the upper middle-class family may not see itself as rich because it does not have enough financial insurance against unpredictable life contingencies. For instance, children or grandchildren could become permanently disabled or unemployed. As a result of such possible uncertainties, the temptation for more is always there—chasing the model of the super-rich, who were earlier defined as having at least 1,000 times more in assets and income than they or their families can anticipate needing in a lifetime. Whether still working or just sorting through the many choices of how to spend leisure time, the rich are usually busy people. Their agendas—for work or pleasure—are crowded. They often choose not to take breaks.

The rich are preoccupied with accumulating surpluses as a hedge against uncertainty. They figure they might need more for a rainy day, particularly given that life expectancy is going up. At the same time, people in general tend to retire earlier than they used to from income-generating work, making calculations of future pensions and Social Security even more difficult. Or the well-to-do may decide to build inheritances for their children, who may in other ways be neglected (because getting rich is so time-consuming that not enough time is scheduled to be with children).

The processes by which the wealthy accumulate assets tilt the global distribution of wealth in their own favor, a self-reinforcing prophecy that makes the world seem to be more in their control than it actually is. For example, during the stock technology boom in 2000, Frank P. Quattrone of Credit Suisse First Boston offered billionaire CEO Michael Dell access to shares of a "hot" initial public offering of Corvis before it came on the market, hoping to lure Dell Computer to his bank. Michael Dell sought to buy 250,000 shares and was sold a pretrading allocation of Corvis shares (about 150,000 shares) at the offering price of $36. The stock went up to $95 as soon as the market opened and closed that first day at $85— a gain of 135% over the offering price.[11] In other words, this opportunity constituted a huge payoff for the possibility of a future business relationship. Although not illegal, this access to stock before it comes on the open market is clearly open only to rich customers, and the normal buyers get the leftovers at a much higher price, which is more likely to make them poorer than richer. Although Dell never became a client of First Boston, this case does illustrate the complex opportunities that absorb the time of the rich and tilt the stock market in their favor.

The surplus income of the rich becomes a trophy of status and power among their peers—accumulation risks becoming an end in itself. The accumulation of wealth is concentration. Rich individuals caught up in this process of concentration at the corporate level can be tempted by the lure of monopolization—the ultimate "certainty." Corporate survival, in an era of turbulent global change, means to shore up reserves as a buffer against competition and inevitable shocks. Socially positioned to believe that will power can help control their own destinies, the rich strive to maximize "certainty" wherever they can, leaving as little as possible to chance. The poor, in contrast, are so dependent on circumstances beyond their control that they usually do not believe they can act to tilt events in their favor.

Despite their financial security, wealthy managers find themselves increasingly running out of time. They often come to view the world as did the Queen in Lewis Carroll's *Alice Through the Looking-Glass*:

> "A slow sort of country!" said the Queen. " Now, *here*, you see, it takes all the running you can do, to keep in the same place. If you want to get somewhere else, you must run at least twice as fast as that!"

Although this sense of time pressure may be true of the poor as well, the rich are more aware of being caught between too many possessions to use and too many financial, professional, and social opportunities. Often overwhelmed with managing their wealth, given the complexity they have helped to create, stress builds up. Hours spent with and for others are reduced. Months and years seem to fly by faster than they think is possible. The rich—and the companies they keep—are caught up in a speed trap partially of their own making. Digitization in the "New Economy," for instance, radically lowered the costs and raised the speed of moving data, making it advantageous for wealthy firms to disperse employees and processes globally.[12] Often, the corporate elite are absorbed in seemingly endless transactions to increase their material well-being and mobility in a world that promises insatiable opportunity for those with the means to take advantage of it. The promise of the "American dream," of becoming whatever you can be, is infinitely elastic, despite real-world constraints that make it impossible even for the rich. But the promise is enough to keep going. Or the greed.[13]

Meanwhile, the poorest of the poor are increasingly left out of the globalization game: Without resources, they fail to attract investments, jobs, or recognition. Without schooling, job training, and work opportunities, they are left in dependent shadow economies. The poor wither like plants without sun and water. They are barely kept alive by accidental spillovers from overabundant gardens nearby ("trickle-down economics"). They are relegated to the shadows, sometimes in shadow countries, removed from the bright lights and economic stimulation of the "casino capitalism" of rich and developed regions.

Casino capitalism is the speculative process of "creative destruction" that governs globalization and targets those areas most easily exploited for quick profits.[14] For example, Microsoft created a computer operating system that "destroyed" the market for typewriters, then tried to extend its monopoly position to the server market and even to video games. Speculative investors finance new innovations. These innovations, in turn, are directed by large-scale corporate production to destroy the old ways of doing things, such as the automobile replacing the horse-drawn carriage or DVDs replacing CDs. This creates economic growth and jobs but often at the cost of a loss of traditions and social stability.

Casino capitalism, of course, works best in nations with casinos and capital. The process thrives on making gamblers of us all. Within the rich countries, the only taste of speculation the poor experience is the lotteries that are used to sell hope to the masses. The lottery is the last, desperate effort to squeeze income from the poor used by states or governments under financial duress. It is the uneducated poor who are most likely to be tempted to play in lottery systems, where the overwhelming odds are stacked against them. There is an emerging danger that global stock markets have been transformed into middle-class lotteries with the same effect—people speculating on letters representing companies they do not really understand. The fact that a few of the "dealers" or gatekeepers at major companies or brokerage houses have been led off in chains for bank and securities fraud merely reinforces the image of the stock market as a rigged casino game for the profit of insiders, notwithstanding the numerous outsiders who got rich during the dot-com boom. Such was the case of Dr. Sam Waksal, founder of ImClone, who was sentenced to seven years and three months in jail for—among other things—telling his daughter to sell $5 million of Imclone stock, knowing the price was about to collapse. After all, the rich can invest in stocks for the long term, weathering deep falls in the market, whereas others are losers who need to take their money out in the short term to meet expenses. The rich created the poor, for example, when former CEO of Tyco, Dennis Kozlowski, pocketed nearly $467 million in stock, salary, and bonuses in the four years he held the job, while shareholders lost $92 *billion* when the value of Tyco shares dropped.[15] Kevin Phillips demonstrates in *Wealth and Democracy*[16] that corporate aggrandizement in the 1980s and 1990s went beyond the extremes of even the Gilded Age and served to frame broad trends of abandoning American workers, communities, and loyalties.

Even the richest of all casino capitalists, Bill Gates, has admitted that capitalism, for all its virtues of dynamism, has failed to come up with a solution to critical problems such as global disease.[17] Clearly, the logic of speculating *for* profit here and now works differently than the logic of speculating *against* disease there and then. Capital prefers to concentrate on multiplying itself. According to the International Labor Organization, in the past 10 years, 54 nations have become worse off economically, and the gap between the richest 20% and the poorest 20% has increased. Capital flows where capital already is or where the return on investment is attractive and the downside risk is limited.

However, capital is not just a question of income but of what your family owns—assets such as a home, job security, and savings. Without assets, a person has no economic security, no health insurance, and not even the means to live in a neighborhood where one has physical security. In this sense, government statistics that focus merely on a set of money income thresholds alone to define poverty leave a lot out. There is vulnerability and social exclusion that this income yardstick alone cannot begin to measure.

The poor watch the global speed trap from a distance. Perhaps they glimpse its glitter, gadgetry, and instant gratification in a James Bond movie on television in a local bar or in the cinema. But they know that globe-trotting Hollywood reality will never be their own. The media amplifies the effect of the increasing polarization between rich and poor. The poor come to view their life chances literally as a question of chance—a lottery game over which they have no hope of gaining any control. Capitalism without capital leaves the poor coming up empty—unless they somehow gain access to capital in order to move toward self-sufficiency.

The major international institutions designed by rich countries to help the poor, such as the World Bank and International Monetary Fund (IMF), are like sprinklers spreading drops of water in a desert: They diffuse the small amount of financial and management support they have over too many targets. It is not that the water is not appreciated. But the efforts of these organizations do little to increase the long-term self-sufficiency of the poor. They may provide public assets in the form of roads, dams, debt relief, or subsidies for microbanks but not the assets for economic independence.

Consider the case of Argentina. On the verge of a deep recession, the head of the Central Bank of Argentina agreed in 2000 to conditions of the IMF to cut the budget deficit from $5.3 billion to $4.1 billion during 2001. With 20% of the workers unemployed, this was not exactly a brilliant time to cut off government spending. In the "Technical Agreement of Understanding," there was a section curiously called "Improving the Conditions of the Poor," which agreed to cut salaries from the government's emergency employment program by 20% and to drop salaries for civil servants by 12–15%, with a provision that meant a cut to the old by 13% in public and private pension plans.[19] Eventually, the IMF even asked Argentina to eliminate its deficit. Argentina's Gross Domestic Product fell by more than 2% in 2001 and dropped further thereafter. In the World Bank's "Country Assistance Plan" for the four years from 2001 to 2005, James Wolfensohn, President of the World Bank, defended the goals of the IMF plan, stating that despite the setbacks, the strategy was appropriate. He even praised the $3 billion cut in primary expenditures to accommodate the increase of interest obligations. In other words, the spigot for domestic liquidity for human needs in the country was being turned off for the sake of paying back creditors—mainly banks based outside of the country. The middle class was shoved abruptly into poverty and rioted on the streets of Buenos Aires.[18]

So the actions of the IMF and World Bank often serve to break down the conditions of self-sufficiency for developing nations with false hopes, increased debt, and antigrowth policies. The government of Argentina bent over backward to accept the recommendations of the IMF, only to push the country deep into malaise. The problem is that the straightjacket the rich policy makers sew for all their poor clients in crisis is often more suitable for another wealthy economy like their own, where there is enough flexibility and buying power to overcome the cuts in government spending. Similarly, the IMF withheld its funds from Ethiopia in 1997 until it changed its budget to be independent of foreign aid, opened its fragile banking system to world markets, and let world markets determine its level of interest rates. The IMF (under the control of the wealthy nations) pushed a dogmatic ideology of market fundamentalism on a poor country with weak markets and banks—a nation trying its best to decentralize funds to build health clinics and schools.[19]

False Promises of Development

Elites from nations that "have it made" often view the world through the lenses of an abstract cosmopolitanism of universal rules they think must apply to all countries at the same time. They forget how their own nations got where they are. To the extent that they believe in the free-market school of Adam Smith, they should consider the shortcomings that nineteenth-century German economist Friedrich List identified in this way of thinking. According to List, Adam Smith's school of thought suffers from three main defects:

> Firstly, from boundless *cosmopolitanism*, which neither recognizes the principle of nationality, nor takes into consideration the satisfaction of its interests; secondly, from a dead *materialism*, which everywhere regards chiefly the mere exchangeable value of things without taking into consideration the mental and political, the present and future interests, and the productive powers of the nation; thirdly,

from a *disorganising particularism* and *individualism*,
which, ignoring the nature and character of social
labour and the operation of the union of powers in
their higher consequences, considers private industry only as it would develop itself under a state of
free interchange with society (i.e., with the whole
human race) were that race not divided into separate
national societies.[20]

Poor countries, according to List, must protect their manufacturing sectors in order to increase the national power of production
and employment. Each country has a distinctive national culture and
society that must be taken into account when creating government
policies. The poor, in short, are not yet developed or strong enough
to focus only on "global values of exchange" in an abstract, "cosmopolitan," free-market sense. The immediate adoption of these values
would assume that all countries share the same starting position in
the global economic competition, which is clearly not the case.

The rich and the poor think differently. Too often, the well-to-
do assume "I accumulate, therefore I am." Too often, the poor assume
" I depend on others, therefore I exist."

The rich—as individuals, as corporations, and as nations—
struggle to position themselves and their offspring to become
self-fulfilling prophecies of success. They increase their own productive power and that of the generation that follows them, taking on the habit of focusing their perception to put "halos" on just
the successful. The halos are projected onto models they would
mimic, up-and-coming winners to invest in for profit, and established circles with whom to network in order to solidify their
own positions.

Studies have shown that if a teacher is given a handful of random names of pupils sitting in a classroom and told that these are
particularly gifted individuals, the teacher will give them special attention, and those randomly selected will actually perform better in
the final testing, given the halos projected on them. Rather than
continuing the habit of projecting halos on their own kind, the rich
in society might risk projecting positive expectations on poor but

potentially competent individuals who would become independent. Again, you get what you pay attention to: more social and economic support for spoiled rich kids or a deliberate effort to bring out the best in disadvantaged children in order to make them less dependent on welfare systems in the future.

How could the wealthy help the poor to become more self-sufficient? By providing targeted social, educational, and financial support. Each school in a wealthy real estate area could be given tax incentives to adopt a school in a nearby poor neighborhood or a "sister" school in a developing country. The established have a long-term stake in helping to transform the willing poor from being passive stoics to becoming active agents who seek to shape their own lives and to create productive power for their own communities and nations. As shall be demonstrated, by redirecting the "halo effect," the well-positioned could help to restore the confidence of the poor in their own human dignity and make them more independent and less reliant on those more fortunate than they are. This process of refashioning social reality to create bridges of educational and job opportunity might slow down globalization. But a slower speed could make the process more sustainable for rich and poor alike—at home and abroad. Poet Antonio Machado said, "Speed kills the soul." We must slow down to become more human.

Consider the proposition that *everyone* might be better off if opportunities were spread more equally. This is not to deny that to really help the poor, you must be self-sufficient yourself in order to show the way. But how we use—and extend—the brief time we spend on earth can be made more meaningful than we once thought possible, given our global reach.

The rich have successfully sped up the global economy to the point that only they have the funds to cope with it, reallocating resources away from the poor to "winners." Productivity in the global economy is increased only too often by concentrating retraining and technology on those who already have work. But the human dignity that is lost in the process, along with jobs and sustenance, makes the high speed of globalization suspect.

The shift in historical momentum from a fossil-fuel-led economy toward a global system led by technological transformation has yet to be accompanied by a widespread recognition of how powerful nations achieved their growth. Many economists maintain that manufacturing is "the engine of growth."[21] If so, how are poor countries to achieve industrialization through manufacturing when 20 large economies lost 22 million jobs in manufacturing between 1995 and 2002, a decline of 11%? Those factory jobs are not apt to come back because of the productivity increases that globalization has wrought through technology.[22] Companies gain market share by outsourcing: it is the workers left behind who suffer.

From Brazil to Russia to China—not to mention the United States—manufacturing jobs are disappearing, and politicians are trying to gain popularity by trying to close the barn door after all the horses have left. The new jobs are apt to be created in the service sector, even in the developing countries. But it is more difficult to raise productivity in the service sector than in manufacturing. And service sector jobs often pay less than traditional factory jobs did. So by skipping the manufacturing sector and moving straight to the service sector, poor countries risk missing the economic growth and wealth accumulation that did so much to make "old rich" nations rich.

The Cold War is over and the rich won, revolting against the state domination of economies in order to reinforce their position. The universal rules of economic and political globalization they have enforced benefit established nations and companies, as well as emerging nations with sufficient assets and productive capacity to tap into the wealth generated, such as China and India. But as we shall discover, these cosmopolitan free-market principles do not work as well for countries and peoples who start off so far behind in the race that they find themselves falling further and further behind. To see how this time-consuming global competition concentrates opportunity, one must first understand how the rich and established live and operate.

References

1. Max Weber, *Wirtschaftschaft und Gesellschaft* (Tübingen, 1956), p. 20.

2. Ralf Dahrendorf, *Lebenschancen* (Frankfurt: Suhrkamp, 1979), pp. 48–50.

3. Jean Jacques Rousseau, *Émile* (London; J. M. Dent & Sons, Ltd., 1933), p. 48 (French original: 1762).

4. Helen Epstein, "Enough to Make You Sick?" *New York Times Magazine,* October 12, 2003, p. 77.

5. Bob Herbert, "Locked Out at a Young Age," *The New York Times,* Op-Ed, October 20, 2003.

6. World Bank, *World Development Report: 2001:Attacking Poverty* (Washington, DC: World Bank, 2001), p. 2.

7. David E.. Dunn, "The Knowledge Divide: Where Some Angels Dare," in *The OECD Observer* (Paris: OECD, 2000), issue 223, pp. 55–57.

8. Sharon LaFraniere, "AIDS Patients in Zambia Face Stark Choices," *The New York Times.* October 11, 2003.

9. World Bank, *World Bank Annual Report:* "Statement of Changes in Retained Earnings for the Fiscal Years Ended June 30, 2003, June 30, 2002, 2001, 2000" (Washington, DC: World Bank, 2003).

10. Richard Robins, *Global Problems and the Culture of Capitalism* (Boston: Allyn & Bacon, 2002), p. 126.

11. Andrew Ross Sorkin, "Banker's Trial Gives Glimpse into Close Ties of Tech Boom," *The New York Times,* October 13, 2003.

12. Harry Barkema et al., "Management Challenges in a New Time," *Academy of Management Journal,* Vol. 45, No. 5, October 2002, p. 916.

13. Frank Portney, *Infectious Greed: How Deceit and Risk Corrupted the Financial Markets* (New York: Times Books/Henry Holt, 2003).

14. Joseph Schumpeter, *Capitalism, Socialism and Democracy* (New York: Harper & Row, 1950).

15. Arianna Huffington, *Pigs at the Trough* (New York: Crown Publishers, 2003), p. 12.

16. Kevin Phillips, *Wealth and Democracy: A Political History of the American Rich.* (New York: Broadway Books, 2002), p. 413.

17. Interview with Bill Moyers, *NOW with Bill Moyers*, Public Broadcasting System, May 7, 2003.

18. Greg Palast, *The Best Democracy Money Can Buy,* (New York: Plume/Penguin Group, 2003), pp. 162–163.

19. Joseph E. Stiglitz, *Globalization and its Discontents* (New York: W. W. Norton, 2002), pp. 25–34.

20. Friedrich List, *The National System of Political Economy,* translation by S. S. Lloyd (London: Longmans, Green and Co.,1885, reprinted 1922), p. 141.

21. John Cornwall, *Modern Capitalism: Its Growth and Transformation* (Oxford: Martin, Robertson and Co., 1977).

22. Jon E. Hilsenrath and Rebecca Buckman, "Factory Employment Is Falling World-wide," *Wall Street Journal*, October 20, 2003.

I

THE RICH

*Who They Are,
and How They
Work and Why They
Speed Things Up*

3 Who the Rich Are and How They Live

The rich are different than us.

—F. SCOTT FITZGERALD

Yes, they have more money.

—ERNEST HEMINGWAY

T*he rich have more of everything, except time.*

The rich can't help themselves. They maximize. They know how to do it. And they do it for themselves. They do it *to* the poor: They don't always mean to do it, but they *do* create the poor. The rich pull investment, skilled people, and resources away from poor areas and target them in winning regions. The way they go about maximizing their interests generates poor people as surely as seed spawns grass. As often as not, their wealth becomes a habit, and they do not even perceive themselves to be rich. Recall that *rich* was here defined as clearly having more than enough assets and income to cover the lifetime needs of your family. Given the explosive developments

43

in technologies, skyrocketing health care costs, and uncertainties concerning security globally, the amount needed to cover all possible future needs of a multigenerational family seems to be elastic—stretching to a limit unknown.

Almost anyone you ask about the proposition that the rich *create* the poor has an opinion. A wealthy neighbor responded, "I don't know much about these things. Actually, I don't *know* any poor." And that is part of the problem. By interacting with the poor, one gives them social and psychological support, which can be as important for human motivation as financial help. Moral and social considerations need to become a part of deciding which products to buy and sell so that we support the poor directly and indirectly wherever possible.[1] Changing such behavior can be counter-intuitive and inconvenient.

We often have difficulty in understanding what we have not experienced. If you haven't *been there*, it is very hard to grasp how those in poverty or out of work perceive the world. Yet we must develop empathy to overcome this lack of experience. Vincent van Gogh was able to paint the perceptions of the poor so acutely because he was one of them. Nevertheless, Hogarth, who was not poor, brings hope: His paintings are crowded with striking images of poverty and what it means to be poor. But imagining what it is like to be poor is not easy, even if we take time to try to understand.

Let us consider for a moment how it is that many wealthy individuals live and operate. They do not have a lot of time or room in their hectic schedules. Any concern they might have for the poor tends to be squeezed out by other concerns. Left alone, the status quo conditions keep the existing poor in their state of poverty and proliferate more poor people. Ignoring the poor, the wealthy help to create them through "the sin of omission"—that is, through not giving the disadvantaged the opportunities for education or upward mobility while acting in ways that serve to increase the differences between the rich and the poor.

* * *

That Bill Gates is the richest man in the world is no accident.

Of the top ten richest individuals in 2002, nine were citizens with significant corporate identities in the United States and, therefore, were well positioned to be candidates for wealth: Gates (of Microsoft), Warren Buffett (of Berkshire Hathaway), Paul Allen (of Microsoft), Lawrence Ellison (of Oracle), and the Waltons (of Wal-Mart)—Jim, John, Alice, S. Robson, and Helen.[2] Of the top 50 richest people, fully half were Americans, six were German, and one was Japanese. The American culture puts more primacy on rich individuals than do the more communitarian Japanese and German cultures. Even more telling, almost all of the richest 50 individuals were from developed countries—except for two from Hong Kong, two from Saudi Arabia, one from India, one from Kuwait, and one from Mexico.[2]

The United States is not only the biggest, wealthiest economy in the world, but it spawns the biggest and best-endowed companies, which dominate global markets and produce the richest individuals. Gates, born in the United States into a family situation that permitted him to attend Harvard University, was in a profound sense "born rich," despite the talents and efforts that later led to his extraordinary achievement. His father was a lawyer, his mother president of the Junior League. He was socially positioned to have the opportunity to study at a good university. When he went to college, he caught the emerging "Silicon Valley wave," which emerged first in the United States with a long-term social and economic impact comparable to the coming of the industrial revolution in England a century earlier. Thus, Gates did not "drop out" of college as much as he "dropped in" to the cutting edge of the information technology (IT) revolution, which he, in turn, helped to develop, to promote, and to exploit through the creation of Microsoft. He converted a small initial investment in his company into a bonanza with innovative business savvy, a relentless workaholic drive, and winner-take-all competitiveness.

Very few people in the world had the "circumstances, the time, and the country" of Bill Gates, who knew exactly how fortunate he was: "I knew I'd been fortunate and wanted to give something back—not lucky in the sense that I found the code sitting on a desk but in terms of the circumstances, the time, and the country I was born in."[3] What he made of his circumstances was unique, but the stars were lined up to bring unique circumstances together, positioning him for immense opportunity.

It is easy to forget just how far ahead of other rich countries in the world the United States is:

- In terms of Gross National Product (GDP), the United States is *over twice the size* of Japan (number 2), which, in turn, is twice the size of Germany (number 3).

- The United States is first on the "Economic Creativity Index" (measured by technological innovation, technology transfer, and the ease of starting up new firms)—again *by a margin of 2 to 1* over Japan and Germany.

- In terms of "global competitiveness," *The Economist* ranked the United States first in 2002, Germany twelfth, and Japan twenty-sixth.[4]

By the end of the economic boom in 2000, the world had over 7 million people with investable assets of at least $1 million. There were 425 billionaires; 274 of them were American. Silicon Valley's dot-com boom clearly raised the stakes: Thousands joined the ranks of the "mass affluent" with $250,000 to $5 million in investable assets. Thus, to stand out in Silicon Valley called for more wealth—but with no taste required. This threshold in "the Valley," crudely called "f___-you money" (that is, enough to liberate a person from ever having to work again), is estimated to be about $10 million—producing a yearly income of some $500,000.[5] Curiously, in the United States only 13% of Americans say they are rich or have high incomes. Yet households with incomes of $85,000 or more are in the top 20% of the population economically and must be considered "rich" relative to anywhere else in the world, even given the rising costs of living, schools, and health care of these upper-income families.[6]

How rich you feel depends on how rich others are around you and how *they* live. If you meet people who have had more opportunities in life than you have had, you may feel "poor" even though, objectively speaking, you have had more opportunity than the overwhelming majority of the people on the planet. You perceive "competitiveness" to be *your* opportunity deprivation, whereas you are actually more competitive and provided with more life chances than most of humanity. There is a heavy "opportunity cost" in the behavior of the rich toward the poor to the extent that economic opportunities are seized and monopolized in a manner that leaves the poor with higher unemployment and greater dependence. **The way you conceive of maximizing your competitiveness can have the effect of diminishing the life chances of the billions of less advantaged people if your strategy is not widely and generously imagined.** But to be so imaginative in thinking about the impact of your actions on others tends to go against the grain of habit that served to make you wealthy in the first place. The rich who have enough to cover their family's lifetime needs are inclined to keep going—aiming to become "super-rich" (having 1,000 times more than they or their families will ever need).

Rich countries that foster individualism produce rich individuals: The more individualistic the culture, the more wealthy individuals are created. Free-market-oriented societies with private property rights provide abundant opportunities for individuals to increase wealth through innovative entrepreneurship, even if some of this risk-taking behavior at times goes beyond the boundaries of the law. Individuals, if not born rich, usually become so by creating, managing, or investing either in small companies that become big or in just plain big companies.

Big, First, and Well Positioned

Being *big*, *first* to market, and *well positioned* in the richest country with the largest domestic market gives an American company a huge edge. Technology has sped up business cycles, particularly in consumer electronics (where a two-month innovation cycle is not unusual). To innovate or to keep up with rapid technological change, countries must have the required resources. Size often provides a buffer against uncertainty. Hiring the best and the brightest individuals is expensive: Big companies can afford it.

Some people, of course, argue correctly that big companies are notoriously bad at accommodating change. The real key to innovation is the emergence of small firms in a rich primordial soup. Cooking up this soup and keeping it simmering at the right temperature is as much an art as it is a science. Then the company grows and becomes large. At a later stage, when its profits head down and competitors streak by, the big company learns to adapt to the cycles of change or to buy up small, innovative firms in order to stay on the cutting edge. Or it goes bust.

The key to economic power is the learning curve. This creates a challenge for big companies. Lew Platt, former CEO of Hewlett-Packard, once noted how incredible the company *could* be if it only *knew* 30% of what it knew. Companies diffuse their knowledge among people and departments, lose their organizational memories, and often act too fast, failing to bring all the knowledge they have to bear on critical strategic decisions. Individuals function the same way: Albert Einstein noted that most people use only 10% of their brain capacity.

Individual and institutional learning capacity defines competitiveness in a knowledge economy based on technology. Those who can exploit and apply new knowledge and trends early and quickly create competitive advantages. These advantages may become permanent and difficult to reverse in the high-tech global economy. How does one compete with Microsoft's operating system? Intel's chips? Nokia's cell phones? Wal-Mart's virtual organization and economies of scale? Unionized supermarket workers in California went on strike in 2003, fearful they would be pushed out of the middle class as Wal-Mart planned to come in and set up 40 supercenters in the state, paying its workers only half the wages and benefits that the unionized workers received.[7] And what about Dell's just-in-time computer business model? Dell saves immensely on inventory costs by putting together the customized computer for each client only after pocketing the customer's payment in advance. These organizations constantly cut costs and learn quickly. Many companies that would compete with them are at the very beginning of the learning curve without the buffer of a large share of the market. To stay rich is to learn fast from failure in order to lose the least.

As we entered the twenty-first century, of the ten largest businesses by sales in the world (led by General Motors, Wal-Mart, Exxon, and Ford), six were American and four were Japanese. Of the largest 45, 17 were Japanese and 15 American: The largest economies sport the largest companies. Of the ten largest banks in terms of capital, three were American, three were Japanese, one was British, one was French, and one was Chinese. With the possible exception of China with four of the largest banks, of the 46 largest banks in the world, none were in developing countries (Japan again had the most with 10, the United States coming in second with 7).[4]

In terms of stock market capitalization, the United States leads second-place Japan by a factor of almost four. Investors seek the returns promised by the security and innovation of the entrepreneurial culture of the superpower over the uncertainties implicit in the communitarian consensus culture of the Japanese economy. And the security of investing in bigger markets seems to spill over to the security of investing in larger private homes.

Bigger Houses with Fewer People in Them

The richest people tend to have the smallest households (population per dwelling). The wealthiest countries average 2–3 people per household. Although the size of the houses they occupy has gone up, the number of people living in them has gone down. Whether this is a consequence of wealth or the breakdown of the family unit is an open question. Between 1970 and 2000, the size of new American houses, for example, increased more than 50%, according to census data. In 1960, only about one in five homes did not have access to a phone inside or outside the house (shared with neighbors, for example), but by 2000, only one in 50 U.S. homes had no access. Between 1970 and 2000, the size of new single-family homes jumped from 1,500 square feet to 2, 200.[8] And the trend of the day for those who can afford it seems to be to tear down smaller and older existing homes in desirable neighborhoods and build so-called "McMansions" (outsized homes) if for no other purpose than to "keep up with the Joneses."

The average household size is shrinking worldwide. Many more houses are being created with fewer people living in them. This is particularly true in "hot spots" of biodiversity where tremendous pressure is put on nature resources and land: Australia, India, Kenya, Brazil, China, Italy, and the United States. Even in areas of slower population growth, the housing boom and urban sprawl threaten the survival of plants and animals as more land, wood, concrete, and steel are absorbed in the construction. [9] (Of course, household size is relative: Increasing housing stock in countries such as India, China, and Brazil is often part of a program of reducing poverty.)

As can be expected, Bill Gates has one of these mansions in an environmental hot spot outside Seattle. The home, worth at least $60 million, has 40,000 square feet of living space, a 30-car underground garage, a movie theater, a 60-foot indoor pool, and a reception hall that can accommodate more than 120 guests. A telling quotation from *The Great Gatsby* can be found inscribed in Gates's library: "He had come a long way to this blue lawn, and his dream must have seemed so close that he could hardly fail to grasp it."[10] Gates—(Gates-be?)—may be another reincarnation of Gatsby, who would reinvent himself American-style with insatiable material dreams of upward mobility. Gatsby is ultimately a tragic muse. At the novel's end, F. Scott Fitzgerald writes: "Gatsby believed in the green light, the orgiastic future that year by year recedes before us." But this self-absorptive vision of the rich monopolist who would entrap our energy, resources, and time with his latest computer games has hidden costs, even as the technical benefits trickle down. The rich entrepreneur would speed up time while taking it from us in the endless green lights of desire and promises of untapped possibilities. "Technology," as the Swiss novelist Max

Frisch once said to me, "is the art of so arranging life so that you do not have to experience it." We must learn to benefit from technology without becoming totally absorbed by it, as are some lonely souls working out of "virtual computer offices" in their basements. Appreciating this balance is the task of one of the most underestimated aspects of economic development—education.

Education Equals Savings and Investment

The smaller the household, the easier it is to have a surplus for savings and investment. Those who have not yet figured this out face a future of financial insecurity. The wealthier the people, the less they seem to be governed by religious mandates, and the more they seem to know about birth control and the cost and responsibility of children. The more educated they are, the fewer children they tend to have. Of course, in countries that would become rich fast, this trend can have perverse effects. In India, for example, female children are more expensive than males: There is a costly dowry system that does not stop with marriage (usually arranged) but continues throughout life because the husband's family may extort more money from the wife's family as the years go by.[11] Male babies are seen as potential economic boons in China as well, where girls are often aborted due to the country's official one-child-per-family policy.

In the so-called knowledge economy, education is perceived to be the key to self-sufficiency and wealth, not to mention power. This is not to underestimate the role of will power (often due to family sociopsychological support) and financial backing in economic success. The richest countries have over 40% of the relevant age group enrolled in postsecondary education, that is, college degree courses, graduate courses, and courses not leading to a college degree. Thus, Canada, the United States, and Australia have 80% or above of young people enrolled in postsecondary education. The poorest countries, however, are the least literate. These patterns are critical in a knowledge economy in which the level of education and skills may determine your lifetime earnings. In the United States, for example, as the twenty-first century opened, average annual earnings ranged from $18,900 for high school dropouts to $25,900 for high school graduates, $45,400 for college graduates, $54,500 to those with master's degrees, and $99,300 to those with professional degrees. An American male with a professional degree earned $4.8 million on average over a lifetime ($2.8 million for a woman), with a college degree $2.5 million ($1.6 for a woman), and $1.4 million with just a high school degree ($1.0 million for a woman).[12]

The richest nations have the highest levels of postsecondary education. This positions them to be able to take advantage of fast-moving economic and technological trends. Moreover, the dominant countries of the nineteenth and twentieth centuries established traditions of economic and scientific education that resulted in the highest levels of innovation and achievement (perhaps due to their cultures of individual, entrepreneurial drive combined with empiricism—a focus on testing for facts.). Thus, in the twentieth century, the United States dominated the Nobel Prizes in economics, physics, chemistry or physiology, and medicine with 148, followed by the United Kingdom (the dominant power of the nineteenth century) with 67, then by Germany with 46 and France with 21. Japan won only five (in physics and chemistry). Not surprisingly, the American superpower and formerly imperial United Kingdom dominated the Nobel Prizes in economics (taking 32 of the 40 awarded). This could be explained by noting that the prizes usually went to economists with achievements in the "Anglo-American model of capitalism" following the lines of Adam Smith. This Anglo-American model has dominated and propelled the twenty-first-century globalization of the world economy (the revolt of the rich) and established its winners and losers, but its bias is of little consolation to those left out—for example, the 50% of India's children who are malnourished.

What the rich learn from their education is to position themselves to take advantage of inevitable change.

As sociologists have demonstrated, the poor usually see life and change as "fate." Typically, they invest in the lottery, often unaware that the odds against winning are overwhelming. In contrast, the rich prefer investments with better odds and where they can have some influence in controlling the outcomes. Consider, for example, U.S. government's selection of Halliburton, the company Vice President Richard Cheney formerly headed, for billion-dollar contracts to rebuild oil wells in Iraq following the U.S. invasion in 2003. No other companies were permitted to bid for the work. The rich believe that life is not fate but more a question of free will: They are constantly making decisions to try to steer their destiny and to limit downside risks. They are also better able to position their children against downward mobility.

In the late 1990s, sons of the top 20% of the American population in income and occupational prestige gained prestigious positions such as doctors and lawyers even more frequently than did their fathers 30 years before. In terms of socioeconomic opportunity in the United States, 80% of the population became more vulnerable, whereas the top 20% became more secure. The average annual salary in America was $32,522 in 1970. By 1999, it had risen only to $35,864. Meanwhile, in the same time period, the annual compensation of the top 100 CEOs of corporations went from an average of $1.3 million to $37.5 million—1,000 times the average pay of workers. Just before the end of the economic boom of the late 1990s, while the minimum wage in the United States was just above $5 an hour, the wealth of Bill Gates was increasing at an hourly rate of $4 million. Professor Robert Perrucci, a sociologist at Purdue University, summarized the growing gap in the United States: "I am concerned about the volatility of a society where 80 % of the people are frozen out of possibilities."[13] Recall that ancient Rome fell in part because of the blockage of upward mobility—that is, when it no longer became possible for a peasant to become a soldier, which was the route to becoming a Roman citizen. It is not a question of maintaining that everyone has to be equal but of reduced class mobility for the "bottom 80%" of the American society. Professor Perrucci used four indicators of socioeconomic class[14]:

1. Social connections (whom you know)
2. Credential capital (from which school you got your degree)

3. Income (or consumption capital)

4. Investment capital (stocks and bonds)

Let us consider for a moment how those who score the highest on these economic indicators live and what that implies for everyone else.

The Truly Rich Are Really Thrifty

Often, the rich are thrifty to a fault, refusing to waste money or time. They attempt to maximize their return on investment (ROI). Although no doubt some of the well-to-do are excessive spenders (such as those paying over $20 million for a "wow" apartment with a view in Manhattan), most know that the way to wealth is through saving, saving, and more saving.[15] They are good at letting others pick up the tab—including the government and their own organizations. Senator Robert F. Kennedy, for example, was well known for never having any money on him. And to avoid having to dig into his own (deep) pockets, when CEO Jack Welch retired, General Electric agreed to cover his $80,000 Central Park apartment in Manhattan, flowers, maid service, the best seats at the Metropolitan Opera, and tickets for the U.S. Open and Wimbledon, as well as lifetime use of the company jet. Meanwhile, those who want to be seen as rich but do not quite have the necessary resources go heavily into debt. They often display their conspicuous consumption in houses, cars, entertainment, and dress. In contrast, the truly rich are more apt to be understated, seeking to be less visible so as not to cause envy. Bill Gates and Warren Buffett dress simply. The wealthy know that to keep from being kidnapped and robbed, they must fit in with the crowd. Aware of this threat, big multinational companies typically pay $1–$2 million annually for kidnap insurance for their senior executives. Privacy becomes the motto of the very rich.

Millionaires in the United States tend not to dress like millionaires, eat like millionaires, or act like millionaires. As Thomas Stanley and William Danku noted in *The Millionaire Next Door* they even tend to be thrifty concerning items such as the watches and shoes they buy.[16] Sam Walton was the epitome of parsimony: Wal-Mart became the largest company in the world in the early twenty first century because he trained his people to "sweat the details" and to find savings through economies of scale wherever possible. In other countries, savings and hard work are also part of the ethos of becoming rich and staying that way. In Australia, for instance, the rich are not to be outdone in the thrift department. Australia's richest retailer, billionaire Gerry Harvey lives in a comfortable but not ostentatious home and goes around the house turning off lights. He says that he doesn't like to spend money. Another billionaire, Len Ainsworth, who made his mark in the Australian gaming machine industry and who still takes a packed lunch to work, noted: "If *frugal, frugal, frugal* were the title of a song, I would be singing it."[16]

Nor are these Aussies atypical. Billionaire Warren Buffett, perhaps the most successful investor in the United States, has a first principle: "Don't lose money!" His second principle? "Don't forget the first principle." Buffett searches for investments where risk is minimized, if not eliminated. Not surprisingly, he lives in the same modest house he always has in Omaha, Nebraska. Modesty is his policy, and he takes nothing for granted.

One of the richest men in India, Azim Premji is a Stanford University dropout (who recently graduated via correspondence courses). He went home to run the family business, Wipro, when his father died. Known for modesty and a simple lifestyle, he always chooses economy class when he flies. He learned that the future is not what happens to you but what you make of it. Experience taught him not to wait for opportunity to come his way but to actively search for opportunities, seize them when you see them, and accept the certainty of uncertainty.

No doubt there are numerous wealthy people who live extravagantly. But this excessive spending cannot be counted on in making economic projections, given the thriftiness that helped to make so many of this group rich in the first place. As noted before, big spenders tend to be those who would be rich—those who would *appear* to be rich, "the new niche." They often live above their means and are heavily indebted. The spending of the "would-be's" makes the truly rich even richer. Clearly, the domestic and world economies would be worse off if these conspicuous consumers did not over-consume. The motor of the American economy is consumption to the point of overconsumption. This has been the engine the world economy has relied on thus far in the twenty-first century. Con-spicuous consumption is better for national economic growth than conspicuous conservation. This may be the key reason that neither the United States nor Chinese governments worry about the conse-quences when they advocate policies stimulating more of their peo-ple and companies to take on debt.

The paradox here is that the rich help to encourage the creation of more poverty either by *not* spending or by spending on the *wrong* thing. Either the capital doesn't flow or it doesn't go where it is most needed. The super-rich do not tend to put their money on po-tential losers or into areas of high uncertainty; nor do they invest in poor regions. Typically, the well-to-do achieve their wealth by re-ducing their costs and by maximizing their ROI. When they spend money, they usually do it for self-gratification, that is, to reward themselves for hard work or success. This money for celebration usually goes to upper-class clubs, hotels, tours, and restaurants and not to the local economies populated by the poor. Philanthropy usu-ally comes as an afterthought and mostly after becoming firmly es-tablished. And the taxing demands of a global economy that has sped up and become more complicated seems to consume the leisure time necessary to think about anything but the business at hand.

Meanwhile, in the neighborhood next door, middle-class be-havior is influenced by television programs in which "the lifestyle of the rich and famous" is overblown. Working-class and middle-class viewers are absorbed by the rented luxury Italian villa, the elegant clothes, and other materialistic trappings of the popular "Joe Millionaire," in which a working-class fellow is made to ap-pear extremely wealthy in order to lure attractive middle-class women seeking rich husbands in the "reality" television series. At the same time, a doorman working for the wealthy Lincoln Tow-ers in Manhattan while living in middle-class Astoria, Queens, proudly proclaims in an interview that he and his wife eat out every day: This cannot leave him much savings from his salary.[17] The image of the wealthy, through no fault of their own, is exploited by the media to inspire the masses to mimic the illusion of wealth, to overspend, and to undersave in order to have a slice of "the good life" before they shuffle off these mortal coils.

Harried Leisure and Time Deprivation

The richer the country, the more often leisure time becomes hectic, if not reduced in quantity. There is money to buy more things but not the time to use or enjoy them. Several houses, multiple cars, boats, jets, and numerous club memberships often lie unused as the wealthy scurry from place to place. This VIP lifestyle of always needing to be doing "something important" becomes fashionable. The commercial "busyness" spreads. Sleep and recreational areas in major cities are constantly threatened by potential conversion to productive purposes.[18] But while consumption patterns aim to mimic an often distorted image of the rich, family budgeting for health insurance and pension security are falling behind.

In liberal economies such as the United States and Australia, individuals cannot count on generous Social Security, health benefits, or unemployment compensation provided by the state. Therefore, their citizens feel driven to accumulate surplus income and assets to hedge against risks in the life cycle and to cover heavy expenses, such as college tuition for children, medical treatment, and retirement pensions. In their high-earning years, these people are motivated to work longer hours to maximize their income in order to fund their self-knitted safety net. As a result, leisure time shrinks and becomes hectic. These financial and time pressures have increased to the point that the "upper middle class" is uncertain when it has really become "rich," that is, wealthy enough to cover the lifetime needs of the extended family.

The global speed trap that results from globalization has greatly intensified what has always been a time crunch for the developed countries. Economists have pointed out the problem: Although income may become infinite (in theory), time remains finite for each individual on earth. For example, super-rich Mark Mobius, perhaps the world's leading emerging market investment specialist, has a number of homes in different countries of the world but never has time to spend more than three weeks in any one of them in a year. He is too busy traveling from country to country, interviewing managers of companies in which he might want to invest. He still has only the same 24 hours in the day as you and I do. Despite the utility of ownership, he can live in only one place and visit only one country at a time. All the rest of his houses are "wasted" on any particular day in terms of his own pleasure. Indeed, they become costs because he must spend part of his leisure time managing assets that he cannot use at the moment. Even if "having" conspicuous wealth is the objective rather than "using" it, the result is the same—stress.

Thus, one accumulates more things than one can use as wealth increases. Leisure time is reduced and becomes more harried as one runs from one place or asset to another. In the extreme case, which comes up more frequently, individuals are driven to work too hard in their youth, ravaging their health as they struggle to save enough for a house, tuition payments, health insurance, and pensions. There is a constant temptation to sacrifice present leisure time for a future cut short. But despite medical advances, the risk goes up of becoming disabled or dying early from a heart attack due to the stress of overwork before one can even begin to tap retirement savings.

In short, rich countries have more goods than the people living there can consume. And they provide less leisure time to enjoy what one has acquired than do poor countries. They are "time-starved." Family meals are cut short, if they do not disappear completely. Job mobility separates family members from each other due to the time pressure of long working hours in disparate places. Friendships become catch-as-catch-can affairs, given this mobility. Life is a constant process of *becoming* with no time left for *being*. Loneliness is the price paid for wealth: establishing a private Walden designed to separate oneself from others. The time to invite others to come and share the wealth is reduced. Recent trends in the United States, for example, show a noticeable downturn in the number of dinner invitations annually per family. There has also been a fall in the participation in voluntary organizations and club activities.[19] The habit of meeting friends for "dinner and a movie" outside one's home cuts the time for interaction (and obligation) to a minimum. Those who do not bother to go out can replicate the experience by renting a videotape or DVD or watching television (which absorbs at least four hours a day in the life of the average American). More likely than not, the huge modern kitchen in the newly built McMansion will be used for heating up take-out food brought in by one of the two working parents. The super-rich may hire someone to bring in the meal, but the sense of fast-food loneliness reinforced by the absence of other family members may be the same. Some suggest that "we *are* what we eat." This also suggests that we *are* what we take no time to eat. Paradoxically, 60% of Americans are overweight (eating too much of the wrong things too quickly is not what human beings require). Stress caused by the fear of losing one's job due to globalization leads to frustration, which is buffered by eating. And other developed countries are following this trend toward obesity. Development can quickly tilt toward overdevelopment.

Indeed, "too much, too fast" may be the main theme of growing up rich—a natural consequence of living in a wealthy society caught in an accelerating global economy that is overstuffed with opportunity. Should economic and educational opportunities become more fairly distributed, perhaps life would slow down. There would be more time for friendship and community. And diminishing gaps between social classes would dampen motives for the resentment and conflict between people.

References

1. Charles Hampden-Turner, *From Poverty to Dignity* (New York: Anchor/Doubleday, 1974).

2. "The World's Richest People 2002," *Forbes,* December 10, 2002.

3. "Saint Bill," *The Economist*, June 16, 2001.

4. *The Economist Pocket World in Figures* (London: Profile Books, 2002), 24, 56, 58, 60–61.

5. "The New Wealth of Nations," *The Economist*, June 16, 2001.

6. David Leonhardt, "Defining the Rich in the World's Wealthiest Nation," *The New York Times*, January 12, 2003, Week in Review, p. 16.

7. Steven Greenhouse, "Wal-Mart, Driving Workers and Supermarkets Crazy," *The New York Times*, October 19, 2003.

8. "In Census Data, a Room-by-Room Picture of the American Home," *The New York Times*, February 1, 2003.

9. Jianguo Liu, Gretchen Daily, Paul Ehrlich, and Gary Luck, "Effects of Household Dynamics on Resource Consumption and Biodiversity," *Nature*, 421, January 2003, pp. 530–533.

10. "A Tale of Two Bills," *Time*, January 25, 1999, p. 52.

11. David Rohde, "India Steps up Efforts to Halt Abortions of Female Fetuses," *The New York Times*, October 26, 2003.

12. Jennifer C. Day and Eric C. Newburger, "The Big Payoff: Educational Attainment and Synthetic Estimates of Work-Life Earnings," *U.S. Current Population Reports*, (Washington, DC: U.S. Department of Commerce, July 2002) pp. 2–6.

13. Felicia R. Lee, "Does Class Count in Today's Land of Opportunity?", *The New York Times*, January 18, 2003, from Robert Purruci, Professor of Sociology.

14. Robert Perrucci and Earl Wysong, *The New Class Society: Goodbye American Dream?* (Lanham:Lanham,MD: Rowman and Littlefield, 2002).

15. Nadine Brozan, "The Price of 'Wow!' Keeps on Rising," *The New York Times*, September 7, 2003.

16. Thomas Stanley and William Danker, *The Millionaire Next Door* (Atlanta, Ga.: Longsfreet Press, 1996), p. 32.

16. "The Reluctant Spenders," Simon Lloyd, *Business Review Weekly* (Australia), May 18, 2001.

17. Nancy Beth Jackson, "If You're Thinking of Living in Astoria: Accessible, Affordable and Highly Diverse," *The New York Times*, October 19, 2003.

18. Staffan B. Linder, *The Harried Leisure Class* (New York: Columbia University Press, 1970), p. 48.

19. Robert Putnam, *Bowling Alone* (New York: Simon & Schuster, 2000).

4 Pyramids of Opportunity

*These unhappy times call for the building of plans . . .
that build from the bottom up and not from the top
down, that put their faith once more in the forgotten
man at the bottom of the economic pyramid.*

—FRANKLIN DELANO ROOSEVELT,
Radio address, April 7, 1937

*In an era of global turbulence, the well-off are positioned to find oppor-
tunities to become richer on the job, while the poor discover more obstacles
than opportunities.*

**To be born rich in a rich country is to be near the top of a
pyramid of opportunity.** From childhood on, rich people have
food, shelter, and access to quality education, leading to desirable careers. Life chances are *not* left to chance but guided toward upward
mobility by family intervention.

Private tutors are often hired to supplement learning in private
schools, where the admission is very selective and tuition is expensive. Freed from the necessity to work during adolescence, the pupil

has the time to master those subjects that are critical to being accepted at the best universities. Moreover, through the family, the adolescent is connected to educated and influential people who serve as models of social accomplishment (It is not just what you know but *who* you know that counts). President George W. Bush, for example, got into Yale University less because of his academic competence than because of his "legacy" of being from a well-known, wealthy family that was positioned to situate him in a place of social significance. Note that the social hierarchy serves to establish the educational hierarchy, which in turn feeds into the political hierarchy of wealthy nations. Pyramids beget pyramids. Of course, wealth alone is not the only basis for hierarchy. The overwhelming majority of faculty who teach at the top 10 universities in the United States received a degree from one of these same 10 schools: Birds of a feather flock together.

But most individuals are not born at the top of the pyramid of social class in a rich country. As Jean Jacques Rousseau said, "Man is born free, and everywhere he is in chains." In *Émile,*[1] Rousseau noted that human beings are socially weak through adolescence and shaped (trapped) by the institutions in which they find themselves. Rousseau argued that all people, rich or poor, confine themselves through the mores and manners of their society. However, the children of the wealthy are better positioned to take creative risks—to explore their intellectual options and other interests almost without limit. At the natural phase of developing independence, the child needs support, structure, and models of excellence. If one is born rich, one usually receives such support. Moreover, the rich network with each other. Clubs of social support are born.

If a person graduates from one of the top 10 American colleges, he or she is well positioned to be accepted into one of the top graduate schools. Graduates from one of the top 10 ranked graduate schools of business in turn receive an average of three to four job offers. If the individual attends a university that falls into the second tier of 10, the number of job offers typically drops to two or three. Only 8% of those who apply are currently accepted at one of the best graduate schools of business, located not accidentally in the Silicon

Valley (Stanford University). With 92% of the applications rejected, this is a very sharp pyramid indeed.

The most prestigious opportunities for social mobility, in short,
are densely clustered in the educational hierarchy within the United States. There are, of course, abundant possibilities for entrance to
other American universities, which typically lead to jobs of slight-
ly lesser status than those more readily available to individuals with
the top educational pedigrees. The wealthy social democratic nations in continental Europe are more open in terms of admission to
quality public universities (although the few private universities in
Europe often mimic the U.S. model). Nevertheless, the social class
pyramid feeds into the educational pyramid and into professional opportunity in Europe, as well.

In Germany, for example, a child is sorted out at 10 years of age
for the university-track *Gymnasium*. Although it is theoretically possible to enter the *Gymnasium* from the non-university-track schools
at a later phase, few manage to do so. Growing up in a well-to-do,
well-educated family that speaks "high German" (rather than the
local dialect) at home and that sets high educational standards for
children tends to socialize youngsters for the university track. And
even though tuition is free at German public universities and there
is government financial support for those from families below a certain socioeconomic threshold, working-class families still find it
difficult to cover the living costs of a university curriculum that
typically lasts from 6 to 8 years. At the beginning of the twenty-first
century, only 28% of German pupils went on to higher education,
with but 16% emerging with degrees.[2] However, from the non-
university-track schools, many Germans go on to socially respectable
technical apprenticeships in over 400 fields.

Contrast this with the "average" student in the richest country
in the world, the United States: The debt that a student typically accumulates by the end of four years of college studies is the equiva-
lent of the average lifetime earnings of a person in India. Even in the
United States, such debt lingers on heavily and can be decisive when
choosing a career, biasing the choice pragmatically toward a job that
pays enough to get rid of the debt. Americans from working-class

families are starting to calculate whether going to college is "worth it" if to do so would result in such a high debt load to be paid back later on. After all, in the years *before* college, the working-class family (that is, a husband-wife family earning under $38,000 a year) has already spent an average of $121,230 to raise a child to the age of 18. In contrast, families earning over $64,000 a year have spent an average of $242,770 to raise a child to the same age.[3]

However, even well-to-do families with seemingly infinite cushions against uncertainty find social positioning for their own children to be increasingly complex. For example, Jack Grubman, former telecommunications analyst of Citigroup, whose salary was $20 million a year in the booming 1990s, reportedly traded a bullish rating on AT&T stock for help (a $1 million donation) from his boss, Sanford Weill, for the admittance of his two-year-old into the highly selective 92nd Y preschool program in New York City. At the time, Grubman wrote in an e-mail message: "There are no bounds for what you do for your children." Later he summed up the philosophy that led to this temptation, which caused him to have to resign his position: "What used to be a conflict of interest is now a synergy."[4]

Of course, historically, this kind of favoritism of the influential for their offspring has always existed. Medieval kings saw to it that their sons were made cardinals while they were still infants, and senior management positions were often assigned as a form of inheritance before the twentieth century. The rich look after their own. But due to the ideological promises in the emerging modern democratic global society, more openness of opportunity is anticipated by the masses, if not exactly fulfilled by the elites in power.

If it is so difficult and complicated for even wealthy families to steer their children through the obstacles to get them to graduate from the best universities, how much time do rich parents have left over to worry about other children in less fortunate countries? If the world economy sputters, unemployment goes up, student admission to top schools becomes even more difficult, and children from wealthy nations have to compete with the highly educated immigrant youth from abroad (i.e., particularly from India and China), who are willing to work for much less. Competitiveness and insecurities in developed societies stimulated by global turbulence block out perceptions of the poor.

War and national security issues push solutions to social and economic problems in rich countries off the agenda, much less the problems of the poor nations. On the same day in 2003 that President George W. Bush asked Congress for a down payment of hundreds of billions of dollars to pay for the war in Iraq and its aftermath, the School Without Walls, a high school within walking distance of the White House, suffered with leaks in the roof and problems with getting electricity. As Americans focused on the war, the proportion of people in the United States living in poverty was up, and income for middle-class families was down. The President's proposed budget called for a plan that would have made it harder for low-income families to get government benefits, such as tax credits and school lunch assistance. It would also have made it more difficult for frail elderly people on Medicare to appeal if they were denied home health care or skilled nursing care. Bob Herbert of *The New York Times* noted that the commitment of the Bush administration to a war and series of tax cuts for the wealthy that undermine the federal budget had the effect of pushing aside issues that define Americans as a just and humane people.[5] *Obsession with global safety absorbs the resources needed for the domestic safety net.* The emphasis on fear eliminates the focus on health care or basic education.

Globalization has complicated the educational, health, and job structures at home as well as abroad, putting tremendous pressure on all human beings, whether rich or poor. More opportunities are generated by globalization in countries that benefit from its money, technology, and information flows. But the governments of these very countries (such as Japan, the United States, and the members of the European Union) are so overwhelmed by the changes globalization has wrought that they are preoccupied with restructuring their own educational and employment systems. Meanwhile "the shadow people" of the least developed nations slip even more into the shadows.

Global competition makes educational and employment concerns problematic by radically transforming the organizations providing jobs. The nature of work has changed, no longer providing assembly-line jobs that once lasted a lifetime (such as at General Motors) with guaranteed pensions and health benefits. Today, health benefits are often lost if one changes jobs, and pensions are too often dependent on the stock market (or even worse, on one company's stock). Thus, in the United States, 401(k) plans are no longer guarantees of comfortable retirement, as demonstrated by the Enron debacle (which gave pensions to management while regular employees lost both their jobs and pensions). Coping with mind-boggling social transformations due to technology is exhausting. Computer literacy is a prime example of this effort to cope with global change. Another is the pressure put on inefficient banking systems by a globalized economy that enables investors to shift millions of dollars with the click of a computer key.

A Sea Change: Getting Rich on the Job

Just 25 years ago, it was usually not possible to get rich on the job. Indeed, until the 1990s, the conventional wisdom was that becoming rich from a job is like looking for gold in a salt mine. The pay was barely enough to keep up with the house mortgage, schooling, everyday living, and health insurance. Apart from the exception of entrepreneurs who started successful companies, wealth came from investments outside the job.

But for the well-positioned, outside investments are no longer so important. As Cornell economist Robert Frank has noted, it is now possible to become wealthy just by what you earn for doing your job.[6] Not counting salaries or bonuses, between 1997 and 2001, the top five executives at the average U.S. company split about $32 million in profits from exercising stock options. Even excluding the top five, at 100 large American technology companies, the *average* employee made $425,000 by exercising options between 1994 and 2001.[7] After the boom, companies were threatened with downturns, putting their pension plans in peril: Executives were rescued while the pensions of workers were cut. Enron had set up "rabbi" trusts to fund deferred compensation for top executives even as the company went bankrupt. Although 5,000 workers lost their jobs and those still at Enron lost $800 million in their pension funds, the year before the bankruptcy, 100 executives and energy traders made off with $300 million in cash, with over $100 million going to the former CEO, Kenneth Lay.[8] Delta Airlines disclosed that special retirement trusts had been set up for 33 executives, given the turbulence of the industry, whereas employees were told their pensions had to be cut so that the airline could lower its costs. Managers at American Airlines received huge pension payoffs as the company fired workers and was threatened by bankruptcy. Cases like these suggest there was systemic corporate greed at the top, not just a situation of isolated incidents: Different strokes for different folks.[9]

The sudden opportunity to become wealthy on the job resulted from two other changes summed up here:

1. The Reagan-Thatcher pro-market, laissez-faire thrust toward privatization and deregulation that dominated globalization

2. The increasing importance of private capital flows relative to public capital—particularly for the developing countries

Private foreign direct investment to poor countries rose from 0.4% of Gross Domestic Product (GDP) to 2.8% of GDP in the late 1990s. Meanwhile, during the same period, aid to these countries fell by 20%.[10] These changes in the latter half of the twentieth century made large corporations and institutional investors the dominant economic players in the world. Innovation was systematized into routine by large oligopolies—a market structure where a few firms dominate an industry. These imperial economic organizations attracted the best-educated people and became the motors of global economic growth and pyramid building.[11] The state was declassed. The international organization became a halfway house between the state and the private sector. The multinational corporation was king. To own shares (or options on shares) was to share in this dynamic global status system.

It was not as much a question of "greed" that led individuals to desire options on shares as part of their compensation at work. Options signified status in a hectic, go-go competitive environment and provided a buffer of wealth. They created a sense of security in case one was fired from the job. Without a credible government pension system, the individual feels pressured to try to get rich as soon as possible when young, so as not to be left out in the cold in "old age." Conventional stereotypes brand us as "old" at 50 —-often passed over in the hiring process by prospective American employers. In the job roulette that emerged in the booming 1990s, freedom meant wealth, and wealth meant security.

Consider the very peak of economic opportunity in the American pyramid. Between December 1994 and December 1996, the annual growth rate of Internet traffic was about 1,000% annually, doubling every 100 days. The rate then dropped to 70–150% per year, but it was hardly noticed because the herd mentality of the U.S. financial markets kept pumping the boom.[12] In this dot-com expansion, not only did the executives of the biggest 100 New Economy-type companies take away great wealth, but the employees of these startups received $78 billion during the boom.[7] Average investors who "lost" money on this stock market bubble basically transferred wealth to dot-com workers or executives.

However, most employees in the United States, much less elsewhere in the world, do not have stock options. They are not at the top of the pyramid of economic status like the top 100 New Economy firms at their peak (such as Amazon.com and Intel). Workers make do as best they can, going from job to job, putting little aside for retirement. The illusion wears thin that the Social Security system of the state will be enough to cover their health and living expenses when they grow old.

Currently, all rich countries confront a financial crisis in their health care and social security systems: Their governments have not put enough aside to cover their people when they retire, given rising health and living costs, particularly considering the aging Baby Boom generation. The concerns of "the gray panthers" (people over 60) increasingly dominate the political agenda of the wealthy countries, with few solutions in sight. Consider the example of Japan in the

1990s, where concerns about pensions was a key factor in blocking any possibility of radical economic reforms to get the country out of its deflationary slump. As a result of the growing focus on health and pension coverage in wealthy countries—not to mention unemployment or national security threats—government elites in industrialized countries are fully preoccupied with the problems of their own constituents. The well-to-do create the poor by pulling all attention and resources toward their own domestic concerns.

Of course, "poverty" is relative, and in absolute terms, the poor were generally worse off a century ago. Upward social mobility for the poor has been fragmented with the speed-up of globalization and the abuses at the top of the corporate hierarchy. Corporate corruption reflects the "profit" to be made by manipulating fast-moving markets, rather than merely making money through more time-consuming changes. **By keeping the poor from becoming wealthier, the rich stimulate the widening of the gap between the well-to-do and the poor, threatening a breakdown in the global system.** As an example of such breakdown, oil workers from various foreign countries who work in Nigeria for various multinational firms (such as the Canadian subsidiary Bredero Shaw of Shaw-Cor Ltd.) are frequently kidnapped by impoverished groups of militants resorting to violence and ransom demands in order to resolve their grievances.

Innovative oligopolies, based on economies of scale that dominate global markets, are largely unregulated. Such power corrupts. And "hedging," as we shall see, may be the ultimate high-speed strategy of building wealth while shifting the risk to others—the poor.

References

1. Jean Jacques Rousseau, *Émile* (London; J. M. Dent & Sons, Ltd., 1933), p. 48 (French original: 1762).
2. OECD statistics cited in "Dummkopf!", *The Economist*, December 15, 2001, 43.

3. "What it Costs to Raise a Child (to Age 18)," *Expenditures on Children by Families* (Washington, DC: U.S. Department of Agriculture Center for Nutrition Policy and Promotion, May 2001 data).

4. Charlie Rose interview with Manhattan Attorney General Elliot Spitzer, Channel 13, December 18, 2002.

5. Bob Herbert, "Casualties at Home," *The New York Times*, March 27, 2003, A23.

6. David Leonhardt, "Defining the Rich in the World's Wealthiest Nation," *The New York Times*, January 12, 2003, Week in Review, p. 16.

7. Joseph Blasi, Douglas Kruse, and Aaron Bernstein, *In the Company of Owners* (New York: Basic Books, 2003).

8. Arianna Huffington, *Pigs at the Trough,* (New York: Crown Publishers, 2003), p. 12.

9. Theo Francis and Ellen E. Schultz, "As Workers Face Pension Cuts, Executives Get Rescued," *Wall Street Journal*, April 3, 2003.

10. The World Bank, *Global Development Finance: Financing the Poorest Countries. Analysis and Summary Tables* (Washington, DC: The World Bank, 2002), p. 1.

11. William J. Baumol, *The Free-Market Innovation Machine: Analyzing the Growth Miracle of Capitalism* (Princeton, NJ: Princeton University Press, 2002).

12. Michael Lewis, "The Vilification of the Money Class," *The New York Times Magazine*, October 17, 2002, pp. 48–49.

5 Corporate Wealth and Hedging

The fox knows many things,
but the hedgehog knows one big thing.

—ARCHILOCHUS
(c. 710–676 B.C.) Fragment 103

T*he rules and opportunities of hedging are different for rich individuals and corporations.*

Pyramids of economic opportunity have become corporate pyramids, and the rich tend to become incorporated to protect themselves. This is in no small part a consequence of the revolt of the rich, led particularly by the Reagan-Thatcher privatization and deregulation policies of the 1980s. The freedom from restrictions first benefited multinational companies: They sped up the global economy, which in turn gained momentum with the Internet-led dot-com boom of the 1990s. Competitive pyramids of influence became more complex. Foreign aid for poor countries was increasingly replaced by private capital flows of direct investment by companies and by portfolio investment of large institutional investors, such as pension funds. Economic, social, and psychological support shifted even faster away from the poorest developing countries (unless they had oil reserves) and was targeted at emerging winners by multinational companies, who silently took over the most powerful position of all in the globalized economy. Indeed, 300 multinational companies account for 25% of the world's assets.[1]

To the extent that world capital and trade markets are deregulated, multinational corporations have more freedom to operate—for better or for worse. Corporations are the powerhouses of economic growth. Countries such as Ireland prosper when they successfully lure foreign companies with tax incentives, competitive wages, quality education, and English language skills. Indeed, Ireland attracts one quarter of the high-tech investment of the United States into Europe, although it makes up but 1% of the European population.[2] Foreign direct investment (FDI) is perceived to be the key to national wealth and higher employment.

Multinational companies in a fast-moving, globalized economy naturally seek to increase their returns and to reduce their costs. Typically, they attempt to concentrate their official earned income in countries with the lowest tax rates. For example, it is no accident that all the major banks of the world have subsidiaries in the Cayman Islands, where virtually no taxes are charged for the business they transact there. Furthermore, corporations often underinvoice where taxes are high and overinvoice where taxes are low. Moreover, sales of multinational corporate affiliates are twice as high as world exports. In the United States, tax burdens on individuals have gone up in the past few decades, while corporate taxes have dropped. In 1965, corporate taxes made up 4% of Gross Domestic Product; by 2000, this number dropped to 2.5%.[3]

Rich individuals can use their knowledge of the legal structure of corporations to find tax loopholes or even to transform themselves into corporations, where the tax burden is lower. As Robert Kiyosaki observed in *Rich Dad, Poor Dad,* a corporation is little more than a legal body without a soul.[4] Specifically, it need not be a "thing" but merely a set of legal files in a folder in a lawyer's office registered with a state government agency. Anybody can play, but only the rich know about it and hire the best lawyers and accountants to take advantage of the rules.

Government administrations dominated by wealthy interest groups push for policy extremes favoring these constituencies so that when legislative compromises are completed, the outcome is still a significant victory for the rich. The tax-cutting strategy of the Bush administration heavily favoring the very richest is an illustration. Although the promise of tax reduction was attractive to many voters who assumed the cuts applied to them, Bush's tax proposals disproportionately benefited the top 1% of income earners in the United States. The message implied was that all good citizens should strive to find ways to reduce the money they pay the government as much as they can. For example, the initial proposal to eliminate all taxes on dividend income would have brought a projected tax savings for the top 1% of income earners to $24,000 for the year, compared with an average annual savings of $226 for the bottom 80%[5] The final law, which cut the tax on dividends from 20% to 15%, had the same effect on a more modest scale. It benefited mainly those who could afford to hold individual dividend-paying stock outside of their pensions. Once passed, the dividend tax reductions were scheduled to be dropped after five years—in place just long enough to benefit wealthy supporters in order to help finance the reelection campaign of President George W. Bush. Meanwhile, the war in Iraq was to be funded separately. Most states in the United States (which are not allowed to go over their budgets) were so short of tax dollars they had to cut back on health, education, and police services of vital importance to the life chances of the poor (never mind the life chances of future generations, who will find their Social Security and health benefits in jeopardy because of the growing national debt). The Bush administration neglected the long-term interests of American citizens for the sake of short-term political considerations.

The administration of President Ronald Reagan was even more extreme in this strategy in the early 1980s. The administration deliberately asked for 10% more for the defense budget than it believed it would need, figuring it would have to lower the amount in a compromise with Congress. The administration's financial "guru" who finalized the proposal, David Stockman, made an additional 10% error. As a result, the U.S. Congress passed a defense budget 20% higher than President Ronald Reagan actually planned on receiving. His popularity was so high that he got everything he asked for without having to compromise as anticipated. Although this spending pushed the Soviet Union off the map as a superpower, one cannot help but wonder whether the Cold War could have been won at a significantly lower cost.

Typically, the rich and powerful prefer to overspend as a form of "insurance" on their policy objectives, rather than to take any chances of failure. For example, when the Bank of New York required a federal bailout due to bad real estate loans, regulators discovered that although the bank's balance sheet showed $33 billion in total assets, it had $36 billion in various "off-balance-sheet" derivatives instruments. As a form of "insurance" for speculators, the rich are sold "derivatives"—or financial contracts based on the volatile swings in value of other financial holdings.[6]

* * *

The corporate elite, whether individuals or companies, naturally strive to hedge their bets. As risks increase in an era of uncertainty and diffusion, hedging becomes even more attractive. Having nothing to fall back on, the poor cannot afford to hedge and, therefore, are more vulnerable to risks. Hedging is a strategy of wanting to have things both ways. If, for example, a certain set of one's stocks goes up, one should have a share of this profit; if, on the other hand, another set of stocks goes down, by selling "short," one should also be able to profit. Such stock hedging is done through "options," which allow speculators to buy ("call" options) or sell ("put" options) a stock at a set price within a specified time period. If hedging sounds too complicated for everyday investors to understand, that is because often it is meant to be. Secrecy reigns where hedging is concerned, and it is a strategy designed for the rich.

Take an example that makes the strategy clear: the Rockefeller family. In the traditional two-party system of the United States, the wealthy Rockefellers surmised that either a Democrat or a Republican would win in any particular presidential election. Therefore, to hedge against the risk of losing family influence in case the "wrong" party won, the Rockefeller family made sure that it had political activists or candidates working in *both* parties. The rich, after all, can stay rich if they preserve the status quo. To hedge against either of two possible outcomes means that the rich win, whether the coin comes up heads or tails. You buy 10 of the best stocks in the world (betting they will go up) and "short" 10 of the worst stocks (betting they will go down): If nothing out of the ordinary goes wrong, you should do well.

Warren Buffett, the most successful living American investor, urged caution. Buffett was suspicious of the popularity of hedge funds, referring to them as "the Holy Grail" and noting that a "hedge fund" is "nothing but a name." Buffett's principle, you may recall, is "never to lose money" (a rich man's strategy if there ever was one). To fulfill this principle, Buffett suggests:

1. Buying only investments that one understands

2. Buying a very limited set of stocks of companies one understands at a moment of discounted value

3. Getting onto the company boards that issue those stocks, or "close" to these companies, so as to be in a position to know best when to buy and sell shares

In short, Buffett believes in leaving as little as possible to chance.[7] What is important is not to mistake the *instrument* of a hedge fund (which may be risky if one is not clear what it is investing in) with a common-sense *strategy* of hedging one's risks against possible loss.

The idea is to figure out how to reduce risks on the downside while positioning oneself to take advantage of gains on the upside. Companies do this by striving for monopoly situations in which they lower risk on the downside by keeping lower-cost competitors from entering their game. This can be done by lobbying the government to get favorable legislation. For example, such lobbying in the Clinton administration led to telecommunications legislation in 1996 that set aside one third of American radio stations for "media consolidation," just as Federal Communications Commission (FCC) rules have resulted in six big television stations that dominate the U.S. market. One company greatly benefiting from this consolidation was Clear Channel Communications, the largest U.S. radio broadcaster, which dominates the radio programming of many regions and local areas throughout the United States.[8]

The wealthy individuals behind Clear Channel are not content with corporate strategies to minimize risks and maximize profits. They also have used complicated but legal hedging strategies to protect and advance their own financial positions.

For example, in 2002, B. J. McCombs, a cofounder and director of Clear Channel, cashed in over half of his stock, worth about $260 million. By using a popular technique among corporate insiders called a *variable prepaid forward* with an unidentified bank, McCombs was able to cash out the shares without officially having to sell them. This silent strategy prevented shareholders in the company from becoming fearful of holding stock because one of the big owners was dumping his shares. The bank pays McCombs cash—about 80 cents per dollar—on the shares, which he promises to sell to the bank over the next couple of years. Meanwhile, McCombs is permitted to vote some of the "sold" shares at the annual meeting of the company; he profits from a certain percentage of the gain if the shares go up in value; and he can defer tax payments until the shares are officially sold. This is just one example of a quiet, sweet hedging strategy available for the extremely wealthy.[8] Of course, it is important to distinguish a malevolent form of hedging such as the Clear Channel case from the legitimate strategy of hedging to preserve what one owns.

To make it easy for the wealthy, a growing number of hedge funds have been organized. These are not "mutual funds" but, in the domestic United States, are usually conceived of as "investment limited partnerships." The investors are the limited partners, and the general partner is the manager of the fund. The greatest advantage of these funds is that they are largely unregulated by the government. The government elite figure that rich investors are smart enough to take care of themselves and will still have lots of wealth left over, even if they do get in trouble. Typically, the tax law requires hedge funds to have a limited number of investors (or limited partners), who must be "qualified purchasers." To be a "qualified purchaser" usually means that the individual must have a net worth of at least $5 million.

What is most interesting about hedge funds is that they can take opposite investment positions at the same time to balance risk and presumably profit from their superior models and techniques, whether the overall market goes up or down.

There is a notorious case of a hedge fund with supreme confidence in its own ability to secretly and dynamically hedge one position against another to reduce downside risks and bring in handsome returns: Long-Term Capital Management (LTCM).

LTCM was the biggest hedge fund in the United States. Made up of some of the smartest people (from expert money managers to Nobel Prize economists), it was organized in the laid-back, wealthy town of Greenwich, Connecticut. This fund hedged billion-dollar bets all over the world, all of which were backed by the ultimate hedge: The fund managers knew they were too big to be allowed to fail by their wealthy investors and even by the government itself. Its speculative investments, added together, ultimately amounted to a trillion-dollar bet that might bring down confidence in the whole global financial system if it failed.

LTCM was the pyramid's pyramid, which attracted many well-heeled institutional investors in the 1990s. The company's founder was John Meriwether, a legendary bond trader with a major Wall Street firm who left under controversial circumstances. He took a group of the best people with him to set up his own company. Meriwether knew that the key to the investment game was legitimacy—attracting the best and the brightest, who would in turn bring in the wealthiest customers like pied pipers. He persuaded two Nobel Prize winners in economics, Myron Scholes and Robert C. Merton, to join him. They were awarded the Nobel Prize in 1997 for—you guessed it—a theory of dynamic hedging. This theory was transformed into a formula for pricing stock options. All symbols that could not be measured were dropped out of this formula, leaving only the level of risk as unmeasurable. Merton then borrowed a brilliant theory of continuous time from a Japanese rocket scientist, Kioshi Ito. Ito needed to plot the trajectory of rockets. So he divided time into infinitely small parcels, which permitted him to smooth it out—the notion of continuous time. Merton figured if two risky positions taken in opposite directions were plotted together over continuous time, risk could more or less be eliminated, or smoothed out, and the investment results would return to their historical patterns.

LTCM took this insight and applied it to investment bets taken all over the world in all kinds of economic sectors. To be a player in the game, the minimum investment was $10 million, and the money could not be withdrawn for three years. Many well-known investment firms joined this unique club, this giant hedge fund, because their managers had studied under either Professor Myron Scholes at Stanford University or Robert Merton at Harvard University, or because they had read their books. The fund was legitimized by their knowledge and reputation. The investors trusted them so much that they did not demand to challenge the fund's secrecy agreement and learn where the investments were actually going, how much was really at stake, or who all the other investors were. The assumption was that this fund understood the risks of the world and could hedge them against each other to find an equilibrium—some kind of peace and security for the investor. Peace from profits. At first, the strategy worked. In the first year, the fund returned 20%; in the second, 43%; and 41% in the third. Then other firms started to figure out what LTCM was up to and mimicked its behavior. Suddenly, there was less room to exploit small market deviations. With the same level of assets, there was less capital. This meant that if trouble arrived, the fund would be much more vulnerable, given its large diversification strategy.

Trouble came. It started with the meltdown of the currency of Thailand, where banks had taken in more capital than they were able to process, given investor enthusiasm with "emerging markets" of hot economic growth. When the large investment institutions pulled their money out, they did it all at once. These unregulated, globalized withdrawals spilled over to other emerging market countries, resulting in the Asian financial crisis of the late 1990s. Then something happened that was not typical of historical patterns and interrupted the assumption of the stability of continuous time—Russia defaulted on its debts. This was something that the models of LTCM in Greenwich had not anticipated.

In the fourth year, the returns of LTCM fell to 14% as others copied its strategy. When the Russian default occurred, LTCM started to go into a tailspin, losing $100 million a day until the breaking point, when it lost $500 million in a single day. LTCM was bailed out by a rescue effort organized by the New York branch of the Federal Reserve Board—a $3.65 billion rescue by 14 banks and brokerage houses. After preaching to the rest of the world about the evils of crony capitalism—that is, bailing out rich, well-connected insiders while letting the masses of people suffer—crony capitalism came to flourish in the United States with the bailout of LTCM.[9] The company was simply too big to be permitted to fail because of the global financial meltdown it could have set off. As economist John Maynard Keynes once observed, *if you owe your bank a thousand dollars and cannot repay it, you have a problem; but if you owe the bank 10 million dollars and cannot repay it, the bank has a problem.*

The super-rich know this principle well: At times, they leverage their risk by betting that the government or other big investors will have to step in and bail them out if the risk goes bad because the investment is so big. There is little to suggest that these large financial risks do much to help the poor. Indeed, when they go belly up, wealthy investors are often bailed out (even while losing some of their money), whereas the masses of the people are struck with a sudden downturn in the economy and loss of jobs and income. It is but a short step from legitimate, although complex, hedge funds to outright schemes of fraud designed to take advantage of those new to the speculative temptations of capitalism.

When governments become corrupt, this same principle of taking huge risks with the money of unsuspecting investors can turn into pyramid schemes, such as emerged in the mafia-ridden country of Albania in the late 1990s. Sometimes called "Ponzi" schemes, one of these investment opportunities, approved by the government, promised investors 20–50% return on their money in a "fund" in six months with absolutely nothing behind it. The managers pocketed some of the money from new investors and paid back the rest as "high interest rates" to old investors. This worked fine until there were no more new investors. Then the house of cards fell down, and thousands of people in Albania lost their lifetime savings. Falsely identifying the shift to "casino capitalism" in their country with mere speculation, Albanians were set up to be taken advantage of. This led to a total breakdown of law and order as people protested violently by breaking into public buildings to look for some return on their investment.[10]

In 2003, two million victims in the Philippines lost over $2 billion in the biggest pyramid fraud in Philippine history. It struck all classes—poor folks, wives of overseas workers, policemen, military officials, and politicians. Some reports suggest that the millions of dollars the police and military officials invested came from funds designated for intelligence work. The interlocking set of pyramid schemes worked since 1998 because of the complicity of banks that accepted huge deposits without asking questions. It all started with simple requests for $750 for investment in Multitel Telecoms Investors Corporation, which used one's person's money to pay off another at a high rate of return until no new investors could be found and the scheme collapsed—along with the lifetime savings of thousands of people who could ill afford it.[11] Global casino capitalism arrives in developing countries without the financial education necessary to cope with it or the regulation to prevent it from taking the poor on a ride to greater poverty.

* * *

Given the spectacular crash of LTCM, not to mention the outright fraudulent Albanian and Philippine pyramid schemes, have hedge funds lost their allure?

Hardly. As William J. Crerand summed up in *Fundamentals of Hedge Fund Investing* (1998), "Pirate ships of old were a bit like today's hedge funds, if you can imagine a bunch of wealthy investors outfitting a ship and sharing the spoils with the crew."[12]

In the towns of Greenwich, Stamford, and Westport, all located in Connecticut, billion-dollar hedge funds quietly and secretly make millions of dollars for themselves and their investors. Of almost 6,000 American "investment partnerships," perhaps a dozen and a half have more than 50 employees. Those with over a billion dollars to manage are in the big leagues. Typically, the fund's manager pockets 1% of the fund's assets and 20% of the profits. One notorious big-league player, Steven Cohen, takes 25–50% of the profit for himself.

Cohen runs SAC out of southwestern Connecticut, a $4 billion hedge fund that has generated high returns even during the down years after the economic boom ending in 2000. Closed to new investors, his firm practices a technique called "information arbitrage"—getting information on the cheap in one place and selling it at a premium somewhere else. SAC is rumored to generate as much as 1% of the trading on the New York Stock Exchange every day. In return, Cohen expects to be the first to get the best information from banks. This includes what is termed the "first call" by a salesperson who has a large block of stock for sale. By setting himself up to get a predominant number of the "first calls," Cohen manages to edge out the competition.

Hedge fund managers often prefer investing to actually running a business. Thus, they are "entrepreneurs" in Harvard Professor Howard Stevenson's sense of "pursuing opportunities without regard to the resources they currently control."[13] Entrepreneurship can be seen as targeted "free-rider" behavior. A hedge fund may grow a lot in the first couple of years, paying off the entrepreneur handsomely at 20% of the profits. Then it may decline for a year or two, with a snowball effect when rich investors pull out fast as they see their returns go down. Because the entrepreneur sees no more payoff, he or she shuts down the hedge fund and starts another, rather than having to work the old one out of the hole with little personal profit. This "cut-and-run" free-rider strategy can hurt everyday workers, who may not even know that their pensions are partly tied up in such hedge funds.

For example, the state of California's Calper's fund of $133 billion put $550 million into hedge funds, including $50 million alone into Andor Capital of Stamford, Connecticut. Most of California's retirees living off the fund are not aware of the potential risk of this strategy. A spokesman for the Pennsylvania State Employees' Retirement System, PennSERS, said that the $2.5 billion (or 12% of its assets) put into hedge funds are invested in "funds of funds."[14]

Hence, super-rich hedge fund managers are able to take their entrepreneurial risks on the backs of relatively poor retirees (i.e., those of California and Pennsylvania) without these former retirees being aware of the risks involved. Secrecy, after all, is one of the critical ingredients of successful hedge funds. There is little government regulation because this kind of casino capitalism is thought to be good for economic growth. Everyone involved is supposed to be sophisticated enough in financial matters to take care of themselves, which is clearly not the case. Nevertheless, efforts by the Commodity Futures Trading Commission in 2000 and the U.S. Congress in 1999 to regulate large commodities-trading "pools" and hedge funds met with successful resistance from fierce lobbying by the industry. Huge amounts of money are paid to lawyers and lobbyists to get the American legislature to do the easiest thing of all—nothing.[15]

Although hedge funds underperformed in the economic boom of the late 1990s, they produced steadier returns than many stock mutual funds in the bear market thereafter, drawing more people to them.[16] The entry price dropped to $100,000 in "funds of funds"— funds that invest in a number of hedge funds. This seemed like the ultimate diversification of risk in a highly uncertain world economy. The false promise of a "risk-free" place for investment attracted numerous unsuspecting investors who were unaware of the high expense costs resulting from investing in a basket of hedge funds. Nor were they aware of the ever-present possibility that one extremely unlikely event (such as Russian default) could totally wipe out their "conservative" hedging and their money.[17]

The hedge fund phenomenon illustrates the complexity of the global speed trap of capitalism: Even relatively well-off investors do not understand what these "funds of funds" really do and often suffer losses accordingly. To be modern, emerging nations set up their own "hedge funds," often with public money or even more precious pension money and over time risk losing it all in fraudulent pyramid schemes or in legitimate but sophisticated financial instruments they do not understand. Collective learning processes cannot keep up with the speed of technological or financial innovation, and the people who lose the most are the poorest people at the bottom of the hierarchy. Working or middle-class investors who understand the least and wait too long before taking their money out set themselves up to lose from such high-risk investments. Powerful financiers deliberately create financial investments so complex that they alone have enough knowledge of what is going on to have a temporary sense of control. The mass of investors, lured by promises of "get-rich-quick" capitalism, set themselves up for almost certain losses. The only certainty is that money invested in such speculative schemes is not apt to trickle down to the poor.

References

1. Noreena Hertz, *The Silent Takeover: Global Capitalism and the Death of Democracy* (New York: The Free Press, 2001), p. 33.

2. Jeff Saperstein and Daniel Rouach, *Creating Regional Wealth in the Innovation Economy: Models, Perspective, and Best Practices* (Upper Saddle River, NJ: The Financial Times/Prentice-Hall, 2002), p. 61.

3. Nanette Byrnes and Louis Lavelle, "The Corporate Tax Game," *Business Week*, March 31, 2003, p. 80.

4. Robert Kiyosaki, *Rich Dad, Poor Dad* (New York: Warner Books, 2000),p.99.

5. Bill Moyers, *NOW with Bill Moyers*, Public Broadcasting System,, March 30, 2003.

6. David C. Korten, *When Corporations Rule the World* (West Hartford, CT: Kumarian Press, 1995), p.200.

7. Robert G. Hagstrom, *The Warren Buffett Way* (New York: John Wiley & Sons, 1995).

8. Andrew Ross Sorkin, "Insiders Cash Out, but Don't Quite Sell," *The New York Times*, April 6, 2003, B10.

9. Allan Sloan, "What Goes Around," *Newsweek*, October 12, 1998, p.32.

10. Thomas Friedman, *The Lexus and the Olive Tree* (New York: Anchor Books, 2000), pp..155–157.

11. Carlos H. Conde, "Investors in Philippine Pyramid Scheme Lose Over $2 Billion," *The New York Times*, March 30, 2003.

12. William J. Cerrand, *Fundamentals of Hedge Fund Investing,* the McGraw-Hill Companies, May 1998.

13. H. H. Stevenson, M. J. Roberts, and H. J. Grousbeck, *New Business Ventures and the Entrepreneur*, (Homewood, IL: Irwin, 1989)

14. Andy Serwer, "Where the Money's Really Made," *Fortune*, Vol. 147, No. 6, March 31, 2003, p. 107.

15. Gary Weiss, "Hedge Funds vs. the SEC: The Industry has Crushed Previous Regulatory Attempts," *Business Week*, March 3, 2003.

16. Martin Gross, "Tame Wolves?" *Barron's,* Vol. 83, No. 9, March 3, 2003.

17. J. P. Daloz, "Are Hedge Funds but a Mere Illusion?," Working Paper, CERAM, Sophia Antipolis, France, February 21, 2002.

6 The Global Speed Trap: Diversifying to Ward Off Losses and Old Age

"If everybody minded their own business," said the Duchess in a hoarse growl, "the world would go round a deal faster than it does."

—LEWIS CARROLL,
Alice's Adventures in Wonderland (1865)

As the rich become more preoccupied with planning for their own life chances, given global complexity, the poor are apt to find it more difficult to find support.

Mark Twain said you should put all of your money in one basket and keep your eyes on that basket. But Twain was an unlucky speculator and lost in most of his impulsive investments. Wealthier folks are taught not to put all of their eggs into one basket. They diversify. This is a defensive strategy aimed at avoiding losses even though it results in merely moderate gains. It is, in fact, the hedging strategy we examined in Chapter Five. The rich prefer to stay rich. Therefore, they look to avoid the downside in their return on investment

(ROI). Meanwhile, the way investments in the poorest countries are structured, these options look more like downside risk than profitable returns. And to go into a country, venture capital needs an "exit strategy" to bring the money home eventually: That is, the venture capitalist makes money not by putting investment in but by taking it out. Such exit strategies are hard to imagine in many developing nations, particularly after the end of the hot era of venture capital, with the popping of the dot-com bubble in the late 1990s.[1]

This chapter illustrates:

- How innovative multinational corporations have sped up economic life
- Why rich people in rich countries will become even more preoccupied with their own pensions, health, and life chances
- The consequence: State foreign aid for the poorest countries is apt to become increasingly difficult to obtain in the future.

The emerging global crises in health, environment, and security from terrorism will not easily be contained by either existing private investment patterns or conventional, democratically based government policies.

How the Global Economy Is Speeding Up

If the wealthy or the institutional investors representing the wealthy (such as large pension funds) notice that their ROI is threatened by uncertainty, much less financial meltdown in a developing country, they will cut their losses and pull their money out overnight. This is what happened in Thailand in 1997. Chasing high returns from "emerging market" stocks, more money came in than the Thai banking and corporate system could cope with. The regulations governing these institutions were obscure, and corrupt "crony capitalism" dominated many transactions. The Thai currency started to lose credibility, and the big pension funds and private investors pulled their money out fast, causing a collapse of the Thai economy, having a domino effect throughout Southeast Asia, and spilling over even to other emerging markets in Latin America and Eastern Europe. The U.S. government and the International Monetary Fund intervened to bail out these economies and to stem the crises but at a heavy cost in terms of loss of economic growth, social unrest, and unemployment because of the stringent conditions imposed by these financial elites.

Globalization has sped up the ability both to invest and to withdraw funds to such an extent that even financial experts and advisors have a hard time keeping up with the volatility of the markets. Previous investments by the wealthy in the development of communications, technology, and financial systems made this speed possible. After all, the largest investments in research and development are done by the big oligopolies (the few firms dominating their sectors of the economy). In the United States, 70% of U.S. investment in research and development (R&D) is made by corporations. Of over 34,000 American firms that spend money on R&D, 46% of the total is spent by just 150 firms. Such investment has increased the tempo of information processing and, therefore, of economic life to such a degree that the human mind can hardly comprehend it. As economist William Baumol noted, in the past 35 years, the "clock speed" (operations per second) of one of Intel's microchips has gone up 3 million percent; the number of transistors embedded in a chip has gone up by 10 million percent; and the number of transistors that can be purchased for one U.S. dollar has gone up by 5 *billion* percent.[2]

It is no secret that Intel maximizes innovation to speed up its chips while lowering the cost per chip to increase its global market share. This ability to outspend its rivals in innovation permits Intel to maintain its competitiveness. But Intel leaves nothing to chance and moved manufacturing plants out of the United States to Malaysia, Ireland, and Israel, where the labor is well trained but significantly cheaper, also permitting Intel to be closer to some of the markets it wants to serve. So chip speed goes up, the cost of information goes down, labor costs are kept low, competitors are kept at bay, and everywhere you look at a computer, there's "Intel Inside." Intel, in short, becomes an ubiquitous brand—spread out everywhere as a high-tech fashion label, surrounding the computer industry as effectively as a medieval moat around a castle.

Nor does this high-speed, innovative processing stop with the computer sector. Electronic commerce also served to speed up the steel industry, accelerating the trend toward a more centralized global marketplace for steel. The supply chain is streamlined by this electronic technology, giving customers real-time information about mill manufacturing. And with speed comes a cut in transaction costs.[3] The result: Too much steel is produced in the world, leading to widespread layoffs and pushing steel workers who cannot learn any other trade so late in life into poverty.

What emerged in the late twentieth century was the "virtual organization": collective learning networks that can almost instantaneously produce and deliver products and services at any time, in any place, and in any variety in order to provide customer satisfaction. By mastering speed, the virtual corporation creates processes so functionally specific and user-friendly that they are irresistible. These organizations aim for fast, targeted, knock-out quality. The future is your future, made to order: You can see it, taste it, touch it, buy it. Wal-Mart, the world's largest company, for example, used the virtual organization model when each regional store was ordered to analyze purchase receipts every week and to reorder customized inventory to offer a variety of some 110,000 choices of goods in different colors, styles, and types at a typical outlet.[4] Nonunionized Wal-Mart overwhelmed its competition, such as the more traditional Sears chain stores, and pushed unions to make a desperate last-ditch effort to hold on to the salaries and benefits of the workers of competitors. Unemployment waxes as competition wanes.

But corporations do not limit their innovative efforts to the private sector alone.

Wealthy interest groups have also quickened the economic tempo by using the democratic voting system to their advantage, keeping the economic game from being regulated: They helped to elect conservatives backed by antiregulation interest groups and organized hedge fund lobbyists. In the process, they facilitated the creation of an accelerated global economy that is spinning out of control. In *Infectious Greed*,[5] Frank Partnoy demonstrates that there is a systemic problem: Global financial markets are out of control. George Soros, the super-rich hedge fund manager, has confirmed this unpredictability of financial markets, arguing that the extreme rules of capitalism that allowed him to become rich from these markets in the first place should not exist in an "open society." Moreover, these rules cause economies in the emerging markets of the poor countries to suffer from both capital outflows *and* from higher borrowing costs.[6] Because money managers sense this growing uncertainty, they often adopt even more conservative, defensive strategies of diversification to assure that their clients do not lose money. And some of these customers have a great deal of wealth at risk.

The stakes in becoming rich have gone up—requiring billions instead of millions. The global speed trap—this high-speed, innovation machine—has made decision making more complex, increasing the difficulty in positioning yourself and your children well in this world. Old-boy networks have been upstaged by dot-com millionaire upstarts in their thirties who themselves have created so-called new-boy networks. The language of the Internet is more quickly absorbed and exploited by the speculative, young techno-elite. The key information that is power is no longer neatly kept for long behind heavy, closed doors.

In short, the young rich are in the fast lane, putting pressure on the old rich to speed up their way of working if they want to compete. As Intel's CEO Andy Grove put it in *Only the Paranoid Survive*, the old elite are becoming increasingly paranoid. Grove playfully suggests a "positive" form of paranoia in order to head off excessive optimism and to be alert to the next new competitor or product in the inevitable process of creative destruction of capitalism. He argues for organizational defensiveness and flexibility to ward off unplanned change.[7]

Of course, in some quarters, these dynamic patterns have met with fierce cultural resistance. Or, put differently, just as some companies thrive on innovation, there are organizations that succeed by relying on the preservation of an historical repertoire. The New York Stock Exchange proudly continues to use real people to do the trading on the floor of the Exchange, rather than becoming fully "digitalized." Habits change slowly. The University Club in New York City still demands ties and no paperwork or briefcases on the dinner table: It tries to slow down the pace of things.

Attention Deficit Disorder: Metaphor for Cultural Disintegration?

As the economy speeds up, becoming more complex, the rich have the resources to cope. They seek out buffers against change and "future shock." Psychotherapists, Zen gurus, exotic vacation spots, and luxury health clubs massage their *angst* generated by the cultural disintegration resulting from the increasing tempo of global innovation. Rather than organizing to slow things down, the rich are preoccupied with the increasing complexity of managing to keep up with the pace of globalization. They seek to postpone inevitable physical losses and death through sophisticated distractions.

The wealthy are torn between too many interests and objectives at once. The syndrome of attention deficit disorder has become a widespread cultural phenomenon—a metaphor for not being able to concentrate very long or to dwell at doing anything. Not only has leisure become hectic, but "hectic" itself has become a normal state of being, a habit. The "power lunch" among the movers and shakers in Washington, D.C. means no time for lunch, given a very crowded schedule. Households with two parents working full time have no "quality time" to spend with their latch-key children. Vacations are skipped or cut short. And individuals spend hours "surfing the Web" to see what is on the Internet or shifting back and forth between a hundred channels on the television set. And the action entertainment on those media has increased to a hectic pace, mimicking technology. Even the music of Mozart and Beethoven is usually played today at a tempo that seems to collapse the space between the notes. In the area of private investment, because stock markets are open somewhere in the world at any given time, global traders find themselves tempted to stay awake 24 hours a day to follow the rapid global shifts of money.

As speed has increased, so has the sense of chaos and unpredictability. Experiments have shown that if rats are overstimulated, they get confused in a maze and cannot find their way out. Globalization seems to be having this effect on all people from all walks of life. Thus, as Harvard economist Benjamin Friedman has pointed out, although 20 years ago there was a high correlation between increased wealth and happiness, today this correlation breaks down. This is largely due to higher expectations stimulated by the global media.[8] To live a simple life is illusive for someone who wants to become rich: Simplicity contradicts the global system and the nature and tempo of the times.

Given the secularization of developed societies, one of the problems is that there is no limit to the desire for upward mobility—socially or economically. In an uncertain global era when anything can happen, what does it mean to be "rich enough" to cover every possible unknown contingency? Human beings threatened with too much change and ambiguity often go for more than they need as a buffer against uncertainty. "More " is clear cut and measurable. Accumulation is concrete enough to understand (that is, the mantra of "the bottom line"). Other philosophical perspectives, which would benefit mankind in the long run, have much less short-term appeal for an individual overwhelmed with change. The environmentalist's focus on anticipating losses, for example, does not seem to be all that attractive. Globalization promises deregulation for the sake of prosperity—the privatization of everything possible. Hence, individuals can maximize their interests without limits to their freedom—economic growth *ad absurdum*.

But how can you keep up with all of the changes produced by accelerating economic growth if you happen to get old and start to slow down? The pension and health concerns of older people are demographically ticking like time bombs, ready to implode and dominate the political agendas of most industrialized democracies.

The Graying of the Rich:
From Baby Boom to Bust

The United States is graying fast. But Europe and Japan are graying even faster: Their older populations are growing much more rapidly than the younger working generations who are assumed to support them. Countries such as Germany, Italy, and Spain are not having enough children to maintain their existing population size. Moreover, inhabitants of developed countries are aging from the middle of the age pyramid (the Baby Boom generation). Large aging populations are already putting pressures on underfunded pension and health systems. The oldest of these, the Japanese, were so concerned with how to fund their pensions that it became politically impossible to agree on the radical economic reforms necessary to recover from a decade-long economic recession. Although other factors, such as heavy debt in corporations and the banking system, played a role in the Japanese slowdown, the concern for funding pensions was critical in diffusing necessary political reforms. The Japanese restricted their consumption out of uncertainty, and young people contemplated having fewer children.

Falling fertility rates are widespread in developed countries, dropping below the replacement rate of 2.1 births per woman. In Italy and Spain, for instance, the fertility rate is only about 1.2. Despite their Catholic cultures, the Spanish and Italians practice extensive birth control and have low rates of premarital pregnancy. The United States escapes this pattern of low fertility because of its large number of immigrants who tend to have large families.

Rising life expectancy is the other major factor in the aging of rich nations. But, as Joseph Chamie, the director of the U.N. population division, observed, "The main locomotive of global aging is fertility decline."[9] This led to an historic reversal, in which people aged 65 or over outnumber children under 15 for the first time in nine countries in the world. In the next 30 years, this trend is expected to encompass some 50 countries, including China.

While affluent societies increasingly worry about their own pensions and health care, developing countries are beginning to age as well. Fertility has dropped not only in China (where government policy assured it) but in Iran, Tunisia, and Brazil. Even in India the median age will rise from 23.7 years in 2000 to 40.1 in 2050, according to U.N. projections. If you imagine the demography of a nation as a pyramid chart, the developing countries have the Baby Boom at the bottom of the population pyramid, rather than in the middle (as is typical of the developed nations).

This pattern gives developing countries grounds for hope. As the large base of the pyramid moves up to middle age—shaped like a Chinese lantern with a fat middle—there could be more than enough workers to support the dependent old and young. Economists David Bloom and Jeffery Williamson of Harvard claim that one third of the East Asian economic miracle that occurred between 1965 and 1990 was due to the fact that the working-age population grew 3.5 times faster than the dependent population.

What if the developing countries do not receive enough trade or capital to keep the large young population employed? A large percentage of these young people are already unemployed. The rich nations are so preoccupied with the complexities of funding their own pensions and health care that they appear to short-change support for helping to educate, train, and employ the would-be middle-classes of developing countries. But if the majority of the populations of the developing countries are denied the opportunities to become self-sufficient or to plug into the global economy, the impact would be felt everywhere in the world.

The results would be destabilizing, if not catastrophic, for all human beings. Millions of unemployed young would try to immigrate to developed countries. Extreme social movements and rebellions would emerge for the sake of survival. Studies such as Seymour Martin Lipset's *Political Man* have shown that the threat of downward mobility among the lower working classes leads to militant, fringe political developments. Frequently in their histories, industrial societies have higher rates of downward than upward mobility.[10] Such was the case with Nazi Germany in the 1920s.

To leave huge numbers of people in poverty would increase the likelihood that they would become infected with diseases that are likely to travel around the world. The long lead times necessary to cope with such health and unemployment dilemmas would make them much more difficult to solve, and the problems are bound to compound with potentially catastrophic effects. And the chances of such an outcome of disintegration are multiplying because in the developed countries, the majority of people have not sufficiently provided for retirement, for the upgrading of their own skills, or for the education of their own children. By necessity, most people find themselves too pressured for time to concern themselves with those even further down the socioeconomic ladder. Increased life expectancy ultimately just adds to the pressure of financing more years of retirement.

Nevertheless, the expectation of living longer has not had much effect on a third of the 76 million American Baby Boomers (born between 1946 and 1964), who have saved hardly anything for retirement. The problems of a lack of savings for retirement and health care, educational deficits, and the neglect of retooling people from lower socioeconomic classes for future job needs will make countries such as the United States ever more self-absorbed.

We live in an "attention economy," and there are only so many issues that citizens—no matter how wealthy and well educated—can pay attention to at any one time. Influential interest groups in developed countries will lobby their governments to focus on *domestic* priorities first—security, economic growth, jobs, modernizing the electricity grid, health care, pensions, and education. Future funding for rebuilding Afghanistan and Iraq is already impeded by building public resistance. Expenses related to foreign countries, including aid or trade, are apt to slip further down on the national agenda if such funding cannot be related directly to domestic issues.

Consider the Social Security system of the United States. By 2018, tax revenues are expected to fall below expenses, meaning that the system will have to dip into its trust fund to pay the benefits promised. By 2042, the trust fund will be exhausted if taxes do not go up or if benefits are not cut: $3.5 trillion would need to be added to keep the system going until 2077.[11]

If both pension and health care obligations are added together, the picture becomes much worse. Given the aging of the Baby Boomers and the rapidly rising costs of health care, Peter Fischer, the U.S. Treasury's Undersecretary for Domestic Finance, claims that the cost of the Social Security and health benefits that the U.S. government has promised will exceed projected tax revenues by $20 trillion! Viewing the U.S. federal government as a gigantic insurance company (with a sideline business in national defense and homeland security), Fischer maintains that "this particular insurance company has made promises to its policyholders that have a current value $20 trillion or so in excess of the revenues that it expects to receive."[12]

The budget squeeze may prove even worse for the rich European countries. They are caught between the need to keep the new Euro currency strong on the one hand and the demand to stimulate lackluster economic growth and job creation on the other. A strong Euro, relative to the dollar, will make automobiles exported from Europe to the United States more expensive. The 3% of Gross Domestic Product (GDP) deficit limit for countries in the Euro system is a straightjacket that is not working. From Portugal to Germany to France, countries constantly threaten to breach the limit. There is pressure in the short run to raise government spending, to head off recession, and to create jobs. And in the long run, there is the financial weight of government obligations for the welfare of aging populations. Consider the share of public expenditures on pensions, health care, and long-term care in the European Union (EU) as a percentage of GDP, illustrated in the following table.[13]

Public Expenditure on Pensions, Health Care, and Long-Term Care in 2000 vs. EU Projections to 2040

Nation	2000 % GDP expenditure	2040 % GDP expenditure
Austria	20.3	26.5
Italy	19.4	23.0
France	18.9	24.3
Finland	18.6	26.1
Denmark	18.5	24.6
Germany	17.5	23.7
Greece	17.4	30.1
Portugal	16.8	23.1

EU = European Union.

How much EU money will be left over to subsidize the economies of at least 10 new (and poorer) member nations that are transitioning to join the EU with full rights in a decade (much less to aid the poorest countries in the world that would never qualify to be invited to join the EU)?

Tensions between aging rich sectors of the population and the underclass *within* rich countries are also apt to grow—particularly as the smaller, younger generations realize that the larger, older populations may use up most of the social security resources. This will force governments to cut benefits for future generations. Such domestic rich-poor conflicts between generations as well as between economic classes leads to political party stalemates that make it difficult to free up capital for investment or grants to poorer peoples abroad, much less to resolve things at home. To the extent that government pensions and medical coverage are no longer sufficient, younger generations will have to turn to private investment or savings—or depend on older, richer relatives. The battle between the old rich and the financially pressed, underinsured young will tilt toward those with financial literacy, leaving the poor behind in both the older and younger generations.

References

1. "Alternatives: The Death of Venture Capital," *Global Investor*, London, May 1, 2003, p. 1.

2. William Baumol, "Free Market Growth and Rent Beyond Land: Henry George Generalized," The Fourth Henry George Symposium, Pace University, New York, October 29, 2003.

3. Bryan Berry, "Great Pain, Great Gain," *Iron Age New Steel*, Vol. 16, No. 1, January 2000, p. 1.

4. R. Isaak, *Managing World Economic Change*, 3rd edition (Upper Saddle River, NJ: Prentice-Hall, 2000), pp. 116–117.

5. Frank Partnoy, *Infectious Greed: How Deceit and Risk Corrupted the Financial Markets* (New York: Times Books/Henry Holt, 2003).

6. George Soros, *On Globalization* (New York: Public Affairs, 2002) p. 123.

7. Andrew S. Grove, *Only the Paranoid Survive: How to Exploit the Crisis Points that Challenge Every Company and Career* (N.Y.: Doubleday, 1996).

8. Benjamin Friedman, "The Moral Consequences of Economic Growth," The Third Henry George Symposium, Pace University, April 3, 2003, New York.

9. "Older and Richer," *Economist.com/Global Agenda* (London: March 25, 2002).

10. Seymour Martin Lipset, *Political Man: The Social Bases of Politics* (Garden City, N.Y.: Doubleday, 1960) and Frank Parkin, *Class Inequality and Political Order* (New York: Praeger, 1975).

11. Fred Brock, "Lost in the Shuffle, a Sign of Strength for Social Security," *The New York Times*, April 13, 2003.

12. David Wessel, "The Economy—Capital: U.S. Promises Are $20 Trillion in the Hole," *Wall Street Journal*, November 21, 2002.

13. Marc Landler, "Europe Strains to Put Laggards Back in Line," *New York Times*, October 27, 2002.

II

THE POOR

Who They Are, How They Live, and Why They Are Dependent

7 Why the Poor Are Where They Are

Through centuries he lived in poverty.
God only was his only elegance.

—WALLACE STEVENS,
The Good Man Has No Shape (1946)

With little income and few assets to fall back on, the poor are vulner-able and usually powerless—even in democratic systems where plutocracy often reigns.

Poverty is a state of being that is hard to get out of on one's own.

To be poor is to be confronted with a deprivation of opportuni-ty. There is not enough opportunity to eat, to drink safe water, to work, to have medical treatment when sick, to have basic sanitation, to feel safe—not enough opportunity to be financially secure. The richest 20% of the world's population consumes 86% of all goods and services; the poorest 20% consumes 1.3%.[1]

To be poor is to be hollowed out. Religion can sometimes fill the void. It offers consolation and attempts to dignify poverty. But poverty is not a question of choice, as religion can be. It is a state of being into which one is usually born. And poor lives tend to be brief. If you happen to be born in Swaziland, Zimbabwe, Rwanda, Malawi, Zambia, or Sierra Leone, your life expectancy is less than 40 years.[2] Even in a globalized economy, one may not "know better" than to remain poor and to believe that one is destined to be dependent on others or on the whims of fortune. In Africa, cataclysmic civil wars keep thousands of people in a state of uncertainty. This trauma is symbolized in the extreme by incidents of cannibalism by soldiers in the Congo, due to a mystical belief that if you eat the vital organs of your enemy, you absorb their powers: Consuming the heart of a pygmy may help you to find your way in the forest and to ward off bullets.[3] Of course, this gruesome tradition also is used to intimidate the poor. Meanwhile, as Congolese society disintegrates around them, some of the 15,000 male students at the University of Kinshasa who cannot afford the daily minibus fare of 75 cents force truck drivers to take them to school (while many female students spend the night in the classrooms). The university's science faculty library has only 300 books, and those are outdated. Such a scarcity is not offset by the pilot program for a minority of students sponsored by United Nations and Cisco Systems—a computer-networking course online, without books.[4]

It is not that poverty is merely a self-fulfilling, negative prophecy (although it is that, too). Poverty implies a limit to perception, a shrunken view of what a person can become, given the material situation in which one finds oneself. The poor become used to living on the margins and tend to take things as they come. They have more time each day than the rich, but they have fewer days.

Consider S, a child in Tanzania. S starts to shake without control in a small clinic. The doctor immediately recognizes convulsions from malaria. But S's mother believes the shaking is caused by evil spirits and that if the doctor gives her an injection, the evil spirits will go through the hole in the needle and spread to more victims. The mother seizes S and runs out of the clinic with her. The staff of the clinic chases after her because they are certain she will administer the traditional remedy to S—putting a blanket over her head and having her inhale the smoke from elephant dung set on fire until she passes out. But nothing in this remedy can eliminate the parasites of malaria racing through S's small body. Fortunately, this true story has a happy ending: The staff manages to persuade S's mother to return to the clinic and to permit the child to be given a Valium suppository to calm her down. She is then given quinine, which attacks the parasites. Soon she is healthy again.[5]

S is a lucky girl. She got to a clinic in time, she saw a doctor who recognized her condition, and his staff was able to return her to the clinic before her mother's traditional belief blocked the therapy that saved her life. Many poor people do not have access to a clinic, to a doctor, or to effective medicine. Yet Tanzania remains a positive exception. Unlike other developing countries, elites have not totally gained control over the health care system in order to tilt its priorities toward their own interests. Researchers in Tanzania created a pilot experiment that caused infant mortality to drop 28% in a single year. Previously, 10% of Tanzanian children died in their first year of life. The researchers investigated to discover which diseases caused death and disability most frequently. Public money was redirected toward those ailments that caused the most suffering but were cheapest to treat.[6]

Tanzania is a very poor country. Its 35 million citizens together had a collective income in 2001 of $9 billion—or about half what Americans spend annually on wallpaper. Yet among the Heavily Indebted Poor Countries (HIPC), Tanzania was only one of six countries that recently met the World Bank-International Monetary Fund (IMF) conditions for debt cancellation (with $3 billion of debt forgiven). This HIPC program led to dramatically higher spending in health care and education in the six countries (the others being Bolivia, Burkina Faso, Mauritania, Mozambique, and Uganda, with a total of $12.2 billion in loans written off for all six). But several are already slipping back into a situation of weak exports and additional borrowing.[7]

What causes the poverty that lands these countries in debt in the first place?

In its annual *World Development Report*, The World Bank[8] identifies the following causes of poverty:

- Lack of income and assets to obtain basic needs (i.e., food, shelter, clothing, acceptable levels of health and education)
- Voicelessness/powerlessness in state and social institutions
- Vulnerability to adverse shocks—(e.g., earthquakes, civil wars, economic recession)
- Absence of *human* assets (capacity for labor, skills, health)
- Absence of *natural* assets (land)
- Absence of *physical* assets (access to infrastructure)
- Absence of *financial* assets (savings and access to credit)
- Absence of *social* assets (reciprocal networks and obligations that can be tapped in times of need; political influence over resources)

Let us consider some of these sources of poverty.

Income Inequality

The good news globally is that over the last 20 years of the twentieth century, the share of extremely poor people in the world (those living on $2 a day) fell from 38% in 1978 to 19% in 1998. [9] Still, the World Bank estimates that a fourth of the population of the developing world—about 1.2 billion people—live on less than $1 a day, the Bank's lower threshold of what it means to be "poor."

It has been shown that developing countries that opened their trading systems to the revolt of the rich—to privatization, deregulation, and free markets—had higher levels of economic growth and greater income levels than those that did not. **The income inequalities stemming from the revolt of the rich in the last two decades of the twentieth century did not result from a decrease in the incomes of the poor countries. Rather, the polarization was driven by a very high increase in the incomes of the** wealthy in the rich countries, creating a larger income gap between rich and poor.)

Despite some "convergence" between the economic growth of the developed and a handful of developing countries (China and India, for example), the gaps between the richest and poorest sections of many nations have become much more extreme. Brazil and South Africa have the highest income inequality: The wealthiest 20% of households are about 25 times richer than the poorest 20%.[10] Actually, given their huge populations, the rapid growth of China and India alone can explain most of the decline in poverty in the past 20 years. However, there was a significant increase in the absolute number of poor in other places in the developing world, such as Africa, Latin America, other parts of Asia, and in the so-called transitional economies of the former Soviet Union (such as Rumania). According to the World Bank, between 1980 and 1998, the increase in the number of poor was 59.3 million in Africa, 26.7 million in South Asia, and 10.5 million in Central Asia and Eastern Europe.[11]

If one considers income in terms of Gross Domestic Product (GDP) per capita, the bottom five countries are Sierra Leone ($470), Tanzania ($520), Malawi ($570), Burundi ($690), and Yemen ($790). Contrast these with the top five: Luxembourg ($53,780), the United States ($34,320), Iceland ($29,620), Norway ($29,620), and Denmark ($29,000).[11]

But one must look deeper. The share of income (or consumption) between socioeconomic classes within countries is important, as well, and reveals some surprises. For example, even though the United States ranks sixth on the overall Human Development Index of the United Nations in terms of the share of income or consumption, the richest 10% of Americans have 30.5%, whereas the poorest 10% have only 1.8%. This is roughly comparable to Burundi, ranked 171 on the Human Development Index, where the richest 10% take away 32.9% while the poorest 10% receive 1.8%. In Norway—the country highest on the Human Development Index—the richest 10% receive only 21.8% of income or consumption while the poorest 10% receive 4.1%.[2] No doubt this is because, as one of the Scandinavian countries, the majority of the population of Norway values social democracy more than increases in economic growth for its own sake, unlike the value priorities of the leaders of the revolt of the rich from the Anglo-American cultures. Yet in this cultural struggle, if what is happening to the middle class is any indicator, social democracy appears to risk being overwhelmed in this competition.

Is the World's Middle Class Disappearing?

Whether you compare income inequality by macro country statistics or by people wherever they might live in the world, the middle class seems to be disappearing. This has ominous implications for political stability, which requires a large middle class.[12]

Comparing 111 countries in terms of the distribution of national income and expenditure, Branko Milanovic of the World Bank and Shlomo Yitzhaki of Hebrew University[13] conclude:

1. Seventy-six percent* of the world's population live in poor countries, 8% live in middle-income countries, and 16% live in rich countries, when *middle income* is defined as countries with per capita income levels between Brazil's $3,470 and Italy's $8,000, and *rich* means equal to or higher than Italy's income.

2. Seventy-eight percent of the world's population are poor, 11% belong to the middle class, and 11% are rich.

3. In Asia, where differences are the greatest, inequality between countries is much more important than inequality in incomes within countries. In contrast, in Latin America, differences between countries are less important, but inequalities within countries are large. The richest region of the world—Western Europe, North America, and Oceania—has a mean income of $10,012, which is three times

---

*The country income statistics referred to are in terms of PPP—purchasing power parity—in U.S. dollars. The data is available from http://www.worldbank.org/research/transition/inequality.

the mean income in Latin America, the second richest area. The poorest region, Africa, has an average income of $1,310 per capita per year.

4. Although the middle-income countries have only 8% of the world's population, 33% of the impoverished of the world live in lesser developed countries—- in addition to the 40% who inhabit the two "poor giants," India and China.

In sum, worldwide income distribution is like an hourglass with an extremely large bottom, a very thin middle, and a larger top. In terms of future global political stability, much depends on whether the middle of the hourglass becomes thinner or whether we can begin to expand it from the bottom.

Of course, income inequalities alone are not enough to explain the conditions that characterize poverty.

Asset Inequalities

Talking to the poor throughout the developing countries reveals a sense of powerlessness, comparing their own condition to slavery or being tied to bundles of straw.[14] Not only is income from work precarious and inadequate, due to seasonal factors in agricultural economies, but any assets the poor might have are threatened as well. Many have no place to sleep, no electricity, no reliable drinking water, no education, no means of transportation, no health care system, no social connections in case of job loss, no pension, and no idea of how to obtain these missing prerequisites to well-being. Indeed, if one visits a developing country and observes the great number of homeless people there, one realizes how precarious the "income" of a day laborer is, *if* he or she happens to get some work. The poor in Ecuador, for example, typically long for each of their children to have a bed, a pair of shoes, a canopy or covering over their heads, some sheets and not to have to sleep on the ground. How we see the problem is skewed by statistical averages in which the relatively high incomes of many in city or coastal areas are averaged out with the extremely low incomes typical of rural areas. Thus, the GDP of the overall country can go up while the people in the isolated, stigmatized rural areas may not be any better off than they were in the past. In India, for example, the wealth created in Bangalore does not spread to benefit the masses of undernourished people in Calcutta or Varanasi—much less those living on the outskirts of Bangalore itself. Economic growth becomes truly meaningful to a family only if some of it can be captured in some kind of concrete asset or tangible form of future financial security.

Assets refer to either something *owned* or to *resources* one can tap into.

A contrasting example may help to illustrate the importance of assets. Mr. A came from Bangladesh to the United States. He and his wife bought a one-family house, where they live with their children. But he has a very high mortgage on the house and no health insurance. When his income as a caterer in New York City dropped by two thirds, due to the recession of 2001, he fell behind on the payments on his house, which he may lose if his income continues to decline. His pregnant wife could no longer afford to see the gynecologist. Conventional economic indicators would not measure what is happening to Mr. A. The fact that he does not really "own" his house and has no health insurance makes him extremely vulnerable in an economic downturn. After all, 68% of the families in the United States do own their own homes. And the median American net household wealth is $86,100 (home equity and total family assets minus consumer debt), with the largest minority group, the Hispanics, having a net household wealth of $11,450.[15] Because neither Mr. A nor his wife has strong educational credentials or social connections to find work in another area, he finds himself without any real assets to function as a safety net in hard times.[16]

Mr. A may not own much but he has automatic access to abundant public resources in a developed country, which he could not count on in a poor nation. These *public assets* include many resources often taken for granted: not only potable drinking water but also secure sanitary systems; a functioning system of law and order that deters civil conflicts or attacks from outside the country; reliable public transportation; a well-endowed public library system; and welfare advisory offices where one can receive information on new training, jobs, or careers. Moreover, Mr. A benefits from a large port city where new businesses and jobs are much more apt to be created than in a landlocked country. Landlocked nations pay up to 50% more in transportation costs than the median coastal nation. This means that to ship a standard container from Baltimore, Maryland in the United States to the Ivory Coast runs about $3,000, whereas sending the same container to the landlocked Central African Republic costs $13,000. Mr. A lives in a center of high job creation, with political institutions that are *potentially* empowering and inclusive. However, in social relationships, there is still discrimination that isolates immigrants. There are few organizations to connect Mr. A into the political system. And the resulting lack of information, education, skills, and confidence give him a feeling of powerlessness. The sad truth is that even in this richest of countries, there are problems most people are not aware of. More children are born into "poverty" in the United States than in any other developed country, millions of workers are without health insurance, and there is an alarming increase in the number of teenage suicides.

And if you happen to live in one of the least developed countries of the world, your sense of powerlessness, insecurity, and ill-being are apt to be even more acute because the poor have no assets to fall back on. Without money today, your disease will take you to your grave tomorrow in countries like Ghana.[17] Indeed, illness is the main cause of pushing poor people deeper into poverty. In tropical impoverished countries (and most tropical countries are poor), diseases such as malaria, hookworm, schistosomiasis, river blindness, and yellow fever are difficult to control because the lack of seasons allows mosquitoes to transmit diseases throughout the year. And if countries are not only tropical but also landlocked, conventional "cures" of improving market-oriented policies and the rule of law will not be sufficient to overcome such geographical locations that facilitate endemic diseases, undermine agricultural productivity, and impede market access.[18]

Of about 4.4 billion people in developing countries, almost 60% lack access to safe sewers, one third have no access to clean water, 25% do not have adequate shelter, and 20% have no access to any kind of modern health services.[19] The problem is that within low-income countries, there is an extreme gap between the better off and the poorest parts of the population. This polarization is illustrated by differences in access to assets, such as health care. Just consider the following statistics.[1]

- In Bolivia, the mortality rate under the age of five among the poorest 20% of the population is four times higher than the rate among the richest 20%.

- In Ecuador, 75% of households among the poorest 20% have no piped water, compared with 12% in the richest 20% of households.

- In Ghana, the richest 20% of the population receives almost three times the public health spending of that received by the poorest 20%.

- In Nepal, the richest 20% receives four times as much public education spending as the poorest 20%.

- In Morocco, regions with better rural roads have much higher girl enrollment in primary schools and twice the use of health care facilities.

To build their assets, low-income families must start at home. Parents must be able to find time from working in the fields or factory to nurture and socialize their children, teach them skills, and help to finance their education. In Nigeria, for example, if you are not educated, you cannot get a job, and being without a job freezes your position in society.[17] Farmers must build assets by investment in equipment that allows them to replace primitive tools and to increase their productivity. When workers migrate to cities, any savings they are able to accumulate tend to be invested in household assets. Often, they cannot get beyond this because the economic opportunities of the poor are constrained by extremely limited markets, particularly in rural areas. "Free markets" do not work well for the disadvantaged—particularly when it comes to meeting health, insurance, and financial needs.[18] With physical isolation, the poor are even more dependent on the public sector than are residents of the cities, toward which public services are usually biased. The rural poor thus find themselves without proper roads, public transportation, or access to good schools, bank credit, or hospital care.

In Ethiopia, chronic food shortages due to recurring drought leave thousands of children starving, despite international assistance. Because the majority of workers in Ethiopia are farmers, they can barely cope with "normal conditions." Well-meaning efforts to break this cycle of drought, famine, and starvation through training in proper farming techniques and in building hospitals and schools have not yet proved to be successful.[19] For generations, Egyptian domination of access to the waters of the Nile kept the river's tributaries flowing by so that the Ethiopians could not access the water in their own country. Because of its strategic position, modern geopolitics favored Egypt (reinforced by the dominant countries in international organizations). But hunger has become so chronic in Ethiopia that the politics of the Nile are finally beginning to shift a little in Ethiopia's favor with the "Nile Basin Initiative" of the World Bank and the United Nations, started in the late 1990s.[20] Without access to the river resources flowing through its own country, no nation has been able to develop—much less become educated or "connected."

The uneducated and disconnected find themselves to be further and further behind in the knowledge-based globalized economy. They find their institutions to be disempowering and excluding. Politically, lower-income groups are usually powerless to organize and press for their interests in society or government. **Often, it is not the absence of democracy but the great diffusion of the democratic system that leaves the poor dominated by the rich.**

Democratic Deficits versus Too Much Democracy

Although the difficulty at the level of administering international organizations and multinational corporations is typically a deficit of democracy, the problem is often the reverse within developing countries. **The rich sectors of the population have much greater access** to the country's assets, such as health care and education, because they are able to use their wealth and influence to lobby for their interests in the democratic political system. The poor have no such lobbies. The rich are better educated and are better able to articulate their interests. They know how to use the media to push their own agenda and to tilt the benefits of the infrastructure their way. In developing countries, where education is recommended but not required (e.g., in India), widespread democracy becomes meaningless if the large poor segments of the population have neither the language skills nor the financial means to participate in a way that can improve their situation.

Wealthy citizens, for example, are more apt to advocate the priority of using public budgets to subsidize higher education. In the United States, for instance, the wealthiest private universities have persuaded the U.S. government to give them the highest subsidies and work-study jobs for their students, whereas the colleges that serve the largest percentage of low-income students receive much less.[21]

The class structure impedes mobility, even in this highly mobile culture. Children from disadvantaged families are not able to afford the expensive private training courses (e.g., offered by Kaplan and Princeton) for college entrance examinations. But even if they are successful on the exam, they usually apply to the less expensive state universities and, once accepted, go heavily into debt. And further down the socioeconomic ladder in the United States, there are thousands of poorer income groups, including:

1. Single mothers on welfare with no job prospects and hungry children

2. Illegal immigrants who live hand-to-mouth working at the minimum wage

3. Many elderly who can hardly survive on Social Security payments and travel by buses to Canada if prescription drugs are cheaper there

4. The homeless who frequent the subsidized soup kitchens and often live in shelters provided by major cities

The mothers on welfare, of course, cannot receive benefits beyond two years without finding a job, thanks to the welfare reform legislation passed during the booming 1990s in the United States, when it was assumed that such jobs would be easy to obtain.

In low-income regions worldwide, resources are pulled away from rural areas to fund hospitals in urban areas equipped to cope with diseases that particularly concern the rich. The healthy privileged groups steer the infrastructure their way, driving the poor into deeper poverty through illness. In Europe, the middle classes get more out of nationalized health services because they are pushier than the poor. In poor countries, a small, concentrated group of elites organizes to make sure that health care budgets are spent disproportionately in cities, typically on expensive, high-tech therapies for ailments, such as cancer and heart disease, which are the ailments that are of most concern to the wealthy. Diseases such as malaria or those stemming from malnutrition among the poor are often neglected. In much of Sub-Saharan Africa, health spending is as little as $10 a year per person, half of which is typically blown on fancy hospitals in capital cities.

Indeed, too much diffuse, direct democracy can have the perverse effect of blocking human development and economic growth if widespread democratization occurs before basic infrastructures are in place. In a study empirically examining the prerequisites for "economic miracles" in the last 60 years, it was revealed that a number of these miracles of economic growth had "post-authoritarian structures" from the past still in place, providing a stable base from which "liberated" economic entrepreneurship could then be launched (e.g., the cases of Germany, Japan, South Korea, Taiwan, Singapore, Chile, and China).[22] Fareed Zakaria, an international editor for *Newsweek*, independently confirms these findings, arguing that more or less authoritarian systems of delegated democracy in developing countries are likelier to result in individual freedom. In *The Future of Freedom: Illiberal Democracy at Home and Abroad*, Zakaria[23] notes that "Over the past 50 years, almost every success story in the developing world has taken place under a liberal authoritarian regime. Whether in Taiwan, South Korea, Singapore, Chile, Indonesia, or even China, governments that were able to make shrewd choices for the long term were rewarded with strong economic growth and rising levels of literacy, life expectancy, and education."

Such wise long-term planning by political leaders, of course, is the exception rather than the rule. The biggest difficulty is corruption. James Wolfensohn, head of the World Bank, said that the greatest difficulties poor countries face are corruption and governability.[24] The world's most stable delegated democracy, the United States, is crucially flawed because of the official corruption that is legitimated by the way campaigns are financed: To have to spend $1 million to become a member of the House of Representatives or more than five times that to become a member of the Senate smacks of oligarchy, not democracy. For example, The U.S. Public Interest Group's study "Polluter Payday" for the 2000 elections compared the political contributions made by the energy industry with the favors that industry would receive under the Bush administration energy bill devised by Vice President Dick Cheney (passed by the House of Representatives in 2003): The return on investment (ROI) for those in the energy industry who had contributed to the Republican political campaign was in total 2,000 to 1.[25] **The ideal of stable liberal democracy where individuals feel that their vote counts in a fair representative system has been eroded by the domination of corporate plutocracy. Thomas Jefferson would not be happy.**

The elite use politics to maximize their own short-term interests and those of their wealthy constituencies. Success taught them that they are rewarded by organizing to have their way. The poor have usually not had such experiences. They are used to being dependent on decisions made by others and often believe that they have very little influence over their own personal fate. They are not demanding enough to get the health care and education they deserve. Rather than acting as agents to improve their worldly condition, the impoverished often seek out the more passive refuge and ritual of religion.

Religion is attractive because of its promise of a better world to come if one is virtuous and devout on the earth. As philosopher George Santayana wrote, the function of religion is "to draw from reality materials for an image of that ideal to which reality ought to conform and to make us citizens, by anticipation, in the world we crave."[26] Religion means hope in situations that otherwise might appear to be hopeless. The shift in the historical cycle toward a widespread manifestation of religiosity in all its forms throughout the world in the early twenty-first century is a symptom, in part, of deep-seated socioeconomic and political crises that many find to be hopeless to resolve. The conflicts in the Middle East between the Jews and the Palestinians and in other regions between the Muslims and the Anglo-American Christians are cases in point. We find ourselves in the stage of civilization predicted by sociologist Pitrim Sorokin, in which turbulent events mark the transition from "late sensate chaos"* (secular, empirical disintegration) to a new era of religiosity.[27]

Wealthy minorities in some developing countries may calculate that they can maintain control more easily by supporting the poor in their religious beliefs rather than requiring them to obtain a certain level of "secular" education. Thus, the theory that only the educated should participate in parliamentary politics for the sake of wise policy becomes a self-fulfilling prophecy for those with financial and educational assets. For the poor, to paraphrase philosopher Jean Paul Sartre, to vote is to vote for voting. **The well-to-do vote for their own interests first, pushing more people into poverty because the infrastructures where the disadvantaged live are neglected in the process.** Subsidies to U.S. cotton growers, for instance, sum to more than three times the amount of U.S. government aid to Sub-Saharan Africa, whereas subsidies within the European Union (EU) for each dairy cow exceed the aid per capita the EU gives to Sub-Saharan Africa.[28]

One of the developing countries has made great strides in some areas while getting bogged down in others, creating a paradox for observers. Examining this "poor giant" may help to reveal exactly how the rich tend to concentrate their investments in established areas, keeping the poor in their poverty elsewhere: the case of India.

---

* *Sensate* is not intended to mean sensational or sensual, but rather empirical, worldly, humanistic, secular.

References

1. Barbara Crossette, "Kofi Annan's Amazing Facts: The True Parameters of the Planets," *The New York Times*, September 27, 1998.

2. UNDP, *Human Development Report 2003* (New York: United Nations, 2003), pp. 239–240.

3. Daniel Bergner, "The Most Unconventional Weapon," *The New York Times Magazine*, October 26, 2003, pp. 48–53.

4. "Light in the Harvard of Darkness," *The Economist*, July 5–11, 2003, p. 41.

5. "For 80 Cents More—Health Care in Poor Countries," *The Economist*, August 17, 2002.

6. "Cheap Cures: Donors Should Give More, but the Poor Should Spend What they Have More Rationally," *The Economist*, August 17, 2002, p. 13.

7. Pete Engardio, "This Hot Potato Just Gets Hotter: As Third World Debt Rises, So Do Hurdles to Forgiving It," *Business Week*, October 7, 2002, p. 68.

8. "Attacking Poverty," *World Development Report 2000/2001,* The World Bank, Washington, D.C., 2001, p. 34.

9. Andrew Berg and Anne Krueger, "Lifting All Boats: Why Openness Helps Curb Poverty," *Finance and Development,* Vol. 39, No. 3 (Washington, D.C., September 2002). pp. 16–19. World Bank statistics based on the value of the dollar in 1985.

10. Nancy Birdsall, "Asymmetric Globalization: Global Markets Require Good Politics," Washington, D.C.: Center for Global Development, Working Paper No. 12, October 2002, p. 4.

11. UNDP, *Human Development Report 2002* (New York: United Nations, 2002), pp. 190, 197.

12. See Aristotle's *Politics* (any edition).

13. Branko Milanovic and Shlomo Yitzhaki, "Decomposing World Income Distribution: Does the World Have a Middle Class?" *Review of Income and Wealth*, Series 48, No. 2, June 2002, pp. 155–175.

14. Deepa Narayan et al., *Can Anyone Hear Us?: Voices from 47 Countries* (Washington, D.C.: World Bank Poverty Group, PREM, 1999).

15. "Wealth Gap is Wide for U.S. Hispanics," *The Wall Street Journal*, November 18, 2003.

16. Anthony De Palma, "What the Economic Indicators Miss," *The New York Times,* April 6, 2003.

17. From *Voices of the Poor*, edited by Deepa Narayan, Robert Chambers, Meera Kaul Shah, and Patti Petesch (2000), as cited in Chapter 5, "Expanding Poor People's Assets and Tackling Inequalities," *World Development Report*, 2000/2001, pp. 83, 240.

18. Ricardo Hausmann,"Prisoners of Geography," *Foreign Policy*, Jan./Feb. 2001, Vol. 122, p. 49.

19. Public Broadcasting System, *The News Hour*, October 29, 2003.

20. Roger Thurow, "Ravaged by Famine, Ethiopia Finally Gets Help from the Nile," *The Wall Street Journal*, November 26, 2003.

21. Greg Winter, "Rich Colleges Receiving Richest Share of U.S. Aid," *The New York Times*, November 9, 2003.

22. R. Isaak, "Making Economic Miracles: Explaining Extraordinary National Economic Achievement," *American Economist* xxxxi, no. 1, Spring 1997.

23. Fareed Zakaria, *The Future of Freedom: Illiberal Democracy at Home and Abroad* (New York: W.W. Norton, 2003), p. 251.

24. James Wolfensohn, president of World Bank, interview with Charlie Rose on Public Broadcasting System, October 30, 2003.

25. Former Congressman Richard Ottinger, "Connecting the $ DOTS," Op-Ed submission to *New York Times*, August 4, 2003.

26. George Santayana, *Interpretations of Poetry and Religion* (New York: Harper and Brothers, 1957), p. vi.

27. Pitrim A. Sorokin, *Social and Cultural Dynamics* (New York: Bedminister Press, 1962), Vol. I, pp 775–779.

8 A Passage Through India

Even if the nine sheep, my home, and all the camels
were drowned; even if I were left without children;
even so it is good that the rain must fall.

—An old Rajasthan folk song

India illustrates why a traditional sense of religious dependence can be used by politicians and those in power to keep the poor content with the status quo. The elitist software sector appears to be the exception that proves the rule.

What strikes one most in traveling through India, a human tapestry of over 1 billion people, is the anchoring in old ways and traditions offset by tremendous strides toward modernity.

Globalization serves to magnify this clash of past and present. One is overwhelmed by the extremes of some of the world's most luxurious hotels and most competitive software companies on the one hand and the massive hunger, begging, and the heavy dependence on jobs in agriculture on the other. India is one of the key countries to examine in attempting to try to solve the dilemma of global poverty because it is home to the largest number of hungry people in the world—233 million, compared with 183 million in Sub-Saharan Africa and 119 million in China (where hunger has been reduced the most).[1] With one foot deep in the past and the other foot in the future, India provides a testing ground to see whether it is possible to bridge the gaps between the poorest and the well-to-do or whether the amplifying effects of technology and the mobility of finance and skilled people will merely produce even greater inequalities.

Emerging Modernity

The cities of Aurangabad and Mumbai provide illustrations of the throbbing coexistence of the old and the new in India. Although Aurangabad benefits from tourism attracted by the nearby ancient caves of Ajanta and Ellora, the city is a model of hope for future self-sufficiency. Despite its 2,200-year heritage and its emphasis on agriculture, it has become a rather modern industrial center. Not only does the city specialize in the production of motorcycles, it is home to some 2,500 companies and has the advantage of lower prices than nearby Mumbai.

Mumbai (formerly Bombay) with a population of over 14 million is targeted to become India's financial center and could fulfill this role, provided that the social class situation can be changed. The city is characterized by a paradox: a bustling, modernized center with an English feel, as well as expensive homes and apartment buildings on the waterfront not far from widespread slums.

Despite attempts at modernization (cows cannot freely roam on the highways and streets there), the traditions and century-old rituals that resist economic development still survive. This becomes apparent when visiting the Hanging Gardens, where members of a religious sect (the Parsis) bring their dead, believing that the flesh should be "recycled" by vultures and the bones left to drop down onto the earth (where they are later treated with lime and chemicals). Pollution resulting from the city's development, however, is killing off the vultures that help out with the burials. The Parsis have been forced to become modernized, resorting to the use of electric crematoriums.

Next to Calcutta, the slums of Mumbai are perhaps the most extensive in India, spreading for miles and miles. Even though some new apartment buildings have been constructed there, it was done without planning for such basics as access roads, lowering the chances of ever having electricity and running water. Such blatant mismanagement of the infrastructure would not occur in the city's wealthy areas. Whether in the old, poor sections or the modern enclaves of the wealthy, frequent blackouts prevail. As in most places in India, the electric lights in the shops of the city are turned on only when customers enter the store to save electricity. Throughout the city, one senses a socioeconomic hierarchy of services, from the bustling, prestigious areas where electricity is least interrupted to the occasional blackouts in the middle-class shops to the massive slums, where electricity may be entirely absent.

For the higher social class, opportunities are compounded; for the poor, vulnerabilities are reinforced.

This vulnerability is not limited to access to water and electricity. A newspaper in Mumbai reported that health care is low in priority in all states. Investment in health has declined from 7% to a mere 5.5% in state health budgets, and most of this money goes toward paying salaries and supporting infrastructure.[2] Furthermore, there is no accreditation mechanism for recognizing or grading hospitals, whether public or private. Nevertheless, government politicians in the capital of New Delhi have been publicly celebrating the commendation for India on poverty reduction by the UNDP's (United Nations Development Program) most recent Human Development Report. But this same report notes that India still has areas of intense poverty, unrelieved by increases in economic growth. Such economic dynamism tends to be concentrated in wealthier areas, leaving underdevelopment to the poor. An editorial in the newspaper *Mumbai*, entitled "Ignominy Index: Indian's Development Slide Show,"[3] notes that poverty reduction does not in itself necessarily translate to improved human development and that successive United Nations reports demonstrate that the people of India seem to be running faster to stay in the same place. They remain pretty much at the bottom when ranking countries in terms of the indicators of human development.[3] The global speed trap threatens India's traditional cultures while forcing its modernized sectors to spin their wheels even faster.

But what exactly are these indicators of human development? One example is the buffer stocks of food in case of a major drought or food emergency. Recall that more hungry people live in India than anywhere else, and almost half of Indian children are malnourished. Frequently food stocks have been stored, but are not delivered to the people who need them. Those people will starve while the grain rots in the storage bin. The government gives excuses such as lack of transportation to bring the grain to the starving.

Despite its success with software, much of India is focused on relatively low-tech approaches to solving problems. The traveler through India initially confronts a scarcity that the residents of India must worry about daily—water. Most regions do not have enough of it when they need it. On the other hand, when the monsoon rains do come, they can turn roads into lakes in a matter of minutes, stopping all vehicles in their tracks and drowning people or sweeping them down storm drains. The visitor never forgets the issue of water, because you cannot drink the tap water. And, growing wary of the source of unmarked bottled water, one feels compelled to buy brand-name water, carefully inspecting the seal to be sure it has not been tampered with. Natives, of course, grow accustomed to drinking the tap water—even if the source happens to be the holy river, the Ganges, where the ashes of cremated bodies flow downstream daily. Water in India is precious for many reasons.

It was the leadership of women that pushed through the project of harvesting rainwater in the state of Gujurat. The idea was to harvest or collect rainwater in the rainy season to use in dry months. Beginning in 1981, the villages of Dahod, Bhavangar, and Amreli began to reap the benefits from this idea. The villagers of Dahod constructed plastic-lined ponds to store the water, and the people have since become self-sufficient in water resources. The key to effective water resource management is "local ownership." Community members contributed 30% of the cost themselves, with the government making up the difference. The model was so successful that the people of Nepal, even poorer than India, adopted the Gujarat approach to rainwater harvesting as a step toward solving their own scarcity of drinkable water.[4]

One of the best known and most widely distributed brand names of safe drinking water in India is produced by none other than Pepsi—the U.S.-based multinational that has discovered an almost infinite market for a product that is extremely cheap to produce. Clearly, it would not be in the business interests of Pepsi if suddenly everyone could drink their own tap water, shriveling up the market for bottled water. Hence, lobbyists for such companies are apt to work to maintain the status quo—assuring the dependence of the poor on purchased bottled water, as opposed to advocating free potable drinking water as a public good.

Reinforcing Poverty Through Religion and Cultural Traditions

The national identity of India depends on maintaining its traditions and religious rituals from the past, which, unfortunately, help to spread poverty. These collective habits not only form the cultural integrity of the country but also furnish its distinctive attraction for tourism. One of the holiest of Hindu cities from this traditional perspective is Varanasi, where pilgrims gather just before sunrise, awaiting the supreme eternal moment when the sun god Indra, the source of life, unites with the sacred, reanimating waters of the holy river, Ganga. Old people come to Varanasi when they know they are going to die in the belief that they will get salvation if they worship there and, even more important, if they are cremated there and have their ashes dispersed in the Ganga. Some people come believing that if they perform a Hindu ritual once in a lifetime in Varanasi, they do not have to perform an annual ritual for a relative who has died. Pilgrimages to Varanasi thus appeal to an economic efficiency of religious practice.

However, in terms of water coming from the Ganga and bathing in the sacred river, 29 cities, 70 towns, and numerous villages dump 345 million gallons of raw sewage a day into the water, as well as 70 million gallons of industrial waste from factories, 6 million tons of chemical fertilizer, and 9,000 tons of pesticides added by farmers.[5] No wonder that praying is such an important part of the ritual.

Traditional transportation systems are a part of India's distinctive cultural charm but block development of efficient public transportation systems for commutation to jobs, stimulating the economic modernization that could alleviate poverty. The narrow streets of Varanasi swarm with sacred cows (harming them brings a 20-year prison sentence), as well as dogs, people, bicycles, motorized and nonmotorized rickshaws, cars, and reckless buses. Bikes and rickshaws often substitute for beds to sleep on at night.

The depth of belief in traditions is epitomized by the respect Hindus still give to the role of the skull-cracker. Honor and fees are paid to this man who cracks the skulls of the bodies of the dead before they are cremated on the banks of the river Ganga, permitting the spirit to leave the body. Such traditions and strong beliefs among the less educated multitudes longing for hope in a life hereafter enforce the acceptance of the ways of poverty. This resistance to change as a mode of coping with daily challenges to survival can have high human costs for minorities in poor communities.

A Varanasi newspaper, *The Hindustan Times*, reported that poverty drove a mother in Orissa (one of India's poorest states) to sell her 45-day-old baby for 60 rupees (about $1.30). This mother was struck with a number of misfortunes. Her husband left her, and she had lost her job at a stone-crushing unit. Fearing she would not be able to feed the child, she sold her daughter to a family from her former workplace (who bought the child out of fear that otherwise, the mother would have thrown the baby away).[6] The same paper reported the murder of four women in the previous ten days. One was stoned to death because she had the HIV virus. The other three were killed as "witches" with the tacit approval of the local religious leader. In poor areas such as Bihar, Orissa, Uttar Pradesh, and West Bengal, it is still quite common that members of a family use the ruse of calling a woman a witch to get to her belongings. These murders were attributed to "extreme beliefs," which can be changed only by radical improvements in education. The poor still frequently seek the advice of medical quacks, who reinforce these irrational beliefs for the sake of their own economic interests.[7]

"Indian Time," Caste, and Aesthetic Design Confront Globalization

Between extreme irrational beliefs and the high-speed, secularized thinking that globalization seems to demand economically lies a vast tradition of deep spiritual and aesthetic resources that constitute the grounds of India's cultural integrity. Three active religions—Hinduism, Buddhism, and Jainism—dominate most of India.

In efforts to move beyond poverty, the Hindu view of time becomes important. For Hindus, time is not "here and now," as in Western existentialist thinking. Rather, time is infinite, forever and big enough for the universe to go about its business of cycles of expansion and contraction. Anything is possible in the long run.* Thus, Hindu time is very different from the fast-moving time demanded by globalization, which increasingly directs where investment and economic growth will go. For many Hindus, time spent with religious traditions is perceived to be more important than quick, modern steps to economic progress.

The Hindus have gods for almost every purpose—Shiva, "the destroyer" and god of "creative destruction," for example, who destroys the old to make room for the new (close to the economic philosophy of Joseph Schumpeter epitomized by today's globalization). The very complexity and elaborateness of Hindu rituals tempts believers into a dependence on the past, on the consolation of

---

*I am grateful to Suren Kaushik, my Indian colleague at Pace University, for this observation.

religion as a way to another life in the next reincarnation. This is reflected in the traditional, elaborate design of many sculptures, paintings, textiles, and artifacts that embody the Hindu tradition but may not easily sell to foreign tourists who have been socialized by globalized media into desiring a more minimalist, modern mode of aesthetic design. Tourists appreciate the workmanship and cave stories of the temples but often not to the extent of bringing home a replica from a world so removed from their own culture.

Beneath these rituals and designs lurks the Hindu caste system that dates back to 1200 B.C. The word *caste* stems from the Portuguese *casta*, meaning "race," "breed," or "lineage (Indians use the term *jati*). In India, there are some 3,000 castes and 25, 000 subcastes, each related to specific occupations. These categories fall under four main "Varnas": Brahmins (priests), Kshatryas (warriors), Viashyas (traders), and Shudras (laborers). The caste system tends to dictate not only occupation but also who one marries and what one eats. "Untouchables" are outside the caste system, some 250 million of them. The jobs that they typically have to take require them to be in touch with bodily fluids, such as cleaning toilets or picking up garbage. Hence, they are deemed impure people, not to be touched.

Caste discrimination continues, despite the 1950 law against it and government quotas that attempt to raise the living standards of the Untouchables by reserving jobs for them in the legislature, government service, and schools. These very government programs stimulate an increase of violence against the Untouchables by members of other castes, due to resentment.[8] Urbanization and economic development can break down caste barriers and benefit Untouchables in the long run. But there are short-term political advantages in identifying with constituencies opposed to undermining this caste tradition. National politicians appealing to religious traditions can reinforce the dependence on religion and the role of the social caste system. This political position encourages the poor to be content with their lot. Without social motivations to innovate and to modernize the economy beyond traditional modes of operating, more poverty will be the inevitable result. The ruling Bharatiya Janata party (BJP) has pushed an agenda of *hindutva*, advocating the creation of a Hindu state in which minorities would be forced to live as second-class citizens if they believe in a religion founded outside of India. Such a Hindu nationalist platform can give extremists an excuse to attack Muslims, leading to increasing social polarization.

Another problem is female literacy. On the macro level, the UNDP reports huge disparities across India's states between low social classes and the rest of the population. Although Rajasthan and Madya Pradesh have been praised as development models, bringing up overall literacy from 44% to 64% in Madhya Pradesh and from 39% to 61% in Rajasthan, in the low social classes, female literacy was only 7% in Rajasthan and 9% in Madhya Pradesh.

Noting that barely 1% of women in India have a college education, compared with about 3% of the men, several Indian professors in the United States have established their own colleges in India to help alleviate this problem. For example, Finance Professor Suren Kaushik of Pace University, New York decided to set up a college for women in Malsisar, his birthplace, a rural village of some 15,000 people surrounded by a desert. Located 150 miles west of Delhi and 120 miles north of Jaipur, the road connection to "civilization" is long and can be rough, especially during the monsoon season. The desert beauty colored by the unique saris of the women working in the fields with very simple hand instruments is offset by the realization of how low their agricultural productivity must be and of how important the education of women will become for their children.

This college was founded in 1999 and now has over 240 women attending classes. It is the only college within a radius of 20 miles and draws young women from the surrounding communities.* With large, modern classrooms and a new dormitory, the development of the college itself is a major human achievement in this rural area where people overwhelmingly live from agriculture. It represents a counter-stroke to the trend of the skilled and educated to leave the

---

*The Mrs. Helena Kaushik College for Women. To contribute, contact Professor Suren Kaushik, e-mail skaushik@pace.edu.

countryside for the opportunities in the cities, symbolized by a number of deserted and dilapidated old *havelis* (or palatial homes) in the village of Malsisar. The college also represents an effort to create a positive model of education at the higher level in order to have a multiplying effect of pulling more girls into lower-level preparatory secondary education in the region. Although the library has a relatively large number of English books, many donated by colleagues, it still lacks subscriptions to English newspapers or magazines, or an efficient Internet connection. Because English is the key language of access to the world economy and a prerequisite for upward mobility globally, it is essential to raise the level of English training and Internet connection. The connectivity level in India is still very low. Fewer than 3% of its population have access to the Internet.

India spends but 3.2% of its Gross Domestic Product (GDP) on education, despite the government's proud proclamation of a 6% target.[8] The government has particularly neglected elementary education, spending only 1.7% of GDP on primary education. Moreover, "free" government elementary schools are of such low quality that even the poor people who cannot afford it feel forced to use some of their precious rupees to try to put at least some of their children in private elementary schools they have to pay for in order to increase their chances for upward social mobility. The educated elites push higher education as their priority in government policy, undermining what should be a basic human right—adequate free education at the primary school level for all citizens. In so doing, the better paid government elite create more poverty, rather than putting scarce resources where they are most needed. Economist Jean Drèze projects that if the present trend of low-income families deserting low-quality government schools continues, the government schools will almost be wiped out within 10–15 years.[9] Yet, education is the key for moving beyond dependence on the agricultural sector, which keeps a nation underdeveloped .

Agriculture makes up some 29% of the Indian GDP but around 65% of the total work force. Ancient ways of cultivating crops still continue to be used throughout the country. But to bring the disadvantaged farmers to a point of potential self-sufficiency and further development, the productivity of the agricultural sector must be raised significantly.[10] Nobel economist W. Arthur Lewis demonstrated that the principal cause of poverty in the developing countries and of their poor factor endowments in terms of trade is that about half of the labor force produces food at very low productivity levels, limiting the domestic market for manufacturing and services.[11] As a nation moves from an agricultural economy to the manufacturing and service sectors, it benefits from a "virtuous economic circle" of "learning by doing" that leads to competitiveness in a capitalist world economy.[12]

When this transformation occurs, there are inevitably two economies within the nation—one modern and one underdeveloped. This transitional "dual economy" between the traditional, underdeveloped rural sector and modernized urban sector leads to prolific begging in the cities, where the contrast between wealth and poverty is the greatest. One must keep in mind that India has no pension or health insurance system. "Retiring," therefore, becomes meaningless for most Indians, except when going to sleep in the evening. In this light, the following brief exchange with an Indian shepherd, who could have been anywhere between 50 and 70 years old, is informative.

> "How old are you?"
> "I don't know . . .
> "I count my sheep and goats every day. Somebody might steal them. But why count my years? No one will steal those!"

For a poor shepherd, there is no need to keep track of one's age. The few sheep or goats are all he has. These are what count.

For the majority of the Indian population, health care and pension systems are luxuries that emerge only in the cities and are reserved for the elite, that is, for a select group of civil servants. Civil servants must be counted as part of the well-off in India, compared with the masses of have-nots. The civil servants are "insiders" who know how to use the system to maximize their own interests. Elected officials, like politicians anywhere, promise much more than they deliver (e.g., "Drinking water for everyone" being one of the slogans). In most cases, they do not run for office out of higher ideals but to enrich themselves. Once elected, most of these politicians direct their efforts toward only their own social class or constituency, and the poor are usually forgotten. As often as not, foreign aid money to the government gets siphoned off to interest groups that can stabilize the power base of elected officials.

Such class differences emerge nationwide in critical areas. A further gap between those better off and the poor is in rates of infant mortality. Despite a general drop in infant mortality in India, it is extremely high in rural areas where poverty is widespread, particularly in the north and center of the country. The areas where immunization rates are high are overwhelmingly concentrated in the south of India—pointing to a gap between better-off people in the south and poorer people in the north and the center of the country. Overall, India spends only 1.3% of its GDP on health.

Public money appears to be more evenly distributed in the tropical, lush, southern state of Kerala ("God's own country"). With the highest literacy rate in India, Kerala is ruled by the Communist party (advocating socialism). This exceptional state has apparently been successful in mitigating the gap between the better off and the poor to a great extent, although the natural beauty no doubt gives poverty a more pleasant aspect, especially because it is distributed here more evenly throughout the region. Strikingly, life expectancy in Kerala is actually longer than in Washington, D.C.[13]

But socialism has its opportunity costs—high unemployment. The heavy unionization due to Communist party leadership limits the number of companies desiring to set up in Kerala, and the natives must seek work elsewhere. Indeed, there is a local joke that if you climb Mount Everest, you will find someone from Kerala at the peak, ready to serve you tea. Many households in Kerala used to have a family member who did service work in Middle Eastern countries and sent back money—an important source of income for this region (until 2002, when restrictions in state policies in the Middle East caused most of the Indians to go home). Nevertheless, in Kerala, as in other parts of India, some of the world's most luxurious hotels are situated in exotic locations but never too far from the shanty towns or huts of the poor, from which they are carefully guarded.

Consider the case of W, a 26-year-old driver, which illustrates the vulnerability of the poor, even in "God's own country." He is one of four children, the youngest crippled and bedridden at home. His father was cheated in a family business by relatives and had to give them the home he had built. When they refused to give his home back after he paid off some of the debt as agreed, he committed suicide. It seems there was some animosity caused by that fact that the father was Christian and the mother Hindu, and it was not a customary arranged marriage. After his father's death, the mother took to cooking banana fritters at a little roadside stand. Because of the family situation, W was not able to continue his education beyond the fifth grade. He had searched for work for two years before he found the job as a driver (and even this was scheduled to last only a short while). His marriage had already been arranged. To seek a better life and economic opportunity, he was ready to leave India for the United States, not recognizing that without a good educational background, mobility to greater opportunities in developed countries is limited. W will most likely be pinned down in a disadvantaged situation in his native country, with few or no opportunities for improvement. Such is the fate of the poor: They get stranded without fallback positions.

High-Tech Bangalore and the Time Warp

India lives in many centuries at once. Again and again, the traveler experiences a "time warp." From the traditional skull-cracker in Hindu circles to the cutting-edge software designer, one perceives contrasting stratum of the living past in going from region to region—even from street to street in the same city. The layers of history are thick and distinct, and one has a feeling of being thrown into a time machine out of control. These extreme differences mirror the world at large and permit the efficient, urban, educated rich to spring decades ahead of their disadvantaged brothers and sisters in the rural periphery. In Bangalore, more than in any other Indian city, this contrast is particularly apparent.

From a sleepy administrative center under the British Raj, Bangalore has been transformed from a pensioner's dream (given the mild climate) into a modern city of 5.5 million people by the low-cost software development information technology (IT) sector. The city appears to be not only modern but almost Western in its commercial sector on MG (Mahatma Gandhi) Road in terms of stylish boutiques and fast-food shops, although the infrastructure of a developing country that has not yet been fully transformed can still be detected.

Criticizing this infrastructure, Azim Premji, one of the richest men in India and CEO of Wipro, a company headquartered on the outskirts of the city, noted how embarrassing it was to have overseas clients visit his office and experience about four power cuts during a one-hour meeting.[14] Observing that large tracts of land were being developed for both commercial and residential use in the area, Premji predicted that traffic would come to a standstill in a year or so, due to a breakdown of the whole infrastructure. He threatened public officials with the possible need for a "dharma"—a people's protest movement, such as the one held several years ago by residents of Electronic City Road in Bangalore, to demand a better infrastructure. It was probably no accident that Premji's political threat of staging a dharma came only a day after the chairman of another successful software company in Bangalore, N. R. Narayan Murthy, failed to talk the civil aviation ministry into flying more international flights out of Bangalore. Thus, **powerful business elites organize politically to create better infrastructures in the areas where they live and work, whereas the disadvantaged are usually not organized enough to demand that government resources go to their poorer regions.**

Clearly, India *as a whole* is much better off with the economic growth engine of Bangalore than it would be without. Software accounts for about 65% of India's IT revenue and for over 200,000 jobs, and about 32% of India's software production is based in Bangalore.

The question is how to get other such IT centers going in India in order to redistribute the growth where it is needed. But to consider this question, one needs briefly to consider how this software Mecca came to be.

After India received its independence from Britain in 1947, it had an extremely protectionist policy that required companies to get government permission for any business they undertook and which discouraged foreign investment. IBM left India when it could not keep over 50% of the ownership of its direct investment. A traditional policy of socialist five-year plans and high tariffs kept India apart from the global economy. But national policy shifted toward trade liberalization under the government of Rajiv Gandhi in the 1980s. In 1986, Texas Instruments received permission to own 100% of a subsidiary. This started a wave of foreign direct investment that sped up after further economic liberalization of the economy following the 1991 foreign exchange crisis. But this liberalization emerged largely in the software sector because government policy makers still focused on protecting steel, textiles, and automobiles—hard "wares." Software was not on the government's regulatory screen. Because it was not dependent on government regulation or capital and no license was needed to manufacture anything not made in a factory, not much attention was paid to the sector. "The best thing the government did was to ignore it," said Rajiv Sahney, working in the Mumbai office of "antfactory," the European high-tech incubator.[15]

Sometimes you get what you do *not* pay attention to.

What was critical to the development of the IT sector in India, however, was the government's creation of the Indian Institutes of Technology (in New Delhi, Mumbai, Chennai, etc.). Based on a national exam competition, it offered fully funded engineering programs starting in the 1950s. So competitive did these schools become that it is now easier to get into the Massachusetts Institute of Technology in Boston than into some of these programs. Just as targeted Pentagon funding of programs at Stanford University was critical to the development of Silicon Valley and of the Internet, so too was the investment in human capital in India by the government vital to create an applied intellectual elite in order to help modernize the country.

Meanwhile, 25 engineering colleges around Bangalore provide the talent needed for the companies there. One large problem is that thousands of Indian engineers come to the United States every year to work, and many never return to India. Also, initially the creative, synergistic IT designs were completed in the United States and elsewhere, and India became the low-cost, high-quality offshore place to service the software needs for these designs. However, this is changing as companies in Bangalore go up the value chain in the sophistication of their software development. Still, India has not yet created a cultural center of creative innovation and synergistic high-tech learning that is able to attract the best and brightest scientists from all over the world. As the CEO of Oracle, Larry Ellison (who made a major new investment in 2003 in India) noted, India has become the center for offshore service for developed countries, and China is the center for offshore manufacturing.

Because manufacturing is the traditional engine of economic growth in industrial revolutions, this does not bode well for India but suggests that China may modernize more effectively. Indeed, China pays as little as 50 cents an hour to automobile workers and could surpass Germany as the world's third largest auto-manufacturing country by 2007.[16] One difficulty for India in this competition is that it is easier to get productivity increases in the manufacturing sector than in any particular service sector. This permits China to use software advances from elsewhere and to apply them to their dynamic manufacturing companies. China also has the edge in terms of the adult literacy rate (86% of those 15 and above are literate, compared with 58% in India) and in enrollments in primary, secondary, and tertiary schools (64% vs. 56% in India).[17] India must find ways to systematically transform its disadvantaged traditional agricultural sectors so that they can join the twenty-first century or the existing inequalities could well become so severe that they will encourage extremist religious national movements that threaten to undermine democratic stability.

India's advantage may lie in entrepreneurship. Indian entrepreneurs founded more than 750 technology companies in Silicon Valley. Indeed, some experts argue that India's home grown entrepreneurs may give it a long-term advantage over a China hamstrung by inefficient banks and capital markets.[18] Many of these entrepreneurs send money back to India, but whether they will ultimately come home to refurbish the dynamism of India's IT sector is an open question. "Brain drain"—with the best and brightest engineers often ending up in the United States—is just one of a number of poverty traps that India illustrates. This is a symptom of the global free market ideology that permits those initially subsidized by the state to leave the country and to seek out higher wages or profits elsewhere. Individuals will naturally tend to go to the places in the world where economic opportunities are the greatest, leaving their responsibilities at home.

Economically, India embodies a paradox. On one hand, the country needs to open its national economy to the global market in order to stimulate trade, foreign investment, and economic growth. On the other hand, this very move toward liberalization can cause wealth to become concentrated or to leave the country altogether. Culturally, economically, and politically, India is a crucible for what development economists have called "poverty traps."

References

1. UNDP 2003 Human Development Report, as cited in *The Indian Express*, July 11, 2003.

2. "Sickness in Health," *The Times of India*, Mumbai, July 19, 2003.

3. Lalita Panicker, "Ignominy Index: India's Development Slide Show," *The Times of India*, Mumbai, July 19, 2003.

4. Suvecha Pant, "Water Management: If Gujurat Can, So Can We," *The Kathmandu Post*, July 8, 2002.

5. Barbara Crossette, "Kofi Annan's Amazing Facts," *The New York Times*, September 27, 1998.

6. "Poverty Drives Mother to Sell 45-Day-Old Baby for 60 Rupees," *The Hindustan Times*, July 11, 2003.

7. *The Hindustan Times*, Op-Ed page, July 11, 2003.

8. Memorandum to the United Nations Calling for an Investigation into Atrocities Against Untouchables of India by the UN Commissioner for Human Rights (July 21, 1997), paragraph 10.

9. Amy Waldman, "India's Poor Bet Precious Sums on Private Schools," *The New York Times*, November 15, 2003.

10. See, for example, S. S. Somra, "Globalization and Sustainable Agriculture and Rural Development in India," a paper presented in conference on "Globalization and Sustainable Development," Mrs. Helena Kaushik Women's College, P.O. Malsisar, District Jhunjhunu, Rajasthan, India.

11. W. Arthur Lewis, *The Evolution of the International Economic Order* (Princeton, NJ: Princeton University Press, 1978).

12. R. Isaak, *Managing World Economic Change*, 3rd edition (Upper Saddle River, NJ: Prentice Hall, 2000), pp. 211–213.

13. "Attacking Poverty: Opportunity, Empowerment and Security," *World Development Report 2001* (Washington, D.C.: World Bank, 2001), p. 4.

14. "Premji Battles the Sloth Virus," *The Times of India*, July 19, 2003.

15. As cited in David Rosenberg, *Cloning Silicon Valley* (London: Pearson Education/Reuters, 2002), pp. 125–126.

16. Keith Bradsher, "China's Factories Aim to Fill Garages Around the World," *The New York Times*, November 2, 2003.

17. UNDP, *Human Development Report 2003* (New York: United Nations, 2003), p. 239.

18. Yasheng Huang and Tarun Khanna, "Can India Overtake China?" *Foreign Policy*, July/August 2003, pp. 74–81.

9 Poverty Traps

*The rich creditor governments that "own and operate"
the principal international financial institutions—such
as the IMF, the World Bank, and the Paris Club—
have failed to acknowledge the pervasive risks of poverty
traps for very low-income countries.*

—JEFFREY SACHS,
Resolving the Debt Crisis of Low-Income Countries
(2002)

T*he global economy sets up a number of traps that poor people cannot avoid without help.*

India demonstrated that significant progress toward modernization runs into deep-seated traditions and obstacles that seem to be locked into the social system. It still remains the country with the largest number of hungry people in the world. India's difficulties typify those of other poor countries. Globalization in the late twentieth century proved that reliance on free markets is the key to wealth. But if the government opens up all rules and regulations at once, the most skilled people and most imaginative entrepreneurs are motivated to leave India for places of greater opportunity and larger markets, such as Silicon Valley, perhaps never to return. Without globalization, India would never have had its stunning successes in the global software business, nor would it have improved its economic growth rate to such an extent. But this very same globalization cannot solve India's "brain drain" problem without government regulation of some kind. The evidence suggests that the reason India and China were able to keep a great deal of their economic gains from globalization may have to do not merely with liberalizing their economies but also with their governments' refusal to liberalize their domestic capital markets. India and China did not want all their money to leak out as fast as their brainpower did. By avoiding what might be called "the financial liberalization trap," these countries buffered themselves somewhat from the downturn in the global economy after the dot-com bust and the events of September 11, 2001, and kept much of their gains. But they are exceptions to the rule(s).

Compare the global economy for a moment with the setting of a number of mousetraps. How are the traps set? By whom? Where are they set? For whom? How does one get caught?

The global elite, the insiders, key interest groups, and their lobbyists help to set the traps. Basically, these actors are motivated to maximize their own interests and those of their support groups through increasing their economic welfare, either by stabilizing or by disrupting the global system in order to make this self-interested welfare possible. Economic growth thus takes on a very specific meaning: These elite interest groups want to maximize their own economic growth, and if it is necessary to maximize their nation's economic growth and wealth in the process, so be it. Therefore, they have to be sure there is a highly motivated working class at home and abroad that can provide the resources, goods, and services that the elite require at a reasonable cost. So the traps that are set have to be established in the developing countries where many of the required natural resources are located, as well as wherever cheap skilled labor is still available—at home or abroad. From this perspective, the working-class poor, for example, are no accident. They serve the agenda of global competitiveness. And the unemployment and underemployment generated by eliminating tariffs and regulations on capital flows keep labor costs down and the work force flexible. Global productivity rises as costs of production, including labor, fall. Poverty rises as wages fall. And some of these effects come from the design of institutions.

The Institutional Trap

The existing institutional setup of most countries rarely targets the needs of the poorest of their people. Moreover, these bureaucracies typically work against creating solutions that would make these disadvantaged people more self-sufficient. As we noted previously, when what seemed like all the money in the world rained down on Thailand in the early 1990s, it became clear that Thailand did not have the institutional or banking infrastructure to cope with all this investment or "hot capital" chasing the highest short-term global returns. Money was distributed to relatives of corrupt elites, who set up unregulated banking subsidiaries until the whole system came crashing down because investors no longer believed in the strength of the currency. As German economist Wilhelm Hankel has observed, while developed countries tend to be "overbanked" (too many banks), developing countries are "underbanked "(too few banks).

A transparent banking system is hard to come by. China, for example, is coping with a series of major banking crises and reported 8,000 cases of financial fraud, totaling some $12 billion in one year alone.[1] **Well-regulated and stable financial institutions are key building blocks for economic development that can provide widespread opportunity to all citizens.**

From Nepal to Mexico, in talking with everyday people, guides, and taxi drivers, one common conclusion stands out in developing countries—people enter politics to enrich themselves. As we noted in the case of India, politicians typically promise whatever they need to in order to gain support; once elected, they use their offices to accumulate wealth, forgetting their promises. The nexus between the government civil service, large banks and multinational companies, and other official institutions keeps this status quo going for the sake of careers and the privileges of all the individuals lucky enough to have landed "institutional positions." This institutional stalemate keeps the poorest countries in a permanent state of welfare dependence from outside the country and creates a situation, at its worst, in which countries caught in this trap will not necessarily benefit from a healthy global market. In this case, **those people in developing countries without the right training and equipment inevitably lose, even if the market "works."** As development expert Nancy Birdsell noted, the preexisting institutional assets of industrialized countries explain much of why 80% of all foreign investment occurs among the these nations while just 0.1% of all U.S. foreign investment went to Sub-Saharan Africa in 2001.[2]

Human beings come together to create institutions in order to satisfy their human needs. Over time, these social arrangements become routines, unconscious habits, and traditions that repeat themselves over and over again, taking on lives of their own. Thus, temples, churches, and governments are born, as well as central banks and entire banking, religious, and educational systems. Once established, they become difficult to change because the people running them build in rules that shore up their own job security and privileges while the populace takes these institutions for granted as a part of the culture. Even if institutions become obstacles to satisfying the needs of the population, the people still tend to believe in them and give them legitimacy—looking at them with awe, usually reinforced through potential military or police force. Indeed, sociologist Max Weber pointed out that the state is the one institution in a country with a monopoly on the use of force. If this is true, how can you make meaningful reforms in the key institution backed by a monopoly of force that can be used potentially to eliminate all opponents?

Consider a simple but not so simple case—Madagascar. The social institutions that developed there were focused on how many cattle a person owned at death: The greater the number, the greater the honor. Therefore, the farmers overgrazed the land and the rain forests with cattle in order to accumulate for prestige at death. The institutional tradition became self-destructive in terms of the people's long-term needs. As the land wore out, more members of the population were driven into poverty.

Or consider the classic case of institutional decay—Italy. The Italians became so exhausted by the turnover of governments due to political wheeling and dealing and corruption after World War II that in the 1990s, they finally supported Silvio Berlusconi for a second time as Prime Minister. In part, the voters figured that as the richest man in Italy, a media baron, he might be able to hold the government together longer than previous prime ministers had been able to. Italy had joined the Euro monetary system and needed strong government leadership to keep up the fiscal responsibility required. But institutional corruption at the top of the government threatened Italy's long-term legitimacy. Berlusconi's successful efforts to pass legislation in order to keep from being indicted while sitting as Prime Minister and his ability to get laws changed to maintain and to extend his media empire did not go unnoticed in the foreign press (e.g., particularly *The Economist*[3]). Then in 2003, Berlusconi suddenly assumed his turn representing Italy at the head of the European Union (EU). The institutional trap the Italians had fallen into was exposed, and the legitimacy of the government continued to unravel.

Of course, the Italian case appears to be civilized in comparison with the murderous reign of Uganda's Idi Amin, who ordered thousands of tribes other than his own killed and had Asian workers expelled in the 1980s. The very same media power that Berlusconi abused in Italy can function to expose megalomaniacs such as Amin, who manipulate existing institutional frameworks for their own whims, no matter where they are in the world. Nor are such policies isolated incidents.

Tanzania's "villagization" program in the 1970s is another case in point. At that time, President Julius Nyerere advocated rural socialism, called *ujamaa* or "familyhood," based on agricultural cooperative living. Nyerere began with voluntary means, then used the state's monopoly of force to move Tanzanians to 8,000 "familyhood villages" (*ujamaa vijijini*), where the government presumably would provide them with water and education and keep an eye on them. By the end of the 1970s, some 65% of the population was deported to these villages. But the water did not arrive, nor did the schools. The people who had been moved then drifted out of the villages to set up their own shelters in the bush. A well-to-do, powerful elite succeed in impoverishing masses of the population despite the nation's natural wealth and beauty. With rich wildlife reserves and other resources, the institutional trap in Tanzania illustrated what journalist P. J. O'Rourke summed up as "How to Make Nothing from Everything."[4] Indeed, between 1970 and 1990, the World Bank records that *zero* foreign direct investment went into Tanzania.[5]

As noted earlier, after the passing of the Nyerere regime, Tanzania was so successful in reforming its institutions and improving its "investment climate" that it is one of only six nations that qualified for outright debt cancellation by 2002, under the recent Heavily Independent Poor Countries (HIPC) guidelines of the World Bank-International Monetary Fund (IMF). To qualify, these countries are forced to spend much more on education and health care. But the global recession caused several of these nations to slip back into a debt trap, due to weak exports or renewed borrowing. Uganda, for instance, which had been a model reformer, had to apply for new debt relief after coffee prices dropped 53% over three years.[6]

In sum, without stable, transparent institutions that appear to be free from corruption, it is difficult to attract foreign investment or to increase economic growth and opportunities of upward mobility for the disadvantaged. Rich and stable countries tend to invest in rich and stable countries. But a vicious cycle of institutional stalemate is often made worse by distortions in the structure of trade.

The Trade Trap

Perhaps the most characteristic dilemma into which developing countries inevitably fall is the trade pitfall, illustrated by Uganda's dependence on coffee. Most of these nations rely on commodities—agriculture or minerals—as their basis of survival. Yet the price of these commodities typically stays flat or declines, compared with the prices of the manufactured goods and services of developed countries. Thus, **a trade gap increases inequality because developed countries produce goods and services that fetch much more money than what developing countries produce.** Developed countries are more capable of creating a diverse portfolio of products and services so that their economies do not become unduly dependent on any one industry or product. And just to add salt to the wound, developed countries such as those of the EU and the United States impose tariffs on agricultural goods and other commodities coming in from developing countries in order protect their own domestic labor forces.

In the period between 1973 and 1995, for example, the World Trade Organization reported that the value of world exports in manufacturing increased six times more than the export value of agriculture and mining products. This was six times better news for manufacturing producers than for those dependent on exporting commodities. Between 1997 and 2000, the export performance of the primary commodity exporters among the least developed countries, located mainly in Africa, was erratic, dropping in 19 of the 26 non-oil commodity exporters. Consider what happened to the price of commodities during this period (the same time frame as the dot-com boom in the United States): Between 1997 and 2001, copper fell by 27%, cotton by 39%, coffee by 66%, gold by 18%, food by 31%, agricultural raw materials by 20%, and minerals, ores, and metals by 17%. Meanwhile, in contrast, merchandise exports from the least developed countries that export mainly manufacturing or services increased by 46%: The least developed Asian countries were prominent in this group, helped by low labor costs and proximity to better-off East Asian nations that served as a source of sales and investment. Of course, oil exporters among the least developed countries were the exceptions that proved the rule, accounting for 40% of all least developed country exports between 1997 and 2000.[7] However, as Fareed Zakaria has noted, "The most difficult task economically is reforming the trust-fund [oil-producing] states. It has proved nearly impossible to wean them off their easy money."[8] The lone commodity of oil is a sticky trap in its own right. In Sudan oil has stimulated war. In Chad, villagers are not too happy with the payment they received for the land where oil was discovered—a fraction of the investment going in to the country, yet driving up the price of each mango tree to $1,000.[9]

If, like most developing countries, you depend mainly on agricultural or mineral commodities for a living, you are stuck with decreasing bargaining power when it comes time to swap what you produce for the manufactured goods you need. This "trade gap" applies not only to agricultural and mineral commodities but to textiles as well—another specialty of poor countries.

Mexico tried to overcome its protectionist traditions and get around the trade trap by setting up the *maquiladoras*—an industrial plant just below the U.S. border that assembles parts from abroad (for example, for cars) and exports the finished products. In the first decade, from 1978 to 1988, the *maquiladoras* grew 14% annually, employing more than 350,000 workers in 1,500 plants. But in this effort to match the standards of globalization, the *maquiladoras* exploited the labor of young women, forcing them to live in dehumanizing slums. Because most of the girls would not have had jobs otherwise, they put up with these depressing conditions. They needed to send money home to support their families. By the early 1990s, the level of Mexican productivity growth had reached double that of the United States, but the average Mexican worker earned only one sixth or less what his or her American counterpart earned.[10] And by the early twenty-first century, many of the *maquiladora* assembly jobs had left Mexico for China, where manufacturing wages were much lower. It is not just Mexico that suffers from an increasingly sophisticated trade trap, due to the global mobility of multinational companies chasing low Chinese wage rates.

Take the case of Mauritius, an island not far from Madagascar that became independent from Britain in 1968. Initially, its economy relied on sugar cane and tourism on its beaches. But the government shifted priorities to plug into the globalized economy, creating an export zone of low taxes and flexible labor laws to attract textile manufacturing companies. However, this focus on just one commodity-based sector left the economy vulnerable to any radical shift in the global economy. After median household income almost doubled in the 1990s, the people from Mauritius became complacent with what they thought were secure jobs in the textile factories. But companies turning out global brands, such as Gap and Calvin Klein, grew so fast that they needed to import cheaper labor from India and China to keep up with the demand.

Literacy in Mauritius climbed to one of the highest rates in Africa, and the government was a stable democracy. The natives who now could afford a house and a little stability in their lives no longer wanted to work overtime, and the textile companies started to discriminate in favor of hungry immigrant workers who would not have to leave early to take care of family obligations. Trade barriers eased worldwide, and India and China flooded the market with their own textiles, putting huge competitive pressure on the one-sector dependent island of Mauritius. Factories closed down. The unemployment rate jumped from 3% to 10% in a decade, and Mauritians suddenly found themselves becoming poor again as the dark side of globalization cast shadows over their sunny climate.[11]

In sum, the trade trap keeps developing countries dependent on commodities and textiles, where prices do not go up to the same extent that they do for high-end manufactured goods or service industries. Frozen into low-paying sectors, when the inevitable global changes come, most of the people do not have the training or resources to adapt and to find other means of livelihood.

The Educational Trap, the Gender Gap, and the Digital Divide

What hurt the Mauritians as the world economy was transformed was the inability to shift their skills and attitudes to the new conditions imposed on them by the acceleration of global business. As the world becomes dominated by the "knowledge economy" due to the amplifications of technology, displacing the importance of not only agriculture but manufacturing as well, people have to retool. Indeed, we find ourselves in an era of lifetime learning. As *New York*

Times reporter Thomas Friedman pointed out, most careers have become a series of 100-yard dashes, rather than the long marathon runs they once were.[12]

Opportunities come quickly and briefly. We must seize them in order to prepare for new jobs. Learning how to learn quickly (to be "quick studies") has become the most critical skill of all. Or, put another way: We must learn how to fail quickly. We must recognize our mistakes quickly so that we still have the time and resources left to adapt and to minimize the consequences of the errors we are bound to make.

The poor do not have as many chances to learn to fail quickly. Rarely are they given second chances ("learning by burning"). They have few assets to fall back on to recover from failure and to finance a new start. One of the huge advantages of the Silicon Valley boom in the United States was that it gave thousands of Americans the chance to fail at innovations and to be funded again and again for second, third, and fourth chances. During the 1990s dot-com boom, venture capital was easily invested in ideas, many of which never became products. But each time, the learning curves of Silicon Valley entrepreneurs sped up and raised the bar of competitiveness. Jim Clark, a Stanford professor, dropped out of academia to create three billion-dollar companies (Silicon Graphics, Netscape, and Healtheon), based on liberally provided venture capital. This generously financed process of collective learning was unique to the United States. Other wealthy countries and peoples did not have the same opportunities, much less those in developing nations. After all, in the United States, if you have not been bankrupt at least once or do not have a debt record you have paid back slowly, you will not have a credit record and will have a hard time getting loans. The American commercial banking system is based on funding those who have recovered from bad experiences. It thrives on the mistakes of others and, therefore, encourages "learning by burning." China seems to have adopted this lending behavior as well, leading to a large overhang of bad debts and an overheating economy—typical results of these financial "learning" cycles.[13]

Reducing gaps in education may be more important than narrowing differences in income within poor countries, according to recent research. Spanish professors Amparo Castello and Rafael Domenech analyzed 108 countries from 1960 through 1990 and found that a concentration of higher education in a small percentage of the population was associated with slower per capita income growth. In contrast, in their study, unequal income distribution did not seem to be strongly correlated with slow growth. Not surprisingly, South Asia and Sub-Saharan Africa are the regions with the most unequal distribution of education, whereas the developed countries have the least inequality of education, followed closely by East Asia.[14] In a study of the 20 most populous developing countries between 1982 and 2001, it was found that the greater number of years of schooling per person correlated with greater economic growth.[15]

The overlap of the educational trap and the gender gap in developing countries is striking. Two thirds of the illiterate in the world are women. And of the women who do work, most are concentrated in the bottom end of the labor market and receive as much as 50% less pay than men in developing countries.[16] Among women, the pitfalls of poverty seem to compound, creating tragic conditions. Low educational levels mean higher fertility rates, and more children often mean higher disease rates, lower family income, greater hunger, housing shortages, and higher infant mortality. If, for example, mothers in Sub-Saharan Africa have no formal schooling, only 30% of them have their children vaccinated, compared with 70% of mothers with a secondary education.[16]

Look at it a different way. If you really want to break down poverty, focus on the education of girls, who then have fewer children, get better-paying jobs, increase the family income, and are more likely to become entrepreneurs, stimulating national economic growth. Studies have shown that gains in women's education contributed most to reducing malnutrition in 63 countries between 1970 and 1995. Indeed, if female farmers in Cameroon or Kenya were given the same schooling and opportunities as male farmers, the crop yields in these countries would increase 20%.[16]

Even in rich countries such as the United States, studies show that low-income parents on welfare impart to their young children only half the vocabulary that children of more affluent parents receive, and the poor admonish their children twice as much as privileged parents, who are more apt to praise their children (giving them self-confidence). Low-income minority children in the United States are three months behind in reading and math skills when they start kindergarten, and they never catch up. By the twelfth grade, African-Americans and Hispanics read only at the level of eighth-grade white and Asian children.[17] Meanwhile, preschool programs that could help to close these gaps are being cut back or slowed down in 23 states in the United States because of constraints in state budgets. Children from low-income households graduating from high school with at least minimal qualifications for four-year colleges enroll at half the rate of their peers from high-income families. And if they do attend college, the low-income students in the United States are much less likely to graduate.[18]

At higher levels of education, 99.6% of the populations of Africa and South Asia did not have use of the Internet by the beginning of the twenty-first century. Clearly, there is a "digital divide" that slows growth rates in the developing economies, compared with those in developed countries.[19] But without an adequate infrastructure of electricity in rural areas, one cannot access the Internet. Although Internet access is strongly correlated with increased growth rates, other priorities are more important than digital literacy in poor countries beyond water, food, and electricity, such as basic health and education.[20]

There is a deeper issue here. Although information technology can have many positive effects in modern societies, such as increasing productivity and distributing medical therapies to remote areas, it can also destroy traditional cultures and ways of being. Even in developed nations, the Internet is not an unmixed blessing because it tempts people to spend more time with computers than with other human beings and provides such sudden productivity increases that unemployment spreads rapidly among older economic sectors, at least in the short term.

The very identity of cultural life in developing countries can be permanently changed, if not undermined, by a preoccupation with computer technology for its own sake. Social critic Ivan Illich wrote about the dangers of "overprogramming," in which knowledge representative of man's "trivialization" by his manufactured milieu overwhelms his knowledge that signifies creative human action on the environment. That is, a human being's sense of confidence in using personal knowledge to be active in creating his or her own distinctive works is forgotten in the absorption of Internet surfing, computer games, and derivative work on the computer. People seek knowledge in sorting through information that exists, rather than creating knowledge through personal experimentation and experience. Illich extends this thesis of crippled learning further to the outside world, arguing that "overefficient" tools applied to facilitate man's relationship to his environment can destroy the balance between man and nature and lead to situations of "radical monopoly," or the dominance of one product exclusively produced by one corporation (Microsoft would be an example).[21]

The danger of merely adapting to the competitive economy is that "globalized" knowledge can lead individuals to become mere specialized functions and vehicles of institutionalized behavior. People become simply accessories of bureaucracies and machines, rather than learning to use technology to free themselves of dependence on the routines of others in order to become more creative and self-sufficient. For example, in Egypt, more educational achievements paradoxically seem to steadily reduce the probability of being self-employed or an employer.[22] Institutionalized education often socializes us to increasingly depend on "experts" to satisfy our needs, undermining our abilities to learn to take care of ourselves. Yet it is all too easy for those who have had the advantage of advanced institutional education to level such social criticism. Millions of people in the world have not even had the opportunity to have access to primary education.

Because some 113 million children in the world between ages 6 and 11 did not even attend school as the twenty-first century began, the international community has set 2015 as the date for achieving universal primary education. After all, adults in Africa and South Asia have completed only an average of three years of formal education, and those in Latin America have completed six years. On average, countries with a per capita Gross National Product (GNP) below $1,200 annually have an average of about four years of formal education. Moreover, simply enrolling children in school does not mean that they will finish or become well educated. Although almost all children enroll in primary school in Madagascar, for instance, only 27% of them reach the fifth grade (only 11% of girls in rural areas). Here the gap between the better-off and the poor is clearly visible. Although 70% of the children in the top two income deciles complete primary education, only 6% of those coming from households in the poorest two deciles make it through.[23] In sum, most people in the world are blocked from access to the highest levels of education, which have become increasingly complex and expensive.

In a knowledge economy increasingly dependent on services, the ability to attend primary school through college has become critical in terms of gaining respectable employment. Education brings self-confidence and the tools to become more self-sufficient in an environment in which people discriminate according to educational background. And those from lower income families who do attempt to become as educated as they can often find themselves going deeply into debt.

The Debt Trap

The educational deficits of the disadvantaged are directly related to the debt their country has accumulated. When Madagascar's debt payments peaked between 1991 and 1995, government spending on education was cut in half. **Poor nations must spend so much to pay off their old debt that they are forced to cut spending on essential public services, such as education, in order to qualify for new financing from other nations or international institutions.** In short, old debt drives away new money and puts poor countries in a permanent cash squeeze.

Due to the debt crisis emerging in the late 1970s, some 40 developing countries (from Mexico and Argentina to Brazil and Poland) found themselves in this cash squeeze by 1982, and many have never recovered. In the 1970s, oil prices shot up. So did multinational bank lending on the assumption that even if the banks did not get the principal of the loan back, they could live off of high interest rate payments. Loans went disproportionately to countries with oil reserves (as they still do today) on the assumption that rising oil prices would be the collateral. But then oil prices fell, and even oil-producing developing countries such as Mexico could not pay back either the principal or the interest on the loans. For the next decade, the creditors did not consider writing off the loans but merely tried to restructure them. Eventually, by the 1990s, they agreed to write off arbitrary amounts—initially one third (in 1988), then one half (in 1994).

Nevertheless, despite these arbitrary debt reductions, 39 countries remained in a chronic debt crisis. They got neither sufficient help to restore economic growth nor a deep enough debt reduction to reestablish normal relationships with creditors.[24] No international system of "bankruptcy" protection is in place for sovereign states to prevent a "grab race" by creditors to get repaid first or to give countries a "fresh start" at economic growth without being dragged down by old debt. Insolvent governments, heavily burdened by servicing their debt, have to cut back on essentials such as health, police, and fire services, undermining stability and public order and making the nation more vulnerable to internal insurgencies and external military threats. Clearly, the least developed poor countries find themselves caught between a rock and a hard place—neither able to pay off the old debt because of lack of economic growth nor in a position (due to their reputation for debt) to attract enough new money to start up economic growth. By 2001, the less developed countries as a group had a total debt stock of $143.2 billion, with annual debt service payments of $4.6 billion. The major source of new debt is official loans, particularly multilateral loans, skewed by the rules established by the rich countries.[25]

But indebtedness is also a cultural issue that can reduce the ability of a country to govern itself successfully.

Cultural Traps and Governability

One of the key dilemmas the poor must fight against is the culture of colonialism that still often remains, however hidden beneath the surface. During the nineteenth and early twentieth centuries, the colonial powers from Europe assumed that peoples in developing countries were so constituted that they react differently from people of European stock. Swedish economist Gunner Myrdal summed up this prejudice: "Their tendency toward idleness and inefficiency, and their reluctance to venture into new enterprise and often even to seek wage employment, were seen as expressions of their lack of ambition, limited economic horizons, survival-mindedness, carefree disposition, and preference for a leisurely life."[26] Curiously, many of the natives of colonized countries passively accepted these views and later created their strongest trade ties with their former colonizers, preferring to do business with "the bastards they know the best."

Of course, the natives learned a great deal from their occupiers. It is difficult to imagine India's modernization without the heritage of British rule and language (even down to driving on the left side of the road) or South Korea's fast development without its mimicking many of the institutions and ideas of the Japanese, who were harsh occupiers indeed. In both cases, whether it was Prime Minister J. Nehru aping the British gentlemen in India or the South Koreans determined to outcompete their Japanese competitors, the developed colonial power set standards of achievement for poor nations to strive for, if not some day to surpass.

More often than not, traditional cultural beliefs get in the way of modernization and adaptation to global acceleration. If cultural traditions are not changed and government policies shifted toward the Anglo-Saxon capitalist model of deregulation, privatization, economic liberalism, and monetary stability, private investments are pulled out and the IMF puts support on hold. When government policy shifted in the early twenty-first century toward socialism in Venezuela, capital was withdrawn, and local opposition forces aiming to destabilize the regime were supported from abroad (from the United States). Yet just before this occurred, even when the "Washington consensus" was followed and Argentina obeyed the demands of the IMF, capital fled because investors anticipated stalemated economic growth, due to the sharp austerity measures imposed.

Cultural dilemmas, in short, are inherited from the past and make it difficult for governments to adapt appropriately to radical shifts in the global environment. Such cultural traditions also determine the degree to which the government recognizes and protects private property.

Property Laws, Legal Traps, Limited Markets

What the industrialized democracies of the world have made clear is that if private property is protected and law and order kept stable long enough for economic growth to go forward, more investment from similar countries is apt to come. After the brutal fall of the socialist regime of Salvadore Allende (precipitated by actions of the CIA, IT&T, and U.S. National Security Advisor Henry Kissinger), the economy of Chile was stabilized and updated by free-market-oriented University of Chicago economists. Notwithstanding massive human rights violations by dictator August Pinochet, Chile then received the political and economic support it needed. The Anglo-American consensus on globalization came to mean "follow us if you want to become successful." Otherwise, bye-bye capital.

But as Peruvian economist Hernando de Soto pointed out in *The Mystery of Capital* (2000), if most of the people in a country do not hold title to private property that is integrated into one transparent system of laws, they do not have access to capital.[27] At most, they sit on "dead capital." In Cairo, for example, most of the people squat on land they do not own. They live in houses but without titles of ownership—those houses are "dead property." Why? Because only the legal concept or representation of the property in a deed or title transforms a "dead house" into living capital that can be bought or sold in the market place or be used as the basis for obtaining credit from a bank or leased as a rental property. In

Western countries, a transparent legal system of property rights is taken for granted and allows individuals to buy and sell property, take out credit, and use such legal representations of property as a basis for starting businesses, buying stock, or sending children to expensive schools. In many poor countries, there is no single, transparent legal system of private property that is easily accessible to most of the population. Maybe the government owns title to most of the property, but no one knows for sure who really does. The property, in short, is neither secure nor liquid.

If 20 rich families own 80% of the property in a country, most of the capital is tied up, and most of the people will not have enough access to property or credit to buy and sell and keep economic growth going. If, on the other hand, property rights in a country are not transparent, such as in transitional economies in the former Soviet Union, one is not apt to buy a house or land there. What if there is no market where one can sell the property if one wants to take the capital out? What if the government decides to reclaim the property for its own uses? **The uncertainty of private property status, the absence of a transparent legal system, and the limitations of domestic markets function as traps for the poor: They have little access to "living capital" or credit. And foreign investors will shy away from investing in property they might not really own or are not sure that they can sell when they want.**

What this means is that the Western rules of free market capitalism constitute the rules of the game for global investment and economic growth. If you cannot join the game, you will stay poor. But if you manage to play, you can move your capital from lower value to higher value investments, become better off, and leave the poor further behind. Therefore, access to this legal system of free market capitalism means greater opportunity for the poor. The question is whether such opportunities will become available based on merely securing the existing markets, contracts, laws, and property owners of the status quo. Globalized markets clearly work well for the rich, who set the rules. But to the poor, these rules must often appear like a giant, obscure lottery system. Next, let us take a look at what the "rules" of globalization are and how they emerged.

References

1. Karby Leggett, "China's Banks Face Growing Threat from Major Fraud," *The Wall Street Journal*, August 4, 2003.

2. Nancy Birdsall, "Asymmetric Globalization: Global Markets Require Good Global Politics," Center for Global Development, Working Paper Number 12, October 2002, p. 13.

3. "Leaders: Dear Mr. Berlusconi,"in *The Economist*, August 2–8, 2003, p. 11.

4. P. J. O'Rourke, *Eat the Rich* (New York: Atlantic Monthly Press, 1998), Chapter 8, pp. 160–198.

5. "Tanzania," *Global Development Finance: Financing the Poorest Countries* (Washington, D.C.: The World Bank, 2002), p. 528.

6. Pete Engardio, "This Hot Potato Just Gets Hotter: As Third World Debt Rises, So Do Hurdles for Forgiving It," *Business Week*, October 7, 2002, p. 68.

7. United Nations Conference on Trade and Development, "The Least Developed Countries Report 2002: Escaping the Poverty Trap," pp. 5-7.–

8. Fareed Zakaria, *The Future of Freedom* (New York: W.W. Norton, 2002), p. 156.

9. Somini Sengupta, "The Making of an African Petrostate," *The New York Times*, Feb. 18, 2004.

10. "The Mexican Worker," *Business Week*, April 19, 1993, pp. 85–92.

11. Carlos Tejada, "Paradise Lost: Textile Powerhouse Learns Downside of Globalization," *The Wall Street Journal*, August 14, 2003.

12. Thomas Friedman, *The Lexus and the Olive Tree,* (New York: Anchor Books, 2000), p. 12.

13. See Kathy Chen, "Cash Flows: Surge in Lending in China Stokes Economic Worries," *The Wall Street Journal*, October 3, 2003, p. 1.

14. Margaret Popper and Michael Mandel, "A Learning Gap Slows Growth," *Business Week*, April 29, 2002, p. 28.

15. S. K. Kaushik and H. D. Vinod, "Human Capital and Economic Growth: Empirical Evidence from Developing Countries," August, 2003 (Working Paper, Pace University, New York).

16. "The Female Poverty Trap," *The Economist*, July 3, 2002.

17. June Kronholz, "Trying to Close the Stubborn Learning Gap," *The Wall Street Journal*, August 19, 2003.

18. Laura D'Andrea Tyson, "Needed: Affirmative Action for the Poor," *Business Week*, July 7, 2003, p. 24.

19. Robert Isaak, "The Digital Divide," in Gabriele Suder, ed., Chapter 7 in *Terrorism and the International Business Environment: The Security-Business Nexus* (London: Edgar Elgar, 2004), pp. 164–182.

20. Charles Kenny, "Development's False Divide," *Foreign Policy*, Jan/Feb. 2003, Issue 134, pp. 76–78.

21. Ivan Illich, *Tools for Conviviality* (New York: Harper & Row, 1979), pp. 65–71.

22. UNDP, *Egypt/Human Development Report 1998/99,* p. 104.

23. Alain Mingat and Carolyn Winter, "Education for All by 2015," *Finance and Development*, Vol. 39, No. 1 March 2002, p. 33.

24. Jeffrey D. Sachs, "Resolving the Debt Crisis of Low-Income Countries," *Brookings Papers on Economic Activity* (Washington, D.C.: Brookings Institute Press, 2002), pp. 257–286.

25. "The Least Developed Countries Report 2002: Escaping the Poverty Trap," United Nations Conference on Trade and Development, UN, 2002, p. 12.

26. From *Against the Stream: Critical Essays on Economics* by Gunner Myrdal, copyright © 1972, 1973 by Gunnar Myrdal. Used by permission of Pantheon Books, a division of Random House, Inc.

27. Hernando de Soto, *The Mystery of Capital: Why Capitalism Triumphs in the West and Fails Everywhere Else* (New York: Basic Books, 2000).

III

THE RULES

10 Origins of the Rules of Globalization

*Economic globalization has become a formidable cause
of inequality among and within states, and the concern
for global competitiveness limits the aptitude of states
and other actors to address this problem.*

—STANLEY HOFFMANN,
Clash of Globalizations (2002)
Reprinted by permission of Foreign Affairs, (July/August 2002).
Copyright © 2002 by the Council on Foreign Relations, Inc.

*How the Anglo-Saxon model of free market capitalism came to dominate
the rules of globalization and why its efficiency can work to increase unemployment and concentrate the benefits of growth.*

Napoleon knew something about globalization. He upset the apple
cart of the conservative balance-of-power system in Europe by changing the rules of war. Rather than aiming for limited objectives with
mercenary soldiers, as was the custom, he went for absolute victory and drafted all able-bodied men into his army. Mobilizing the
masses behind his extreme ideology that identified with the common man, he changed the way the world worked. Never mind the
slaughter of millions on the battlefields of Europe as a result of his

strategies or that he left his own country on the brink of starvation by the time he was overthrown—all radical globalization shifts have their opportunity costs.

The conservatives came back, of course. Under the careful balancing act of the British (who would always shift to the weakest side to keep the balance), the balance-of-power system was restored after Napoleon's defeat and functioned well to keep general stability intact until World War I. British hegemony (or domination) was built initially on the strongest navy in the world.

Fast forward a century: The British ability to set a socioeconomic and political standard created the legitimacy for one rather narrow interpretation of Anglo-Saxon thought that was to dominate globalization in the late twentieth century. Man is defined, by this view of Anglo-Saxon liberalism, as economic man, *homo economicus*. This vision of man was translated into the "revolt of the rich," by a woman, Prime Minister Margaret Thatcher. Her conservative victory in 1979 called for replacing what she called the "Nanny State" that "coddled" individuals from the cradle to the grave with an "enterprise culture" of risk and reward. In her electoral manifesto, she identified the two major problems of the British economy as "the monopoly nationalized industries and the monopoly trade unions."[1] Her successful war against these two institutions helped to shape the rules of the globalizing economy, magnified by the election and similar ideology of President Ronald Reagan in the United States in 1980. To understand how the ground was prepared for the acceptance of this conservative revolution and how it was nurtured by the historical development of industrialization, one must turn briefly back to the nineteenth century.

Protecting Comparative Advantage: Making the Most of What You've Got

In the latter half of the nineteenth century, the British came to dominate in the economic sphere. Already by the end of the eighteenth century, the British had the highest agricultural productivity in the world. Fifty years later, agricultural efficiency had increased to the point that over half the British working population were freed from the traditional agricultural sector to go into other lines of work—manufacturing and services. This meant that fewer and fewer people were needed to produce food. The Industrial Revolution resulted when the British used these manufacturing opportunities to introduce new ways to make the same old things.[2]

At this time, a lobbyist for British industrialists, David Ricardo, conceived of the influential theory of "comparative advantage." He took the classic, eighteenth-century liberal economic ideology of Adam Smith of maximizing individual interests as the way to national wealth and extended it to the principle of specialization in the division of labor: Do what you are best at compared with everything else, and your niche will make you more competitive, bringing prosperity as a result of your specialized competence. Assume, for example, that Britain could produce both wool *and* wine more *efficiently* than Portugal. If Britain were even *more* efficient at making wool than wine, Britain should concentrate only on wool and trade it for Portuguese wine. The British focused on their own economic interests, particularly those of business—and the state became increasingly less important in comparison.

Across the ocean, the Americans were learning by doing. Entrepreneurial efforts of families were starting to produce major companies. In the late nineteenth century, to help the nation become more competitive globally, the government kept trade policy protectionist until the major companies became competitive international businesses. Thus, the Americans built up the steel business as a basis for their own future hegemony. What Mira Wilkens termed the "American invasion" era was in full swing—led by entrepreneurs such as George Westinghouse, George Eastman, John D. Rockefeller, Andrew Carnegie, Henry Ford, Samuel Colt, and J.P. Morgan.[3] As in the British case, the political stability of the state became a springboard for entrepreneurial risk taking in the United States. This business activity flowed from a cultural belief in the importance of individual freedom and hard work, based on the protection of private property.

What is often forgotten is that the Anglo-Saxon theory of comparative advantage was combined with protectionism for the sake of large industrial interests to create what the French later called "national champions" of economic growth. German economist Friedrich List, who spent some time in the United States when his ideas had become too controversial in his native country, also argued in *The National System of Political Economy* that protectionist policy should be used for Germany. [4] Although accepting free trade in agriculture, List advocated carefully protecting the manufacturing sector until the "power of production" of the nation could be brought up to the standard of international competitiveness.

British philosopher John Stuart Mill made a similar argument for the sake of what he called "infant industries." In his *Principles of Political Economy* (1848), [5] Mill maintained that the only case where protectionist duties (trade tariffs) can be defended is when they are imposed temporarily. Mill thought this exception would apply particularly in a young and rising nation that had hopes of "naturalizing a foreign industry" found to be suitable to the circumstances of the country. He argued that the superiority of one country over another in a particular sector of production often comes only from that nation having begun that business sooner. Given this comparative disadvantage for a young nation desiring to start a new industry, it cannot be expected that individual investors, risking almost certain loss, will introduce a new manufacturing product and bear the burden alone until producers have refined their processes up to par with the competition. Hence, Mill concluded, the incubation of infant industries must initially be protected by state tariffs.

Anglo-Saxon capitalism starts with enough freedom from government regulation to be able to maximize individual and corporate interests. **But to develop a national economy with high economic growth, the state is called on "temporarily" to protect infant corporations until they are mature enough to compete globally. This rule becomes particularly important if jobs in manufacturing continue to disappear the same way that jobs in agriculture have been eliminated as the economy becomes increasingly dominated by the service sector.**

During their hegemony in the nineteenth century, the British had another state advantage: controlling the world's key reserve currency—the pound. Domination of world currency markets was one reason the island of Great Britain was able to cover its current account deficits at home with "invisible" financial services abroad. It is in the British business tradition not to look too closely at where the money comes from (the offshore banking services of the Cayman Islands, for example), as long as it keeps coming.

Despite the shift in hegemony from Britain to the United States in the twentieth century, the rough-and-ready rules of Anglo-Saxon capitalism were the same—what really counts are economic freedom and economic incentives for growth. These rules encourage individuals and companies to maximize their own interests and specializations, supported temporarily in the case of new industries by the government. The role of the state is to provide a strong military, a stable currency, and a predictable framework of law and order.

The "Fixing" of Exchange Rates

The transfer of hegemony or domination from Britain to the United States was completed during World War II. The British asked the Americans for helped when the Royal British Air Force was threatened by the Nazi *Luftwaffe*. U.S. Secretary of State Cordell Hull calculated what it would take to break the back of the British empire financially after the war. This was the basis for the Lend-Lease Agreement of 1941, providing the arms and loans the British needed (but no soldiers) for a stiff price. To the victors go the spoils. When World War II drew to a close, the delegations of the United States and the British sat down in Bretton Woods, New Hampshire to set up the new global economic system. The consequences of the Lend-Lease Agreement gave the United States the upper hand. American negotiators pushed for short-term lending on "hard" banking terms for the International Monetary Fund (IMF) and for limited development loans through the International Bank for Reconstruction and Development (the future World Bank) to go to countries destroyed by the war. The key international reserve currency became the dollar, fixed to the 1934 price of gold at $35 an ounce.

British economist John Maynard Keynes, who represented Britain, argued that unless more money was made available than the Americans proposed, the world economy would enter a deflationary period because the poor countries would not have enough cash to be able to compete globally. Given the tight, conservative U.S. position at the talks, this seemed like a reasonable prediction. But Keynes was proven wrong: The deflation did not come. The United States ended up contradicting its own initial tight money policy, circumventing the Bretton Woods agreements in order to bankroll economic growth in the 1950s and 1960s, largely for what the American government perceived to be strategic national security reasons. Thus, the Marshall Plan of 1948 ($20 billion in grants and loans) was used to rebuild Western Europe as a buffer against possible Soviet aggression. And in the 1960s, President Lyndon Johnson kept printing dollars to cover the cost of the Vietnam War and the "Great Society" domestic programs. The great inflation that was to dominate the 1970s had been launched, which would put those with fixed assets in the US in a different economic class than the people without.[6]

But these rules that the Americans had imposed and were now violating were all too transparent. General Charles de Gaulle started dumping all of France's dollars and buying up gold, saying that the Emperor had no clothes. This astute economic strategy set up the French nation with enough in reserves to be able to afford Prime Minister Françoise Mitterand's expensive socialist experiment in the early 1980s.

By 1971, the United States had only a third enough gold to back up the outstanding dollars, forcing President Richard Nixon to decide unilaterally to take the dollar off the gold standard and to let it "float." Now a dollar is as good as you think it is. That paper IOU in your pocket is just a piece of paper based on a lot of belief. Currencies have become bets placed on the short-term futures of the national (or regional) economies that they represent. As money became not just paper but credit cards and blips on computer screens, not only did the world economy speed up, but the uncertainty about the value of any of these symbolic commodities increased as well.

Oil Cartels and Petro-Dollars

If the value of paper money seems flaky and actually decreases during a period of inflation (such as the 1970s), it makes sense to buy something concrete—houses, gold, or "liquid gold" (oil). At this point, the rules of the global economy get a little complicated. Rationally maximizing one's economic interest to an extreme can lead to a market structure in which a few firms dominate an industry (oligopoly). This trend seems to contradict the concept of Anglo-Saxon capitalism—to free up individual competitors in order to generate more economic wealth through free market competition. But, as with infant industries, an exception is made for the domination of a few firms in an area deemed to be critical to the national interest, such as the oil, energy, or telecommunication sectors. The "Seven Sisters," or multinational oil companies, are an example. Exxon, Texaco, Mobil, Standard Oil of California, Royal Dutch/Shell, and British Petroleum controlled both the production levels and the prices throughout the 1950s and 1960s. The public good of reliable oil supplies to rich countries is assumed to outweigh the costs of the oligopolistic oil cartels formed to supply the oil.

The developing countries where the oil was being extracted had a different view of "Anglo-Saxon" oil cartels. The Organization of Petroleum Exporting Countries (OPEC) was formed to force multinational companies to share control of the oil industry by Iran, Iraq, Kuwait, Saudi Arabia, and Venezuela (later joined by Indonesia, Algeria, Libya, Nigeria, Ecuador, Qatar, Abu Dhabi, Sharjah, and Gabon). The breakthrough for OPEC came when Libya (under Colonel Muammar al-Qaddafi) persuaded a new independent oil company, Occidental Petroleum (led by an ambitious Armand Hammer), to go along with its demands in a tight oil market more or less at the same time the dollar began to float. In 1973, OPEC took advantage of the war in the Middle East to quadruple oil prices. Since that time, the oil industry has been "managed" by *two* oil cartels—the oil companies on one hand and OPEC on the other. The result was stability of supply for the developed industrial countries dependent on imported oil. What about the less developed countries that had no oil?

The recycling of "petro-dollars" was handled by the free market system: Oil-producing countries of OPEC would take their windfall profits from the steep increase in oil prices in the 1970s and deposit them in short-term, offshore (tax-free) bank accounts. These offshore banks would then turn around and lend the money at a high interest rate to developing countries so that they could buy oil or even lend the money to the developed countries, where it initially came from.

When David Rockefeller, head of Chase Manhattan Bank, found out about this, he too wanted in on the game. So Chase Manhattan began to loan large amounts to developing countries, particularly those with untapped oil reserves, such as Mexico, on the assumption that even if the country could not pay back the principal of the loan, the lending bank could live well from the high interest charged. The banks assumed that the price of oil would keep on going up and, therefore, the collateral behind the loans would be safe. At the same time, Marxist-oriented economic advisors from Cambridge School of economics in England were advising countries such as Mexico to take on as much debt as possible because when it became impossible to pay back the loans, Mexico would "have the banks by the debt," and the U.S. government would have to step in and bail out the banks or the banks would have to write off the debt to avoid a global financial crisis. This actually worked out in the long term just as the Cambridge School economists had predicted. By the early 1980s, the nine largest U.S. banks had lent out three times the amount they held in equity to developing countries. But the price of oil fell. Poor countries such as Mexico could not pay back either the principal or the interest on the loans. The "debt crisis" in the developing countries was in full bloom.

What is striking is that both David Rockefeller and the radical Cambridge economists were in agreement concerning these large loans to developing countries. The "rule" seems to be:

If companies (e.g., banks) are big enough, and the country is rich enough, corporate managers and investors can use the government as the ultimate insurance policy to bail them out if speculative risks go wrong.

Technically, this is called *moral hazard* because the more that companies and investors use this rule, the more high-risk speculative investments they will make, and the less stable the global economic system will become. For the poor countries, debt crises are not fun because they are not easily able to borrow any new money once they can no longer keep up with their payments. The wealthy investors, companies, and international institutions that encouraged them to take on the debt in the first place often do not have to suffer the consequences of the failures—*if* they are big enough players in the global economy.

Meanwhile, small players, such as Equatorial Guinea in Africa, have to wait until they are "discovered" by the big, wealthy players. For years, oil companies searched for oil off of the coast of Equatorial Guinea and found nothing. Then in 1992, an American firm from Texas struck oil and cut a one-sided deal (i.e., some 60% going to the Texans) with a representative of the local government, who said: "A little bit of everything is better than everything of nothing." Since that time, Exxon-Mobil has used an oil boom to enrich the ruler of Equatorial Guinea, President Obiang Nguema Mbasogo, largely at the expense of the majority of the population of about a half a million who live on less than $1 a day. These absolute poor have little potable drinking water or electricity and the highest rate of malaria in the world. No newspapers or bookstores are to be found in this country, which is run on the principle of nepotism, not democracy. President Mbasogo (who killed his own uncle in a coup to seize power) has purchased a number of elegant private villas in the Washington, D.C. area, including one for which he paid $2.6 million in cash. In terms of the governing ideology of globalization, Equatorial Guinea is a model, achieving the highest rate of economic growth in the world. There is even a "Houston Express" flight between Houston, Texas and Equatorial Guinea. And because the United States wants to have an alternative oil supply outside of the Muslim world or OPEC, Equatorial Guinea is the first of several African states expected to provide as much as 25% of the oil the United States needs in the near future.[7] Therefore, we can expect the world's second largest corporation, Exxon-Mobil; the world's richest country, the United States; and the government of the world's fastest growing country, Equatorial Guinea; to continue this cozy relationship while thousands of absolutely poor people in Equatorial Guinea grow in number.

The world economy thus provides different strokes for different folks.

Democratizing Investment Banking

These rules of globalization become even more intriguing.

Inflation ran rampant in the 1970s as oil prices went up and the dollar became "unfixed" like a floating crap game. Large brokerage houses such as Merrill Lynch wanted to get in on the go-go game of hot money (or liquidity) that was quickly recycling around the world. Donald Regan, CEO of Merrill Lynch, decided to "democratize" private investment banking. No longer would you have to be a millionaire to enter this traditional business privilege for those with deep pockets. You could start by depositing a mere $20,000 (and take out $19,000 the next day if you needed to). The idea was to attract many more people to Merrill Lynch accounts and for Merrill Lynch to get a small percentage of *any* financial transaction the client would make in his or her life.

Middle-class citizens were lured into sophisticated investment opportunities previously reserved for the wealthy. Later, widespread financial scandals dealing with insider trading in brokerages and hedge funds suggested that the odds still favored the wealthy and that the markets were liberalized faster than the government regulatory system could keep up with (provided that the overseers really *wanted* to regulate these high-powered economic growth machines, which remains an open question).

What was so attractive about the revolt of the rich—this deregulation of all markets for the sake of economic growth—is that it promised everyday citizens in developed countries the chance of becoming better off by being able to participate in the game of "casino capitalism" without government interference. Lots of money would be circulated and "bet" on new investments, businesses, and stocks, and this "supply" would then increase "demand": Economic growth would take off.

And it did.

The revolution in financial services was complemented in the United States with high-tech and telecommunication innovations, institutional deregulation, entrepreneurship, and management training. These developments resulted in remarkable economic growth and created what can be called the *limelight effect* of American economic dynamism—the tendency of other people in the world to mimic the United States, once the focus is concentrated on success there.[8] The rising interest rates of the early 1980s brought down the high inflation rate (peaking at 13%) and set the stage for an American wave of economic and technological development, hyped by defense spending that more or less caused the Soviet Union to implode. The end of the Cold War in 1989 meant that only the rules of Western, neoliberal capitalism were left standing in the world economy. This put the United States at the top in the "soft power game." People risked their lives to get into the country; to study or to invest there; to set up factories; or to copy American styles, technology, or entertainment.

However, this also led to a backlash against American cultural domination and U.S. policy in the Middle East, culminating in the September 11, 2001 terrorist attacks. Following a short wave of sympathy for the victims, there was a pervasive negative world reaction to American domination and unilateralism, amplified by the massively unpopular U.S. war on Iraq in 2003. This "cultural" war (based, of course, on oil and strategic interests, as well) was predicted by Professor Benjamin R. Barber, in his *Jihad vs. Mc World* (1995), in which he noted that the carrying power of the popular American culture among the masses, illustrated by Walt Disney, McDonald's, and MTV, had to do with their characteristics of being light, fast, and simple. This culture spread fast globally, initiated by the media (cartel) consolidations of entrepreneurs such as Rupert Murdoch and Ted Turner.[9] In the 1990s, CNN seized domination of the market for worldwide news, and Disney-ABC as well as SONY/Columbia Pictures grabbed large market shares of global entertainment. "Soft" cultural power and entertainment combined with "hard" monopolistic-seeking power of telecommunications and the media conglomerates to dominate and to define social reality. Social reality is steered by subjective knowledge—the image of the world that one believes to be true. This image determines human behavior. Information is meaningful to the extent that it produces changes in the image, which is why domination of the media is so important. Just consider the role of "herd perception" in predicting swings in the stock market.

Thus, a key rule of globalization is that **the global marketing of culture and products depends on control of the media and on the speed and simplicity of the message.** The *image*, or subjective knowledge, underlies the behavior behind global trends. *Knowledge* in this sense is defined as a significant change in the image brought about by messages one receives from the media. Sometimes we call this the *"ah-ha" phenomena*—recognition that something is different than we expected.[10] For example, let us assume that I believe the U.S. dollar is going to increase in value. But I read an article pointing out that because the United States has an external debt of 25% of the Gross Domestic Product (GDP) and a current account deficit of 5% of the GDP, the dollar will fall unless Americans save a lot more or foreigners buy much more in U.S. goods and services.[9] Then I might well say "ah ha! The dollar is going to fall, not rise." And if enough people come to this same recognition in the world at the same time, the dollar will fall even more than it would have otherwise. The media can coagulate the subjective perceptions of what Thomas Friedman called the "electronic herd," who in turn use their investment behavior to push the existing "objective" trends to extremes.

The rich who do not own media conglomerates themselves can buy access to them in order to broadcast their own images—advertising their products, their political candidacies, or their cultures. The poor have no access and no opportunity to compete in this arena, despite the national success of the prolific movies of "Bollywood" in the middle-income sector of India. What about other businesses? How did trade rules emerge that are so biased toward the advantage of Anglo-Saxon players in the game?

Trade Rules

After World War II, the U.S. Congress dominated rules of world trade with its "veto power." When an international trade organization was proposed to complement the IMF, Congress turned it down. Afraid of another international government bureaucracy on trade like the one already established for money, U.S. conservatives pushed for a voluntary commercial agreement, the GATT, or General Agreement on Tariffs and Trade, which came into being in the late 1940s.

Basically, the GATT embodied the theory of comparative advantage, with a tilt toward necessary adjustments for domestic stability (in basic industries such as steel, textiles, shoes, and cars). Monitoring 90% of world merchandise trade, the GATT was able to stimulate industrialized countries to reduce tariffs from more than 40% to less than 5% from the time it was founded until it was replaced by the World Trade Organization (WTO) in 1995. The WTO converted a commercial treaty (the GATT) into a governmental body that serves major corporate interests, which can be headquartered in any country.

The trade rules of the GATT were basically adopted by the WTO and are skewed heavily in favor of rich countries with lots of comparative advantages to use in international bargaining. For instance, the "principal supplier rule" of GATT negotiations required that the initial bilateral request for a tariff reduction on a particular product could be made only by the exporter of the largest volume of that product to a second country. If this tariff reduction were accepted (i.e., swapped for a reduction in tariffs on another product proposed by the second country), all member nations of the GATT would benefit because the reduction would be applied to all. Clearly, only nations rich enough to be the principal supplier of a product could even play in this commercial game, and everyone else was dependent on the consequences of what emerged from this "rich man's club." If all you had were bananas, a bit of bauxite, and tourism, like Jamaica, you were out of luck in terms of bargaining power.

For a long time, agriculture, one of the largest sectors of commodities of particular importance to the economies of the poor countries, was excluded from the GATT. Later on, textiles and footwear-products—also vital to developing countries—were excluded, as well.

The United States received a broad waiver for agricultural products for strategic, political, and social reasons, as did the Common Agricultural Policy of the Europeans, once their European Common Market (now the European Union) came into being.

The world trade rules set up by the rich nations freed up global markets for the areas in which they had dominant comparative advantages while protecting their own vulnerable economic sectors, such as agriculture and textiles, from the competition posed by low-wage, poor countries.

This rule would have been well understood by Adam Smith, who wrote in *The Wealth of Nations* (1776): "Civil government, so far as it is instituted for the security of property, is in reality instituted for the defense of the rich against the poor, or of those who have some property against those who have none at all."[10] Nations, after all, have their "sovereignty" protected by international law. What this means in practice is that the law and order of the status quo of existing contracts should be maintained without interference from outside the nation. Of course, it is always the haves who have contracts, not the have-nots.

After the end of the Cold War in 1989, the importance of protecting "private property" with stable law-and-order regimes became even more critical for international investment and economic development. Countries could no longer play the United States against the Soviet Union for possible economic subsidies (as nations from Egypt to Italy had done in the past). What happened at home, in the domestic political economy, became critical in order to make an emerging economy appear to be a budding capitalist winner, rather than a fading socialist loser.

Four key rules of economic "transition" emerged:

1. Economic liberalization—legally protect the right to private property and bring in market competition.
2. Macroeconomic stabilization—control inflation, limit budget deficits, create a convertible currency.

3. Privatization—transfer state property to private hands or, for corporations, *socialize* the costs and *privatize* the gains.

4. Do all of this as *quickly as possible.*

In the early 1990s, these four rules were the key to economic reforms that economic advisor Jeffrey Sachs urged on Poland. They needed to reform quickly—"shock therapy"—Sachs argued. The rationale is the same that would apply if the British decided to shift from driving on the left-hand side to driving on right-hand side. You can't exactly introduce this change gradually by just putting trucks on the other side of the road and permitting cars to continue to drive on the same side as usual. He noted that if the Poles chose to privatize at the same rate as the British under the policies of Prime Minister Margaret Thatcher—five firms per year in the 1980s—it would take several hundred years to privatize the 3,000 Polish industrial firms owned by the state.[13] In short, the speeding up of the global economy required nothing less than shock therapy.

Experiments with rats overwhelmed by too much stimulation at once (electric shocks) show that the rats go crazy. This is sort of what happened in Poland. At first, the reforms showed some success in small retail businesses and the small industrial sectors, as well as in trucking and construction. But the large industrial sector was more resistant to reforms, despite the government's effort to give away a certain number of shares in the companies to the citizens. Prices shot up as Polish consumers scrambled to buy Western goods. Privatization increased economic growth and the range of choice in society but at the cost of losses in jobs and social security. The legitimacy of the government came under overwhelming pressure exerted by thousands of displaced people. Little of the $25 billion of aid pledged to Poland by the 24 richest nations in 1993 reached the average Poles: Advisors got some of the funds, some was never sent (due to risks of helping out such small businesses), and a lot went to projects that benefited the donors rather than the people to whom the money was supposedly donated.

In Russia, of course, the shock therapy strategy hit even more resistance. Beginning with Mikhail Gorbachev's concept of *uskrenie* (the need to speed everything up), the reformists' blueprint ran up against the traditions of the Russian soul, which thrives on a slow, Anton Chekhov concept of time—represented by the unhurried charm of nineteenth-century upper-class Russian society. Moreover, capitalist entrepreneurs were hard to find for this speed race toward privatization. Hence, the managers appointed to run the state firms to be privatized tended to be either old, corrupt party oligarchs or young Russian mafiosi. The new transparency in the society shocked the people when they learned of the pollution, sickness, inflation, joblessness, rise in birth defects among newborns, and drop in Russian longevity. As U.S. Deputy Secretary of State under President Clinton Strobe Talbot put it, Russia needed "less shock and more therapy."

The rules of rapid privatization and economic liberalization favored the big over the small and the fast over the slow. Traditionally, the private businesses that create most of the new jobs in the world start small, as family affairs. The natural process of companies developing from workshop to factory to national corporation to multinational corporation sped up after World War II, leading to oligopolies that concentrated direct investment in metropolitan centers, or "metropoles." This, in turn, meant that metropolitan centers or high-tech "hot spots"(such as Silicon Valley) attracted and concentrated the venture capital, the brains and skilled labor, and the modern infrastructure, leaving the periphery or outlying rural areas underdeveloped.[14]

The speed trap of globalization pulls all critical resources— from money to brains, from technology to media and markets—toward metropolitan and high-tech centers and away from poor, rural areas of the world.

While skilled labor, money, and market attention focused on the metropolitan and high-tech sectors, all other locations and market sectors were rendered passé: Unemployment and underemployment characterized the majority of areas being systematically underdeveloped as a result of the overdevelopment of the metropoles and high-tech hot spots. The most competitive and well-paid people flocked to these overdeveloped centers, where media attention helped to lift their careers and corporate images. What sped up this process of con-centration was the evolution of the New Economy at the end of the twentieth century, which added a few new global economic princi-ples of its own.

From Scarcity to Ubiquity: Digitization and the Falling Cost of Information

The New Economy refers to the radical reduction of the cost of in-formation and the ability to transmit it quickly through the devel-opment of computer applications, digitization, and the Internet.

Digitization is merely the translation of all information —whether spoken or written—into ones and zeroes for almost instant, clear transmission to anywhere in the world. A phone call from New York City to Paris sounds just like someone is talking in the house next door. Such fast and easy transmission spawned information markets.

In *Future Wealth*, Francis McInerney and Sean White note that the first "iron law of information" is that "cheap information *always* chases out expensive information."[15] At the Graduate School of Man-agement in Grenoble, France, for example, all books have largely been replaced by reading material online, which costs the students *noth-ing*—a very good price, particularly if you are a student. It is the price (nearly free) and speed that explain why e-mails are replacing first-class letters and why the postal service is reducing its staff and becoming desperate for business. As a consequence, you can spread information or advertising anywhere in the world much more easily. Something spread around everywhere you look is *ubiquitous*—like dandelions in the spring or goose droppings where lots of geese hang out. Conven-tional economic laws suggest that if something is available every-where, its value must decrease because it is abundant, not scarce.

This is where the New Economy changed the rules of the glob-al economy. *Ubiquity* can actually *increase* the value of a product or service. Think about Coca-Cola or Microsoft software; Intel chips or the United States dollar. These products are distributed everywhere in the world and gain in value as they proliferate because they become "brand names" and are perceived to be reliable and available.

However, Coca-Cola, Microsoft, Intel, and the U.S. dollar are products produced and marketed by the big, powerful organizations, which overwhelm most of the competition that the small try to set up.

Ubiquity is making something available everywhere: Powerful organizations and wealthy individuals can afford to do this, creating "brand names" that drive out the local competition.

Consider another example. The best-selling painter of the twentieth century was Picasso. And guess what? It is not because Picasso painted only a *few* pictures (as did Vincent van Gogh, for example) but because he painted *so many*. Picasso's paintings became so ubiquitous that every museum or gallery *had* to have one to remain or to become respectable. With so many of his works available, he became instantly recognizable around the world. It helped, of course, that he was an excellent and original painter and that his product had a distinctive character. But being so readily available was also a shrewd marketing device. It is notable that Picasso would pay restaurant bills by doing a quick sketch on a paper napkin.

Meanwhile, lesser known painters, who may be superb artists but have very few paintings to show, are starving from lack of recognition in the global "attention" economy.

Attention is as scarce as information is abundant, giving a huge comparative advantage to those with brand names or with the ability to dominate the media in order to create such branding.

Those who create such a brand naturally try to pin down the property rights to it with copyright and patent laws. The organizations behind the brands lobby to see that these rights are enforced throughout the world. The agenda of these branding organizations was successful when the WTO replaced the GATT in 1995. In this transformation, the legal framework of the WTO was expanded into services and intellectual property rights by the GATS (General Agreement on Trade in Services) and the TRIPS (Trade Related Aspects of Intellectual Property Rights). Dominant, wealthy technological economies led by the United States pushed to lock up the rights to software innovations and Internet-related business designs that their companies had spent so much money and time in developing. These companies had been forced into marketing certain goods or services for free, given the global drop in cost of information flows. Now they hoped customers would eventually "follow the free" to the point of being lured into becoming loyal, paying clients and that the WTO would help them out with this objective by enforcing intellectual property rights.

What happened to Benjamin Franklin's principle that technological innovations of any kind should be shared freely with mankind? Clearly, Franklin in the eighteenth century had no idea that technology would become the leading sector in the U.S. economy, just as Adam Smith could not have conceived of the dominant role of large, multinational corporations. Franklin's perspective supports the principle of equity of access to the latest technologies—particularly in the pharmaceutical sector, which transcends mere economic interests and concerns the life chances of millions of human beings. Wealthy governments are slowly coming to respect this principle in very limited cases.

Initially asking for absolute protection for intellectual property and patents, the U.S. government modified its position to make an exception for generic drugs to treat AIDS, malaria, and tuberculosis so that these drugs would become affordable in developing countries devastated by these diseases. (This makes the optimistic assumption, of course, that the generic drugs are not siphoned off and sold by corrupt middlemen before they get to the sick.) Nevertheless, in general, protecting existing patents and copyrights is a prime objective of countries that have developed them, regardless of the consequences for the low-income nations. The argument is that without this protection, the pharmaceutical companies would have no motivation to make the large investments necessary in basic research to discover new medicines and therapies. That a certain percentage of all proceeds from such new discoveries should go to alleviate suffering among the disadvantaged would be an ideal rule for the future, but such a principle has yet to be accepted and is apt to face fierce corporate resistance.

Rich countries and companies use all available legal means to protect their patents and inventions, regardless of the social consequences. The only exception is to permit poorer nations to use generic equivalents of their drugs for a very few critical diseases under strict conditions. The WTO is the main vehicle for enforcing these legal protections of corporate patents.

Most WTO claims are settled by panels of experts behind closed doors. Those who bring claims are usually representatives of major industrialized countries on the behalf of major corporate groups. Because the appeal process demands a universal vote on the part of 146 countries (including the country bringing the claim), the closeted experts call the shots.

In his book, *When Corporations Rule the World*, David Korten summed up what he called the "actual functions" of the three key Bretton Woods institutions that established the rules of globalization: "The World Bank has served as an export-financing facility for large Northern-based corporations. The IMF has served as the debt collector for Northern-based financial institutions. GATT has served to create and enforce a corporate bill of rights protecting the rights of the world's largest corporations against the intrusion of people, communities, and democratically elected governments."[16]

As we have seen, the rules of the Bretton Woods system have been dominated by the United States, both in their formulation and in efforts to circumvent them (that is, by undermining the fixed-exchange rate system and increasing U.S. tariffs on steel, textile, and agricultural imports). The American democratic system has granted the corporation as "persona" many of the same constitutional First Amendment and property rights as individuals. Corporations are free to spend as much as they like to promote their viewpoints, even if they overwhelm the media. Corporate property (including intellectual property) is protected in the courts and by important international institutions. Large companies have become virtual innovation machines that increase the pace of economic change and attract the most investment.[17] The new financial order multiplies the wealth of the technology-oriented companies, which can use New Economy technologies to amplify all they do, leading to what Yale economist Robert Schiller refers to as "the winner-take-all effect."[16] "Corporate democracy"(sometimes pejoratively referred to as "crony capitalism" in developing countries) has become the order of the day.

But how, exactly, do these constantly evolving rules of the world economy affect the poor in developing nations?

References

1. Daniel Yergin and Joseph Stanislaw, *The Commanding Heights* (New York: Simon & Schuster, 1998), pp. 92–124.

2. W. Arthur Lewis, *The Evolution of the International Economic Order* (Princeton, NJ: Princeton University Press, 1978).

3. Mira Wilkins, *American Business Abroad from the Colonial Era to 1914* (Cambridge, MA: Harvard University Press, 1970), p. 6.

4. Friedrich List, *The National System of Political Economy*, translated by S. s. Lloyd (London: Longmans, Gree and Co., 1885), reprinted 1922.

5. John Stuart Mill, *Principles of Political Economy,* ed. by J. Ashley, (London: Longmans, Gree, 1909). Originally, 1848.

6. Wilhelm Hankel and Robert Isaak, *Modern Inflation: Its Economics and Its Politics* (Lanham, MD: University Press of America, 1983. German version: *Die moderne Inflation* (Köln: Bund-Verlag, 1981).

7. CBS, *60 Minutes*, November 16, 2003.

8. Robert Isaak, *Managing World Economic Change: International Political Economy* (Upper Saddle River, NJ: Prentice Hall, 2000) 3rd edition, p. 246.

9. Richard Hack, *Clash of the Titans* (Beverly Hills, CA: New Millennium Press, 2003).

10. Kenneth Boulding, *The Image* (Ann Arbor, MI: University of Michigan Press, 1956).

11. "Flying on One Engine: World Economy Report," *The Economist*, September 20–26, 2003.

12. Adam Smith, *An Inquiry into the Nature and Causes of the Wealth of Nations* (1776; New York: Modern Library, 1937), p. 674.

13. Jeffrey Sachs, "The Economic Transformation of Eastern Europe: The Case of Poland," *American Economist* 36, No. 2 (fall 1992), pp. 4–5.

14. Stephen Hymer, "The Multinational Corporation and the Law of Uneven Development," in *Economics and World Order from the 1970s to the 1990s*, ed. J. Bhagwati (New York: Collier-Macmillan, 1972), pp. 113-140.

15. Francis McInerney and Sean White, *Future Wealth* (New York: St. Martin's Press, 2000), p. 26.

16. David C. Korten, *When Corporations Rule the World* (West Hartford, CT: Kumarian Press, 1996), p. 181.

17. William J. Baumol, *The Free-Market Innovation Machine* (Princeton, NJ: Princeton University Press, 2002).

18. Robert Shiller, *The New Financial Order: Risk in the 21st Century* (Princeton, NJ: Princeton University Press, 2003).

11 How the Rules Rule the Poor

The mere mention of a "cartel" usually strikes fear in the hearts and wallets of consumers and regulators around the globe. Its members are the world's leading foreign aid organizations, which constitute a near monopoly, relative to the powerless poor.

—WILLIAM EASTERLY,
The Cartel of Good Intentions (2002)

T*he poor are set up by the rules to remain dependent while the rich are aided in maintaining their way of life.*

Poor people in poor countries suffer the consequences of the rules of the world economy set by the rich countries every day. Consider, for example, two telling international events of September of 2003[1]:

Trade ministers from 146 nations met in Cancun, Mexico. They held talks to assess the Doha Round of trade tariff reduction discussions launched in Doha, Qatar two years before. The guiding idea of the Doha Round of the World Trade Organization (WTO) talks was presumably to raise the prospects of the economies of the poor nations. But remember who set up the rules. The developing countries had appealed to the wealthy countries, such as the United States and the European Union (EU), to lower tariffs against the agriculture and mineral commodities on which many of the poor countries' livelihoods depend. The response by the United States and the EU was to ask the developing countries to lower *their* tariffs in order to liberalize their markets and increase global trade. This alliance between the developed countries was not concerned that the playing field is not exactly "level" for rich and poor countries in terms of comparative advantage. Their initial starting positions give a huge competitive edge to those most prepared to benefit from the new globalized economy.

A protest movement gathered in front of the place in Cancun where the world trade talks were taking place. One of the protesters was a 56-year-old rice farmer, a former president of the Korean Advance Farmers Federation, who wore a sign: "The WTO kills farmers." He stabbed himself in the chest and died in the hospital, leaving a handout behind in which he stated that he had tried but failed to organize opposition to economic forces that had become "waves that destroyed our lovely rural communities."[2] The WTO talks later collapsed, leaving the status quo in place. Meanwhile, another event was unfolding that also illustrates how developing countries suffer the consequences of the rules established by the wealthy.

Argentina defaulted on its $2.9 billion debt payment due to the International Monetary Fund (IMF) after both sides could not agree on the terms of a new three-year aid program. For most of the past decade, Argentineans acceded to stringent IMF demands, only to see their economy sink into deeper malaise. The Argentinean government staked out a tough bargaining position against the governments of France and Italy, who sought to protect their companies and investors in Argentina. The government of Argentina lost in these negotiations. Thus, Argentina joined Iraq, Somalia, Liberia, Zimbabwe, and Sudan—the group of countries in arrears with the IMF. Never mind that the bargaining position is not exactly level between an economically depressed Argentina and two of the richest countries in the world, which help to set the rules in the IMF.

What both of these examples have in common is the starting position of the poor in negotiations: A take-it-or-leave-it bargaining stance by developed countries typically pushes the poor even further into dependence.

As Thucydides observed in ancient Greece, **the powerful exact what they can, and the weak grant what they must.**

How to Increase Poverty with Trade

In Mali, where the per capita income is $270 annually, cotton is a critical raw commodity to export for economic sustainability of the people. The native people grow corn and millet to eat and produce unprocessed cotton to export. With a level playing field in trade, Mali could develop a stable economy to match its democratic system.

However, the trade rules are tilted to create more *poverty*, not more wealth in Mali. The U.S. government subsidizes its own farmers to grow cotton. Without having to compete with these American subsidies, the income for cotton producers in Mali would go up 30%. The government in Mali can't afford to subsidize its own cotton production.

In terms of global agricultural production, the picture becomes even darker for countries such as Mali because the EU and Canada subsidize agriculture more than the United States does. In fact, the developed countries subsidize agriculture to the tune of a billion dollars a day, making it extremely difficult for developing nations to compete with them.

In Mali, there is a saying: "The hand that gives is always higher than the one that receives." But this is not the principle of the global trade regime. A focal point of developing nations at the WTO talks in Cancun was to push the WTO to lower the cotton subsidies granted to largely rich American cotton farmers that prevent cotton producers in poor countries such as Mali from maintaining themselves.

The difficulty is that farmers in wealthy nations correctly argue that without subsidies, many of them will go broke. There are tremendous domestic political pressures on the side of developed countries coming up against the threat of survival perceived by many developing nations.

Mali is not alone. Consider Senegal. The World Bank demanded that this developing country cut its tariffs by 90% as a condition for receiving further financing. The WTO required Senegal not to limit its imports. The people in Senegal could be closer to self-sufficiency if they could afford to eat the chicken that they themselves produce. But subsidized frozen chicken imported from the EU in Senegal is half the price of home-grown chicken: The people of Senegal cannot afford to buy their own. They are becoming more dependent, less self-sufficient, and, hence, poorer.

Or consider Ethiopia. The United States provides generous "food aid" in the form of surplus *American* wheat, corn, or beans on a regular basis, to the point of undermining the economic ability of the Ethiopians to grow and sell their own wheat, corn, and beans. The rules (in this case, American laws) say that the United States must send its own home-grown food for aid, rather than spend cash on foreign produce in all but very exceptional cases.

American agribusinesses use high technology and efficiency to overproduce, given their ability to count on selling at least some 20% of their food as food aid at government subsidized prices. Almost 70% of the farm subsidy payments by the U.S. government go to the largest 10% of producers: It is a corporate welfare program. However, it also keeps American farmers employed, increases their income, and maintains the value of their land.

Meanwhile, Ethiopian farmers cannot earn enough selling their crops to pay for this year's harvest or the space to store it, not to speak of the loans needed to plant next year's crop. The cycle of famine and poverty in Ethiopia is preprogrammed by the existing rules. (Recall that international organizations support Egypt's restriction on the use of most of the Nile's water by Ethiopia, where the Nile originates.) And the welfare mentality of dependence is continually subsidized by the American food coming in, leading Ethiopians to expect and accept it, rather than motivating them to try to stand on their own feet. Thus, American farmers continue to produce much more wheat than they need. The U.S.

government buys much of their wheat to ship to Ethiopia and other developing countries as food aid to get rid of the surpluses. The Ethiopians are socialized into consuming American brand products. And the cycle of poverty is deepened and made inevitable for the future.[3]

One might think that Mali, Senegal, and Ethiopia are possible exceptions to the rule. But how does one explain the statistics? During 1960–1969, Africa's average share of total world exports was 5.3% and of imports, 5.0%. Compare this with 1990–1998, when the African share of world exports dropped to 2.3% and of imports, 2.2%.[4] Of course, many factors could explain this decline, apart from the existing global trade rules: the restrictive nature of Africa's own trade regimes, high costs of transport, the distance of the region from major markets, and the slow growth of per capita income. But substantial efforts made by African countries to liberalize their economies in the 1990s do not change the fact that Africa is poorer today than several decades ago, as measured by world market share of exports and imports. Naturally, poverty, as always, is relative because world imports and exports as a whole have risen significantly during the past few decades. But the existing trade rules seem designed more to increase the gap between the poorest countries and the rich ones than to bridge it.

Moreover, without the barriers of protectionism, the United States, Germany, France, Japan, and the East Asian "tigers" could not have become wealthy and powerful. These barriers included such means as government-targeted subsidies for firms and for R&D (research and development), export subsidies, import substitutions, and government regulations to bolster the domestic savings rate and keep down the cost of capital for local companies.[5] As journalist Tina Rosenberg noted, free trade is a religion, and religions come with hypocrisy.[6]

Powerful economic states became so by protecting their markets until they were ready to compete globally. But the existing "free trade" rules block developing countries from following this strategy. Meanwhile, rich countries take protectionist exceptions to the rules in order to lock in their global position.

Not able even to protect their commodities, the poorest developing countries hardly stand a chance of modernizing their economies beyond dependence on agriculture and natural resources. Not surprisingly, between 1960 and 2002, there has been a long-term downward trend in nonfuel commodity prices. Indeed, the commodity price recession of the 1980s was more severe and more prolonged than that of the Great Depression of the 1930s.[7] A clear link between dependence on the export of these primary commodities and the incidence of extreme poverty is well known but often ignored by richer nations. Over the last three decades of the twentieth century, UNCTAD studies confirm that the long-term decline in the price of primary commodities, relative to the price of manufacturing, undermined the terms of trade of the world's poorest commodity-exporting countries (including Bukina Faso, Burundi, Chad, the Democratic Republic of the Congo, Ethiopia, Guinea-Bissau, Madagascar, Malawi, Mali, Niger, Rwanda, Sierra Leone, Sudan, Tanzania, and Zambia).[7]

Check out the Congo, for instance. Here, miners dig up coltan by chopping down huge chunks of rain forest, which serves as the habitat for the Mbuti people (pygmies), who live by hunting, gathering, and trading. The wireless world of the rich depends on coltan. It is refined in the United States and Europe to become tantalum powder, a conductor of electricity vital for the capacitors used inside miniature circuit boards installed on almost all laptops, pagers, personal digital assistants, and cell phones.

To illustrate the social consequences of this resource dependence, miners in the Congo buy temporary "wives" (teenage girls) for the price of a kilogram of coltan, which can fetch up to $80 (compared with the 20 cents the average worker in the Congo takes home daily). Almost anyone with a shovel can dig up coltan, which is often near the surface. The profit from its sale is so high that it stimulates perpetual civil war and bands of armed predators. According to the WHO, the monthly toll of "avoidable deaths" in the Congo averages about 72,800. And not just human beings suffer from the coltan trade. In the Kahuzi-Biega National Park alone, a population of 8,000 eastern lowland gorillas has been reduced to about 1,000 as some 10,000 miners and traders use the gorillas for food or as bait to trap other animals.[8] For the Congo, the rules of globalization have straightforward consequences: **The greater the number of laptops and cell phones sold worldwide, the greater the violence, the more sparse the rain forests, and the fewer gorillas and pygmies will survive.**

Thus, the rules of the free market often become perverse. Without effective rule of law and a government that can keep a balance between environmental sustainability and growing economic markets, free market ideology alone can spell disaster. Rich countries are in a position to continue to protect their own vital resources and sectors, imposing agricultural tariffs averaging over 40% (and on some products, above 300%) on the least developed countries. And this does not include nontariff barriers applied by developed nations. Consider the case of EU regulations banning the import of foods with aflatoxins—toxic fungi in maize and groundnuts that possibly retard the growth in West African children who consume these products. The World Bank has calculated that this health regulation costs Africa $750 million annually in exports of dried fruit and nuts. Perhaps because of the EU regulations, the life of one European citizen is saved from aflatoxin poisoning every two years. This must be weighed against many African lives that are dependent on the export of these commodities: Without their livelihood from this trade, the Africans have little sustenance or medical treatment and are apt to die young from malnutrition or endemic disease.[9]

The international community has taken the special needs of poor countries into account in some exceptional arrangements in the past. But with rising global competition, existing multinational agreements to buffer the harsh effects of free markets for trade in the poorest countries are coming to an end. For example, the Multifiber Arrangement, which regulates the $350 billion of world trade in garments, is scheduled to expire in 2005. Millions of families in Bangladesh and other developing countries that depend on the garment industry will be devastated economically. In a Muslim nation of 140 million such as Bangladesh, with rising crime and a strong conservative Islamic movement, the timing of the expiration of the trade quotas could not be worse for regional stability.[10]

Left to the free market rules alone, large corporate lobbies dominate the globalization agenda to the point that thousands can die from the results. The most notorious case is the pharmaceutical lobby. Until August 2003, the conservative Bush administration supported the U.S. pharmaceutical lobby's demand that the patents on expensive medicines should be strictly enforced and that no cheap generic versions should water down these profits, no matter what the consequences (i.e. epidemics of devastating diseases in African countries).

Fortunately, this time the Anglo-Saxon free market model did not prevail. The pharmaceutical companies of the EU and Switzerland accepted an accord with African leaders that enables poor countries to import generic versions of expensive drugs to fight AIDS, malaria, and tuberculosis from countries such as India and Brazil without violating the trade laws protecting patent rights. The United States officially backed down. But governments in developing countries courting the good will of the United States, such as in Guatemala, choose to let their people die rather than to distribute inexpensive generic drugs to treat AIDS, even when these drugs become available. The Free Trade Area of the Americas (FTAA) initiative of the U.S. government was targeted to maximize profits for pharmaceutical companies at the potential cost of thousands of human lives.[11] The pressure of thousands of protestors at the FTAA governmental negotiations in Miami, Florida in 2003 helped to slow down, if not to derail, this proposal—at least temporarily.

The question is, **How many lives in poor countries must be at stake before exceptions to the globalization rules of the rich are enforced for the sake of human needs? Poor people do not have effective lobbies.**

Recall the strategy of the rich countries at the WTO meeting in Cancun—to demand tariff reductions from the developing nations before a discussion of agricultural subsidy reductions could take place. Otherwise, the American Trade Representative, Robert Zoellick, threatened to go ahead with his declared strategy of bilateral agreements between the United States and other countries, circumventing the WTO. To counter this strategy, Brazil and India, among others, created a "Group of 22" alliance of developing countries. This initiative inspired other groupings of developing countries to hold firm in opposing the approval of trade-enhancing measures on investment, antitrust, and transparency on government procurement that the Europeans and Japanese demanded before they would talk about agricultural tariffs. The talks at Cancun broke down. Everyone left before any agricultural subsidy reductions could take place. The so-called victory for the Group of 22 was a hollow one because the United States went ahead with its plan to make bilateral deals with 14 countries, with additional countries lining up for their own deals with the United States because the WTO failed to get them any relief. It was more in the interest of American governmental elites than those of the low-income countries to have the talks break down, given the rising protectionism in the United States before the presidential election of 2004. The EU, on the other hand, had put all of its chips on a WTO compromise. Pascal Lamy, the head negotiator of the EU, called the U.S. strategy of cutting separate deals outside the WTO (which would not have any benefits spilling over to poorer nations in the world) "a form of bilateral imperialism."[12] Meanwhile, the EU farmers were no doubt relieved that their agricultural subsidies were not going to be cut—a politically convenient outcome for developed countries all around.

How Free Capital Flows Can Create the Poor

But the developing countries are not just disadvantaged by the existing trade rules. The demands by the IMF to force poor nations to open their borders to free capital flows can also devastate the least developed countries economically.

Or, to put it another way, is it a mere accident that the three developing countries to come out of economic globalization the best in the past decade are those that went against the rule of opening national borders to free capital flows—China, India, and Malaysia? These countries (successfully) countered the uncertainty of the casino capitalism of "hot money" globally with government controls of capital.

Trade in goods is concerned with known quantities. The odds are stacked against the poor because of what they produce. In contrast, financial markets deal with uncertain, unknowable investment risks. Hot money seeks high short-term returns and flows to stable countries with predictable regulations during periods of global crisis.

The world has become an instant, spontaneous auction of financial markets open somewhere every hour of the day. Most investors do not know what really lies behind the acronyms of companies listed on stock exchanges or which direction financial markets are going. The stock exchanges of the world are huge global casinos. Big money is placed on short-term bets, largely by institutional investors of pension funds, who avoid investing in the most risky, least developed countries. Wealthy investors can hardly keep up with the tempo and complexity of global financial markets. The lower-income people without access to expert advice have no chance at all.

Recall that the IMF was set up to lend countries short-term money to cover crises in their balance of payments (that is, when more is paid out by domestic residents than is received from foreigners). But the United States is the only member of the IMF having enough votes to constitute veto power. Hence, the IMF becomes a front for American policy: It has shifted away from its original limited job to focus on economic development through free market fundamentalism. This "religious" belief in free market assumptions paradoxically pulls the U.S. government ever deeper into international situations where free markets break down in crisis, leading it (as chief hegemonial babysitter) to intervene much more intensively than it had ever planned.

Consider the 1997–1999 crisis in Asia, for example. The Asian crisis began with a currency meltdown in Thailand that spread to Indonesia, South Korea, and other states on the periphery. It was hard to tell whose plane would land in the country in crisis first— the jet of representatives from the IMF or that of the U.S. Secretary of Treasury and his assistant. Their (joint) recipe was to let the currency float, raise interest rates to attract capital, and cut government spending in order to lower government budget deficits. And there were many more conditions (aimed particularly at banking systems from Thailand to South Korea) to this "straightjacket" that countries needed to put on if they wanted IMF money. But instead of being counter-cyclical (that is, pumping more money into a system in crisis, as the U.S. Federal Reserve does in the United States when recession looms), the IMF policies were pro-cyclical (accelerating the existing trend). These policy demands served to dry up domestic liquidity, short-circuit economic growth, and push the countries on the periphery deeper into recession.

As financier George Soros has noted, the IMF used a recipe designed to combat excesses in the public sector (i.e., government spending) for a global crisis caused by excesses in the private sector (i.e., hot money chasing high returns in emerging economies, followed by capital flight when the currencies imploded).[13] The IMF initially appeared to succeed in Thailand and South Korea, only to fail miserably in Indonesia and Russia, where its efforts to bail out the banking systems came to nothing and investors lost millions. Weak banking systems, obscure regulations and property laws, imperfect information, corrupt managers, and barriers to getting credit or to gaining rapid access to large markets were factors often overlooked by the IMF. Privatization with the absence of institutional infrastructures (such as corporate governance) does not have a positive effect on growth. As Nobel Prize economist and former World Bank economist Joseph Stiglitz summed it up, "Russia's oligarchs stole assets, stripped them, leaving their country much poorer."[14] The well-positioned, in short, created more poor.

Developed countries can afford counter-cyclical policies in times of financial crisis to pump money in where it is needed; poor countries in crisis on the peripheries of the world economy are hit with money-draining policies enforced by the IMF, developed country governments, and global investors.

The default of Argentina on its loan to the IMF in 2003 is one result of how established institutions with lots of money at their disposal create poverty with free-market, straightjacket policies. By following the recipes of the IMF, Argentina sank into deep economic malaise. That its government became satiated with this no-win policy and overplayed its hand in bargaining with the IMF is hardly surprising. The Argentinean sense of a negative self-fulfilling prophecy had just gone on for too long, undermining all hope for the future among the population.

George Soros predicted that the capital flight (in the form of "resident lending," portfolio investment, and private credit) from emerging economies since 1997 is "structural" or permanent, rather than transitory, as the free market fundamentalists claim. He argues that the risks of investing in or lending to countries on the periphery or of holding their currencies have gone up. And because such risks involve higher borrowing costs, the rewards for such loans or investments have gone down.[13] The unsuccessful behavior of the IMF has reduced its credibility to the point that it has forced private capital out of the poor countries that need it most, driving up the cost of capital for even the most successful companies from the emerging market nations and making it extremely difficult for them to compete globally. **The gap between rich and poor is being systematically increased by the institutions of the well-to-do.**

This structural shift of money away from the countries that need it most is reflected in the statistics on global foreign direct investment (FDI; direct investment abroad in factories or plants). FDI fell all over the world by 41% in 2001, then by 21% in 2002. In the developing world, which faced even more extreme declines in other private external capital flows, FDI went down 23% in 2002—with the steepest declines in Africa (41%), followed by Latin America and the Caribbean (33%).[15] The uncertainties resulting from the September 11 terrorist attacks and wars in Afghanistan and Iraq no doubt helped to intensify this global shift since 1997 away from high-risk investment in the poorest developing countries.

Investment flees from uncertainty and seeks transparency. Dead capital comes alive when laws and rules permit it to be converted easily. Most Third World capital stays buried.

Investment flows to places where private property rules are clearly spelled out and people hold clear titles to property, meaning it can easily be converted to "capital" by rental, sale, or as a basis for credit. As noted earlier, in many of the developing countries, real estate is what Peruvian economist Hernando de Soto calls "dead capital" because people do not hold title to property. De Soto estimates that the total value of real estate held but not legally owned by the poor in the Third World and in formerly Communist nations is at least $9.3 trillion. He concludes that in the Western developed countries, in contrast, "masses"(such as squatters on unclaimed property) have been transformed into "individuals" through formal property rights, which render those with property interests accountable.[16] Consider the example of real estate moguls, such as American Donald Trump, with the name recognition and credibility to borrow a lot and to pay just 10% down in order to amass prime properties and accumulate huge wealth. If some disaster occurs on his properties, of course, he or his company can be held accountable.

In the seventeenth century, John Locke illustrated the principles of the rights of "Life, Liberty, and Property" with what in effect was the natural right to "Property, Property, and Property," in his *Two Treatises of Government* (1681). Similarly, in the twenty-first century, Hernando de Soto found the key to individual potential to be ownership of the title to real estate that can be leveraged to create "capital" in his *The Mystery of Capital* (2000).[16] "Freedom" under the rules of Anglo-Saxon-oriented globalization begins and ends with the state's protection of individual property rights. Money, trade, and property polarize the rich and poor on the one hand, but they constitute the means to individual opportunity and meaningful state sovereignty on the other.

Poor countries can gain short-term advantages from capital controls. But in the long term, they lose foreign investment—just as free trade over time may bring them more economic growth than would continued protectionism. The ultimate questions: Who gets the lion's share of the economic growth and investment? Who owns what and can "leverage" capital?

The Competitiveness Mantra: Consolidate, Raise Productivity, Downsize, Outsource

Globalization, guided by the Anglo-Saxon principles, not only deifies private property; it puts a premium on the value of competition. This blueprint (favoring those with lots of property contracts) constitutes what can be called the ideology of corporate social Darwinism: The rules of society should be set up to maximize the profits of the best organized and funded "national" teams, which prove themselves on the global fields of competition. Innovation leads to power and wealth. To succeed in a global economy, there must be tolerance for big and fast organizations. These nationally based cartels, conglomerates, or multinational companies will bring the nation greater market share within their sectors and, in the process, raise the GDP and employment at home.

The consequences of this grand vision, however, do not live up to its promises. Using the strategy of what Bennett Harrison, in *Lean and Mean*,[17] called "concentration without centralization," the big multinational firms consolidate power through global networking. These organizations reduce in-house operations to "core competencies" by downsizing their personnel, outsourcing peripheral activities to low-cost labor sites at home or abroad (usually without benefits), computerizing and automating to increase productivity, and creating mergers, acquisitions, and strategic alliances in order to counter potential global competition.

This model generates unemployment and underemployment in the process of "creative destruction" in both rich and poor nations as the obsolete and unneeded are let go. It makes it impossible for poor countries to create multinational firms sophisticated enough to compete.

For starters, the unrestrained competitiveness model assumes that the social ideal is export-oriented growth in order to capture the maximum global market share, thus increasing employment at home. But because the world is one system, when one country builds up export surpluses, another must necessarily run trade deficits. Just as the global economy was subsidized throughout much of the post–World War II era by the printing and distribution of U.S. dollars, so too has the recent global economy been subsidized by huge U.S. trade deficits allowing other countries (e.g., China) to run large trade surpluses. But just as the dollar's value fixed to gold was eventually undermined by this extravagant liquidity, bringing down the money system, so does the extreme American trade deficit threaten to undermine the world's trade system. Protectionism has come home to roost in the United States: Unemployment near 6% is pushing toward European levels without European-style safety nets to catch those cast aside. With a huge external debt and a rising current account deficit (trade deficit plus interest payments on old government debt), the U.S. currency is pre-programmed to go down, putting pressure on Americans to save and on foreigners to buy lots of American goods and services. Income mobility stagnated beginning in the 1970s, and the real pay (adjusted for inflation) of workers in the United States in 2003 was lower than in 1973. The real value of the legal *minimum wage* in 2003 was lower than in 1968.[18]

Meanwhile, in the early twenty-first century, the conservative elite in Washington D.C. set a tone of permissiveness for the big, the powerful, and the wealthy to consolidate their positions. For example, pushed by the lobby for the media conglomerates, Republican Michael Powell, appointed head of the Federal Trade Commission, proposed in 2003 that a single media giant could expand its "penetration" in the United States from reaching one third of all American television viewers to almost one half of viewers. The U.S. Congress diluted the proposal after the Senate rejected it while facing a Presidential veto. Yet the overriding rationale of market efficiency through size—up to the point of irrefutable monopoly—is still perceived to be legitimate.

In the global arena, where anarchy reigns, domination is determined by the deep pockets of network cartels such as CNN and Fox. Poor countries have little chance to compete in this competitive game.

This can be illustrated by the need for such big media companies to advertise in the world's largest domestic national market. A 30-second spot on the highest-priced, most watched American TV show costs close to half a million dollars ($455,700, to be exact). The prices for 30 seconds on the next two most popular shows are $445,000 and $418,750.[19] And if a company wants to advertise during the Super Bowl, it costs over $3 million per minute.

As Silvio Berlusconi, Italy's media baron, has demonstrated, domination of the national media is not merely an economic act; it is a political act. Social reality is transformed into a game dominated by plutocrats. Journalist P. J. O'Rourke put it as follows: "If most people are broke, that's great for the wealthy few. They get cheap household help, low ancestral-manor real estate prices, and no crowds on Martha's Vineyard. This explains the small, nasty plutocracies in impoverished countries."[20]

When one looks to developing countries where state-run telecommunications and media are being privatized to go along with the Anglo-Saxon rules of globalization, the negative impacts on the small firms and poor individuals become clear. State-run telecommunications have a monopoly and are therefore able to socialize their costs and to benefit from economies of scale. To diffuse information technologies to increase the competitiveness of small and medium-size businesses, governments of poor countries are encouraged to privatize their telecommunications sector (along with transportation and energy). But when they do so, they discover that even if the infrastructure is provided through private companies, this is not sufficient to increase the competitiveness of small firms. In fact, these small businesses often become poorer as their local telephone bills go up. Demand for the telecommunications services does not follow supply of the infrastructure because of the increased cost in outlying rural areas, the lack of quality there, and insufficient content to attract customers. In the northern and northeastern regions of Brazil, for instance, no procedures are used to screen for defective parts in telecommunications; there are few technical regulations and no consumer surveys. Although the government of Brazil reduces the costs of telecommunications for registered small businesses (compared with homes, where the cost is higher), most of the small companies are not registered, so their local telephone services are counted as "domestic" and go up in cost.[21] Thus, although the costs of the upgraded telecommunications infrastructure are socialized (supported by the general population), the profits are privatized (going to the new, large "cartelized" private companies).

The privatization of state-run companies socializes the costs through society's infrastructure while privatizing the profits for the largest, most competitive organizations. This further impoverishes the rural areas and the people on the periphery.

Not only have the basic services of developing economies been cartelized by large, private concerns, but the foreign aid bureaucracies aimed to help developing countries have become costly, cartelized organizations, as well. Former advisor to the World Bank William Easterly notes that the global aid bureaucracies constitute a "cartel of good intentions." This cartel is made up of the United Nations Conference on Financing for Development, the World Bank, the U.S. Agency for International Development, the IMF, the United Nations, and the Inter-American Development Bank. Like all cartels, the aid cartel thrives when customers cannot find alternative suppliers and have little chance to complain, just as OPEC dictated severe terms to its oil customers during its peak in the 1970s.[22]

A case in point is Niger, which wanted debt forgiveness and new loans. The World Bank and IMF requirements forced the understaffed government offices there to spend 15 months preparing a participatory Poverty Reduction Strategy paper. This included not only a 14-point World Bank check list (the Comprehensive Development Framework) stretching from lumber to labor practices, but also a Financial Information Management System report, a report on Observance of Standards and Codes, a Medium Term Expenditure Framework, and a Debt Sustainability Analysis for the Enhanced Heavily Indebted Poor Countries Initiative. Niger's report was 187 pages long. It had to itemize spending for 2002–2005, including the annual cost of detailed items down to the level of sensitizing population to traffic circulation.[22]

Good business practice would require the aid bureaucracies to "keep it simple, stupid!" But each well-intentioned, well-paid aid organization adds its own regulations (reaffirming its own need to exist), making for a regulatory morass that would challenge even the best educated and best staffed government seeking funding. Meanwhile, the many at the bottom of the society become poorer while the exhaustive paperwork is being filled out.

Indeed, the developing countries have adopted a much simpler approach to support themselves—money sent home annually by immigrant workers in developed countries. From such family members working abroad, poor countries receive about $80 billion—*twice* as much as they do from foreign aid and *ten times* as much as they do from private investment.[23] But restrictions on immigration by developed countries due to the fears of terrorism and of domestic unemployment may complicate even this last source of finance for low-income nations, despite the growing need for immigrant workers in most aging rich nations whose native populations are shrinking.

The rules of globalization set by the wealthy are extremely complex and make it difficult for individuals in any country to cope—particularly for the poor, who lack education, opportunity, and resources. The acceleration of change due to the process of globalization has only made things worse. To become competitive, organizations must become quick while still having a large enough size to benefit from economies of scale and to "socialize" some of their costs—that is, to pass them on to others. A social reality has been created that is characterized by increasing uncertainty in the name of freedom on the one hand and by the search for security on the other. Plutocracy reigns. Meanwhile, even in developed nations, social safety nets are being trimmed back for the disadvantaged who can't make it or who fall behind because of lack of opportunity, bad luck, illness, or old age. Let's examine some of the trends that make up this social reality and will structure our life chances.

References

1. Scott Miller and Neil King, "Poor Nations Bristle over New Push," and Michael Casey, "Argentina Ends Standoff with IMF by Defaulting on $2.9 Billion Debt," *The Wall Street Journal*, September 10, 2003, p. A22.

2. Elizabeth Becker and Finger Thompson, "Poorer Nations Plead Farmers' Case at Trade Talks," *The New York Times,* September 11, 2003.

3. Roger Thurow and Scott Kilman, "Bitter Harvest: As U.S. Food Aid Enriches Farmers, Poor Nations Cry Foul," *The Wall Street Journal*, September 11, 2003.

4. S. Ibi Ajayi, "What Africa Needs to Do to Benefit from Globalization," *Finance and Development*, Vol. 38, No. 4 (Washington, D.C.: 2001), pp. 6–8.

5. R. Isaak, *Managing World Economic Change*, 3rd edition (Upper Saddle River, NJ: Prentice Hall, 2000), p. 252.

6. Tina Rosenberg, "The Free-Trade Fix," *The New York Times Magazine*, August 18, 2002.

7. "Commodity Export Dependence, the International Poverty Trap and New Vulnerabilities," *The Least Developed Countries Report 2002* (UNCTAD, 2002), p. 138, 142 143.

8. Blain Harden, "The Dirt in the New Machine," *The New York Times Magazine*, August 12, 2001.

9. Kofi Annan, "Best Hope for Least-Developed Countries," *Presidents & Prime Ministers*, Vol.10, No. 3 (Glen Ellyn: May/June 2001), pp. 18–19.

10. Peter Fritsch, "As End of a Quota System Nears, Bangladesh Fears for Its Jobs," *The Wall Street Journal*, November 20, 2003.

11. Nicholas D. Kristof, "Death by Dividend," *The New York Times*, November 22, 2003.

12. Neil King and Scott Miller, "Cancun: Victory for Whom?" *The Wall Street Journal*, September 16, 2003.

13. George Soros, *On Globalization* (Cambridge, MA: Public Affairs/Perseus, 2002).

14. Joseph Stiglitz, *Globalization and Its Discontents* (New York: W.W. Norton, 2002), p. 160.

15. United Nations, "World Investment 2003: FDI Policies for Development: National and International Perspectives," New York and Geneva: 2003, Chapter 1, pp. 3–5.

16. Hernando de Soto, *The Mystery of Capital: Why Capitalism Triumphs in the West and Fails Everywhere Else* (New York: Basic Books, 2000), pp. 35, 54.

17. Bennett Harrison, *Lean and Mean: The Changing Landscape of Corporate Power in the Age of Flexibility* (New York: Basic

Books, 1993), pp. 9–12. Also see David C. Korten, *When Corporations Rule the World* (West Hartford, CT: Kumarian Press, 1996).

18. *NOW with Bill Moyers*, Public Broadcasting System, November 21, 2003.

19. David Goetzl and Wayne Friedman, " 'Friends' Tops Ad Price List', *Advertising Age.* (Midwest region edition), Vol. 73, No. 39, Chicago: September 30, 2002, p. 1.

20. P. J. O'Rourke, *Eat the Rich* (New York: Atlantic Monthly Press, 1998), p. 236.

21. Renata Lebra La Rovere, "Diffusion of Information Technologies and Changes in the Telecommunications Sector: The Case of Brazilian Small and Medium-Sized Enterprises," *Information Technology and People*, Vol. 11, No. 3, pp. 194–206.

22. William Easterly, "The Cartel of Good Intentions," *Foreign Policy*, July/August 2002, pp. 40–41.

23. "A Lifeline for Poor Nations," *Business Week*, November 24, 2003, p. 28.

IV

CRISIS
AND
SOLUTIONS

12 Global Crises We Will All Face

*As forests have been felled and aquifers drawn down;
as the atmosphere has filled with toxins and the oceans
have been fished to exhaustion; and as the climate itself
has begun to talk back, holding up a mirror to our
profligate ways, the world has seen the dangers
of business as usual.*

—KOFI ANNAN,
Beyond the Horizon (2002)
© 2002 Time, Inc. Reprinted by permission.

T*he growing gap between rich and poor will aggravate interrelated crises,
such as overpopulation, epidemics, unemployment, illiteracy, environmental
degradation, civil war, and the loss of legitimacy of American hegemony.*

Every day, each individual has a part in the social and environmental construction of the world. But much of the time, most of us do not perceive this sense of agency, this ability to influence global outcomes, this responsibility for our immediate surroundings. Rather, the existing Anglo-Saxon rules of globalization seem to encourage us to "let things go" (*laissez-faire*) as a part and parcel of deregulation, privatization, and individual freedom. There seems to be an unrealistic, optimistic assumption that if all the regulatory shackles came off, we individuals would create so much economic growth that prosperity and peace would be the inevitable results. But as we have seen, this reasoning has led to an economic and corporate Darwinism that gives the power to those who start with the most advantages and the easiest access to assets. If the rules in the globalized economy are not changed and continue to push the gap between the rich and poor to new extremes, we are bound to magnify a number of global crises that will undermine our way of being.

Assume that things stay more or less the same. Some of the major crises we can expect are overpopulation; epidemics; extreme educational inadequacies; unemployment; deficiencies in what we call "democracy"; political instability; environmental disasters; the proliferation of chemical, biological, and nuclear weapons; and the further unraveling of the legitimacy of American unilateralism. If the growing chasm between the wealthiest and the poor were eliminated tomorrow, many of these problems would be alleviated, although not eliminated. Otherwise, these crises will intensify and feed on each other, leading inevitably to global disintegration and war. The elements that make up these crises are all part of one, interrelated global system. The stakes are enormous. Let's consider these potentially explosive problems one at a time, as well as their relationship to the dilemma of wealth and poverty.

Too Many People in the Wrong Places

Some commentators in wealthy countries throw about figures in the billions of dollars without thinking twice, as though a billion does not mean much. For instance, in its annual list of the 400 richest people in the United States, *Forbes* notes in passing that their average net wealth was $2.4 billion and that all together, they are but one Bill Gates (valued at $46 billion) away from being worth $1 trillion.[1] These huge numbers are too large for the human mind to grasp easily, but they seem to give hope—as though there were an infinite amount of wealth to be tapped into. But when it comes to global population, the well-positioned cringe when they are told that the number of people now stands at 6.3 billion and is headed for 9 billion by 2050. These numbers are also hard to conceive of, but they conjure up an image of despair—even of fear. Too many people suddenly appearing on the doorstep of the rich could, after all, reduce the quality of life: the masses, the pollution, the disease, the suffering, and *the lack of space* would be an overwhelming shock. So the wealthy countries set up immigration barriers to try to limit the numbers moving in from outside. When the Europeans, for instance, are told that the population of India increases more in a week than in the European Union (EU) in a year, they become reluctant to increase the number of immigrants permitted to migrate permanently into the EU. Never mind that fertility is dropping below the replacement rate in many European countries.

In terms of population increases today, according to the United Nations Population Division, six countries account for half of the growth: India—21%; China—12%; Pakistan—5%; and Bangladesh, Nigeria, and the United States—4% each.[2]

However, in the coming 50 years, the United Nations projects that almost all of the growth in the world population will be in developing countries with close to a billion extra people being added to the least developed countries. This takes into account the plagues and epidemics that will be most likely to counter the projected population increase.

By 2050, the world's population growth will shift to the countries least able to afford it. Meanwhile, the rich will have fewer children, smaller families, and longer life expectancy than the poor. The global population will age faster than ever before. There will be many more old people in wealthy countries, whereas developing countries will be younger, with the least developed countries being the youngest. Global inequalities of income among individuals will increase.

Rich nations, in short, have used their resources to help create more old folks in rich countries and many more young people in poor countries. New medical technologies (initially often very expensive) will extend human life to perhaps 120 years for the wealthy in developed nations. Meanwhile, by failing to provide sufficient support and training in developing countries, through the *absence* of funding for family planning programs, the wealthy will contribute to the proliferation of populations in places on the earth where the resources are the scarcest. This means that more of the resources of the wealthy should be going to help educate and employ the young in developing nations and to create healthy environments for them. But, at least in terms of government priorities, this is not the case, especially when developed nations seem to be having difficulty funding and caring for their own aging populations.

The Anglo-Saxon free-market school has little to say here because the very old and the very young are perceived to be drags on national economies, rather than productivity-enhancing: Cut the regulations; drop the fringe benefits. Corporate Social Darwinism reduces the welfare state further and leaves the youngest and the oldest to the lottery of chance. The market is the Holy Grail that must be defended above all other priorities. As economist William Baumol has shown, globalization has put oligopolies in an "arms race" competition to co-opt and to routinize innovation in order to survive. What he calls the "free market innovation machine" does not leave these firms much time to consider social consequences.[3] Time is money. And the pressures of profitability on corporate gladiators is perhaps no more keenly felt than in the pharmaceutical industry, where their marketing calculations have to consider the potential cost of losing thousands of lives if low-priced drugs do not reach people infected with contagious, terminal diseases in time to contain global epidemics.

The Spread of Plagues and Epidemic Diseases

In its most extreme form, Corporate Social Darwinism means cutting health benefits and letting the weak and ill die. That way, the strong, the competent, and the well-positioned companies can remain competitive and dominant, representing the best of "the species." Although this principle is no doubt simplistic and overstated, it does characterize a trend of cutting back corporate benefits for the sake of competitiveness in the United States. And, in response in part to the resulting globalized competitive pressures, health care support is being trimmed in other developed countries as well. As always, in developing countries the health situation is much worse. For example, with about 40 million people infected in the worldwide AIDS pandemic, global funding for medicine is severely challenged with the problem of equity, because the poorest nations most affected have the least access to the needed drugs. But this is the tip of the iceberg.

Life expectancy in the 42 so-called Highly Indebted Poor Countries (HIPCs) averages a mere 51 years, largely due to the deadly mix of tropical diseases and poverty. In contrast to the temperate ecological zones typical of the rich countries, 39 of the 42 HIPCs are tropical or desert societies.[4] Nor do the problems end with tropical diseases in developing nations. The seven countries most infected with the HIV/AIDS virus—Botswana, Lesotho, Namibia, South Africa, Swaziland, Zambia, and Zimbabwe—are expected to have their populations reduced by 19% lower than otherwise by 2015 and by 36% lower than they would otherwise be by 2050.[5] In Sub-Saharan Africa, you have a 50/50 chance of being one of more than 300 million people who live in extreme poverty on less than $1 a day. The main causes of illness and high mortality rates here, as in other developing regions, are apt to be malaria, tuberculosis, childhood infectious diseases, maternal and prenatal nutritional deficiencies, and HIV/AIDS. The World Health Organization Commission on Macroeconomics and Health estimates that $30–$40 per person in these developing countries would be the minimum cost for essential treatments (including those to fight AIDS). This sounds small compared with the $2,000 in per capita annual health spending in high-income countries. But attaining the recommended minimum of $30 will be a difficult reach from the current $13 per year per capita spent on health in the poorest countries.[6] Will it happen? Not likely, even given the multimillion-dollar contribution of Bill Gates toward curing malaria.

Consider an incident that is suggestive of where money from the wealthiest government—that of the United States—is *not* apt to go. In 2003, the George W. Bush administration announced it would stop payments to the Reproductive Health for Refugees Consortium because one of the seven charities involved was linked to abortions in China: Marie Stopes International. The doctors and nurses in the Marie Stopes organization work in slums in Kenya and other developing countries to fight AIDS, rape, sexually transmitted diseases, and the genital mutilation of girls. *New York Times* reporter Nicholas Kristof investigated the consequences of this policy shift. The results he uncovered could be devastating for women in developing countries. The United States cuts in funding led to the elimination of planned outreach programs to aid Somali and Rwandan refugees. The Bush administration's objections to the activities of the Marie Stopes International in China are difficult to understand because the organization distributes condoms there to reduce the number of abortions, which seems consistent with American policy. Kristof notes that although the Bush administration undoubtedly perceives its policy in terms of abortion and sex as well as appealing to its domestic political base, the change in the policy will clearly result in the death of women and children in the shantytowns of Africa.[7]

The problem here is that faith-based, ideological first principles can get in the way of the effectiveness of policies that are finally carried out. The actual results of such policies can have perverse effects, even contradicting the intentions of the first principle, which seems to be the situation in the Marie Stopes case. Anti-abortion is a faith-based ideological principle. Free markets first, before all else, is another principle for "true believers." Such ideological principles may make sense as starting points. But they can also result in empirical disasters if not modified to be adapted to each particular culture where they are applied. The deeper philosophical belief from which these principles stem is an American conviction that there must be *universal* principles that can be applied anywhere in the world, regardless of the particular cultural context or economic conditions of a particular place. The rules of globalization (as illustrated in the free market fundamentalism of the International Monetary Fund [IMF]) must be understood in terms of this American longing for universal principles.

Fortunately for the sake of the sick in developing countries, in the case of the protection of intellectual property rights and corporate profits, the "first principles" were relaxed by the Bush administration: The U.S. government consented to the 2003 EU-Swiss-African agreement to permit third countries to provide generic drugs for AIDS, malaria, and tuberculosis at prices poor countries could afford without violating the patents on the brand names of these drugs. But this is the exception, not the rule. Many developing nations (such as Guatemala) do not distribute the drugs where they are needed, even if they do become available. The most likely outlet for such generic drugs that are legally allowed to be "cloned" in third countries will be the black market drug trade, given the high unemployment in developing countries and the propensity of corrupt officials to make a profit on the side. Only an increase in employment and economic growth can help to overcome this petty corruption that has such disastrous consequences for the lives of those who are ill.

The Rapid Global Spread of Unemployment and Underemployment

The Anglo-Saxon domination of globalization has increased world economic growth rates in boom times. But this same global creative destruction has left countries having the most open money and trade systems with the greatest exposure to unemployment and underemployment in times of economic slowdown. This, of course, includes the United States.

Since 2000, the International Labor Organization estimates that the number of unemployed in the world increased by 20 million, reaching a total of 180 million by 2003. This hit women and youth the hardest because they are most vulnerable to economic shocks. And the progress made in reducing the number of "working poor" (workers who live on $1 a day or less) in the late 1990s was reversed—to total 550 million.[8]

Recall the fanfare of spreading democracy, privatization, and free market activity in Latin America in the past decade. Latin America and the Caribbean were the hardest hit with unemployment in the economic slowdown since 2000 and September 11: Almost 10% are now jobless, with youth unemployment going to 16%. In Sub-Saharan Africa, the increase of joblessness was less, but the unemployment rate is still over 14% and rising. In the Middle East, youth unemployment was extremely high in Syria, Algeria, Bahrain, and Morocco. The general unemployment in these regions went into double digits in many countries, given a fall in GDP growth from more than 6% in 2000 to 1.5% two years later. In the "transition economies" (that is, those transitioning from state-controlled economies to democracy and free markets) in Eastern Europe, the unemployment rate is pushing 14%.[8]

A government's openness to free trade and markets in the globalization era increases economic growth in boom times but rapidly increases vulnerability to joblessness and underemployment when the economy turns down—particularly in developing countries. Free markets can become free falls.

Globalization in a downturn leads to rising unemployment and underemployment (in all countries—rich and poor alike). "Jobless recovery" characterizes the productivity-led economic growth of the twenty-first century. In the United States, output per worker went from 1.5% growth in 1992–1996 to 2.6% between 1996 and 1999 to over 4% from 2002 to 2003.[9] Under President George W. Bush, more jobs were lost than under any President since President Herbert Hoover in the Great Depression. For corporations, to compete in the accelerated world economy has meant to restructure and downsize. Workers face the constant threat of unemployment or underpaid, insecure employment. This is not just a question of economic deprivation. Studies show substantial psychological costs for both individuals and their families everywhere in the world in terms of depression, stress, and loss of self-esteem on the part of the unemployed.[10]

To add salt to the wound, a lot of the jobs have been "offshored" to developing countries that pay much less. Back-office jobs at the

Bank of America go to India for one fifth the labor cost. And to cut wages even further, information technology (IT) service providers headquartered in India are opening offices in Hungary, Poland, and the Czech Republic, tapping into a German- and English-speaking work force closer to the European markets that is abundant but educated. German multinational corporations, in turn, look to Romania and Bulgaria for cheaper IT workshops.[11] By 2015, Forester Research predicts that 3.3 million services jobs in the United States will move offshore, some 500,000 of these being in computer software and services.[12] But this hollowing out of employment in developed countries due to the transfer of jobs to developing countries will still not be nearly enough to meet the rising demands for work in any of these countries.

Globalization provides companies with the tools to systematically seek out cheaper labor abroad, creating unemployment at home. This is how the well-to-do create poorer workers domestically. Some of the wealth trickles down to places where the education and infrastructure are developed enough to catch the drops.

The Education Crisis: Elite Hierarchies Confront Desperate Demands for Tools and Open Access

The Anglo-Saxon model of globalization is targeted to expand democratic liberal capitalism worldwide, which demands high levels of mass education and increasingly skilled human capital to function. Education is inherently hierarchical. But *access* to education should *not* be hierarchical. There is a crisis if there are physical or financial obstacles preventing clearly qualified students from being accepted to study at the best universities in the world. Practically speaking, to gain entrance to the best universities in the United States, for example, a student seeks out private tutors while already attending expensive private preparatory schools or public schools that depend for their quality on high real estate prices. Here the observation of nineteenth-century political economist Henry George applies: The value of real estate rises much faster than the wages of workers, impoverishing them. Skyrocketing tuition costs in most American universities add to the problem. In European countries, students can study at most public universities practically for free, but overcrowded conditions lead many to try to spend some time studying in the United States as well.

Why is there *a crisis*?

We live in a knowledge economy. *What* you know is beginning to count almost as much as *who* you know. Educational degrees are slowly becoming mere driver's licenses when looking for a job and moving from one job to another. What you know and specialize in beyond the credentials is what counts. The dominant software companies in the world see their most valuable "assets" walking out of the door each day and have to create stock option bribes to hold on to their most gifted employees (despite a temporary glut of IT workers in some places). There are still not enough highly educated and skilled people within any particular country to fill the top positions. The best and brightest workers know this and are ready to use their mobility to their advantage. Moreover, not enough people are being trained for the critical job slots.

Each country has its own kind of educational crisis. Many have to recruit specialized talent from abroad to keep their economies functioning. Technological knowledge and the global economy are developing so fast that it is almost impossible for any but the most sophisticated and well-financed educational institutions to keep up with latest state of the art in any particular field.

The rich countries push the envelope, raising educational standards for success to ever higher levels of achievement and making it difficult for developing countries to match (the prestigious engineering institutes in India are the exception). Not surprisingly, the lowest primary enrollment as a percentage of the relevant age group is in some of the poorest countries of the world: Niger, Bukina Faso, Ethiopia, Mali, Burundi, Sudan, Eritrea, Guinea, Chad, and Mozambique.[13]

By raising the standards and cost of higher education in the richest parts of the world (particularly in the United States), the wealthy create an educational divide with the poorest regions,

contributing to poverty, unemployment, and a comparative lack of learning opportunities.

The high-tech dimension of the globalized economy has made education more vital than ever before. To become competitive, a country must be "wired," or technologically hooked up to globalization. Whole regions of humanity risk becoming shut off from such development and are becoming increasingly dependent on others. Thus, Africa is only a marginal player in global trade, responsible for less than 2% of world exports and imports, and the share of foreign direct investment it is able to attract is declining. In terms of their own social construction of reality, this chronic dependence has made African economies predominately *externally* centered and *passive* internationally.[14] The role of education is to transform passive pawns into active agents of human development, innovation, and productivity. Africa and other developing regions in the shadows of the world economy are still technologically illiterate and are passive and dependent, rather than active and self-sufficient. In his classic *Economic Backwardness in Historical Perspective*, Alexander Gerschenkron[15] showed that each nation can discover its own unique path to development in order to catch up with others (demonstrating how the "later comers"—Germany, France, and Russia—tried to catch up with industrialized Britain in the nineteenth century). Each national culture can find distinctive ways to diminish backwardness that tap its very discontinuities as potential strengths.[14] But the current sophisticated wave of globalization appears to require outside help for developing countries to enable them to organize and to finance their unique competitive advantages.

The faster the acceleration in the global economy, the less the time the rich have taken to understand the unique paths needed to transform the poor from their dependence and passivity. High levels of technological education provide the only way out, the ultimate lifesaver of development for desperate people. But the well-to-do are mainly concerned with their own people and their deficiencies.

The rich usually leave nothing to chance when it comes to their children. They start with the best prenatal care, best preschools, best nursery schools, best private or public secondary schools, and best tutors to be sure their children get into the best colleges and universities.

Relative or absolute poor families start with little or nothing. They cannot compete. Their numbers will increase greatly because it is in the illiterate areas of the world where the population growth is highest. And they will ultimately die young or become increasingly dependent on those who are better off. The rich, with their good fortune, power, and education, bear the most responsibility in the world: They are responsible for millions of silent orphanages globally without being aware of it. There is a continuing trend to ignore the growing educational deficit because it is a "soft" problem, rather than a "hard" problem (like military weapons).

Education is being short-changed among the poor wherever you look—in rich countries or in the ones that are poverty stricken. This educational handicap contributes to a massive democratic deficit, reinforced by corporate elites who have the decisive voice in state policies and economic decisions. The real power has shifted to the multinational corporations, which are at the cutting edge of change, even though politicians have used the terrorist war as a means to try to bring back power to the executive authorities of nation states. National governments are merely reacting to forces they cannot control, and a growing democratic deficit is one of the inevitable results.

From Corporate Oligarchy to Chaos

The ancient Greeks understood that power corrupts and that absolute power corrupts absolutely. The democratic deficit resulted from the increasing replacement of state power with corporate power: It has become the most critical global crisis. In the twenty-first century, not only the reputation of government elites but also the legitimacy of corporate power has been undermined by greed and scandal, along with the technological prowess it promised. Government scandals have been followed by widespread corporate misconduct. Both state and corporate institutions have lost the respect of the masses. If both states and corporations become incapable of maintaining loyalty, this leaves the real possibility of chaos. People everywhere are beginning to realize that corporations *cannot* rule the world by themselves, even if they want to. Michael Hardt and Antonio Negri argue in *Empire*[16] that large transnational corporations have effectively surpassed the jurisdiction and authority of nation states and that the notion of the autonomy of the political has disappeared. But the legitimacy of the corporation, the Federal Reserve Board, and the international organization (IMF, World Bank, World Trade Organization) risks going the way of the nation state.

This all leads us back to a postmodern version of the classic Greek cycle of government. First there is government by the one—a strong executive power embodied in one person or authority that begins with a benevolent objective: to maintain and enforce global law and order. But the oligarchic few, the wealthy, powerful, economic and technological elite at some point or another determine that the government by the one is inadequate, incompetent, or corrupt. Even if successful, the government by the one may ultimately be seen as a threat to their own power by the oligarchic elite. In the postmodern version, government by the one is not overthrown but merely "displaced" or "bought out." This velvet glove strategy shifts the power to the oligarchic elite, who then use the government of the executive "one" as a front. But these powerful few overstep their limits, as well, with boundless greed, undermining their legitimacy. As the corporate elite, for example, increase their own salaries and pension benefits by millions while firing thousands of workers in their own firms, belief in their integrity and reliability is undone. In the global political economy with its increasing transparency of information flows, such greedy behavior is quickly revealed (nothing can be kept secret any longer). Journalists help ambitious politicians to bring down the members of the corporate elite who have overstepped their legal or ethical limits, undermining the legitimacy of corporate power. These journalists represent either democratic ideals or what Aristotle referred to as "mob rule" (scandal-mongering—desiring only to bring down those at the top who have gotten too big and successful). Their outlook is often too limited to find a balanced solution to public problems. Some might argue that this is not their job, but if they are not part of the solution to the democratic deficit, they are part of the problem. American journalist Walter Lippmann is dead— along with his balanced, critical, philosophical wisdom in defining the public interest.[17]

Nor do we appear to be training Walter Lippmanns for the future. Philosophy, as such, is passé in the United States. Philosophers who have anything to say about contemporary political and cultural reality typically have left philosophy departments for comparative literature departments (e.g., Richard Rorty), just as the existentialists left the academy in France (Albert Camus), Germany (Martin Heidegger), and Ireland (Samuel Beckett) in the 1950s and 1960s. In the cultures of France or Germany, philosophy still carries weight in the media, but these countries may be the exceptions. Who has or takes the time today to read what they write? The globalization and computerization of society have taken away the leisure time required for such reading. If leisure is the basis of culture, we seem to have given it up for a high-tech, competitive rat race.

Few people know any more what democracy really means, what this vague notion signifies. This is true, despite the enthusiasm for a populist notion of democracy in transitional economies leaving authoritarian state control behind (as in *some* countries in Eastern Europe). Only a small minority of any particular democratic population knows the difference between direct democracy and representative democracy and, for example, why a "mixed" form of government is necessary to preserve stable political systems that protect the rights of minorities. Even fewer know that Aristotle's ideal of *politea*—the proper mix of aristocratic power and democratic power—requires a large, educated middle class in order to come into being and to be maintained. Aristotle's *Politics*, after all, is not exactly required reading for high schools and colleges in the world. Without understanding Aristotle's reasoning, those who would have democracy end up becoming impatient for direct democracy. This longing to vote on everything directly can spill over easily into what Aristotle called "mob rule" (that is, a populist majority overwhelming all minorities) *unless* all voters in the direct democracy are provided with enough education by the state to be able participate in an empowered town meeting or parliament in a wise and informed manner. Such education and informed participation is particularly important in an extremely complex global political economy in which citizens are expected to vote on issues as well as on candidates.

Representative democracy, as it is practiced in the United States at least, has become a form of plutocracy at the federal level and loses legitimacy to oligarchy by the day. Just try running for Congress and see what it costs. The founding fathers of the United States Constitution would turn over in their graves if they knew the extent of influence of money in the American political system (although Benjamin Franklin warned that such interest group corruption would one day undermine the stability of his beloved republic). And as to the prerequisite of a large, educated middle class, that social reality is also threatened in the United States.

In the last decades of the twentieth century, up until 1996, the bottom 80% of the U.S. population found their incomes staying more or less the same after subtracting for inflation, whereas the top 20% saw their incomes go up significantly. This had the effect of hollowing out the middle class. The brief respite from this trend with the spread of more income to lower class workers in the late 1990s boom was reversed when the tech-dot-com bubble burst. In the state of Alabama, one of five now live in poverty, the illiteracy rate approaches 25%, and low-income people pay three times the taxes that the top-income people pay. Republican Governor Bob Riley attempted to reform the state tax system with a plan to place the biggest taxes on the wealthy and the lowest taxes on the poor. But the business elite and conservative constituencies did a television blitz, distorting the issues (most citizens receiving their news only through the TV) and causing the majority of voters in relative poverty to turn down the complex tax proposal, which was very much in their own economic interest.[18] After reaching a decade's low in the United States at the turn of the century, the poverty rate recently has gone up again (to over 34 million people), and many more jobless folks are finding their way to the soup kitchens. In

Virginia, there are rural areas where people live in shacks without running water. This is the richest country in the world. Just imagine being poor in the poorest countries.

There is a model of democracy to consider, of course, and that is Switzerland. But even here, banking greed got in the way and has undermined the legitimacy of the Swiss model in the eyes of global public opinion (e.g., the perception that any corrupt dictator or mafia boss can stash money of dubious origin safely away in Swiss banks). This is a shame, because the Swiss model has much to recommend it, particularly for small, "neutral" countries seeking a balance between forms of direct, cantonal local democracy and the minimal level of federal authority necessary to function effectively in the global political economy. The smaller the size of the democratic state, the more that direct democracy can be used within a framework of representative democracy. In the United States and in European representative democracies, most of one's political time is spent doing whatever one can to get the attention of the influential elite in order to get that elite group to act in one's interest. In Switzerland (with an average of 3–4 elections in the local canton each year), citizens are consulted regarding a number of issues on which they can vote (on 66 federal issues in the 1980s, for example).[19] In an era of global political cynicism when people do not believe their votes count anymore, the Swiss model and recipe of reverting as many decisions as possible down to the local level where every person's vote counts could bring back political confidence if this system was popularized so that people all over the world knew about it. This assumes that the state subsidizes the education of its citizens to make them competent and comfortable with this greater direct political responsibility. Of course, that the Swiss show a propensity to elect right-wing politicians to protect their existing culture and political system is regrettable and can be explained by massive immigrant migrations in Europe. The Swiss are also extremely protective of their environment and try to maintain a sustainable community (that is, one that works to satisfy present needs without undermining the ability to satisfy the needs of future generations in the process). But whether the Swiss model would work in a large, nuclear-armed state with a strong ideological position is debatable. Even a partial move toward the Swiss model, however, could mitigate the neglect of environmental problems that is typical of such powerful, ideological governments.

The Environmental Crisis

Most people and nations fail to consider that what they do or don't do can have an immediate (as well as long-term) impact on the environment, taking the ecosystem's fragile existence for granted. The more that economic processes speed up, the more people are apt to be distracted from thinking about their dependence on the environment. There are exceptional groups, such as Green Parties, Green Peace, and local environmental coalitions, but they have difficulty getting their message through (unless they attach themselves to another ideological constituency, as did the German Green Party).

Another problem is complexity. Environmental issues are complicated,[20] and they are often described in terms of potential *losses*, not potential *gains*.

Who wants to be bothered by complicated topics that anticipate losses? Most people in the Western world are caught on the hyper treadmill and do not want to invest the time to ponder on ways to reduce pollution.

Combine the natural human temptation to neglect the environmental basis on which we depend and the inclination to ignore the poor, and you get overpopulated cities, deforested rain forests, unbreatheable air, undrinkable water, eroded soils incapable of sustaining crops, maldistribution of critical resources, unemployment, overwhelmed government bureaucracies, armed conflict, and chronic poverty—in short, a growing ethos of care*less*ness. The wealthiest 20% of the world population consumes almost 60% of the total energy, compared with just 4% of the energy consumed by 50% of the people.

Rural-to-urban migration accounts for some 50% of annual city growth in developing countries. People flee the countryside for greater opportunities in education, jobs, health care, and other social services. In shifting to urban areas, population growth lowers the ratio of capital to labor—"capital shallowing." This, in turn, reduces per capita economic productivity. If a population expands rapidly, dependence ratios increase, making it harder for households to educate children and to pass capital on to them. With large numbers of uneducated youth who cannot be productively employed, the country cannot compete in the global economy.[21] This is the dominant trend for most developing nations.

The paradox in the developing countries is that not only does the rise in population growth put more pressure on renewable resources and decreasing supplies of necessities, but those poor countries with an abundance of natural resources are the most apt to suffer from armed conflict and civil wars.[22] And war is the ultimate polluter.

The scientific results may be uncertain as to what extent environmental problems from the United States (the greatest present emitter of greenhouse gases) and the developing countries (the greatest projected future emitters) lead to permanent global warming (or cooling). The U.S. failure to ratify the 1997 Kyoto accord to require nations to cut the emissions of gases linked to global warming made it easier for the Russians to decide not to ratify the treaty. Although 120 nations have ratified the international agreement, it takes effect only when enough countries have approved it to account for 55% of 1990 emissions from the industrialized world. And without the US or the EU and Russia this threshold cannot be met.

What is not uncertain are the increasing radical swings in extreme weather conditions worldwide. And the poor are least able to recover from droughts, hurricanes, floods, and other natural disasters. Multiply the number of energy blackouts experienced in the developed world to get a sense of what low-income countries must experience. And just consider the future projected scarcity of energy supplies alone.

Environmental degradation is just a symptom of a breakdown in global stability that affects rich nations as much as poor nations. Powerful countries are increasingly drawn into the civil conflicts of the poor, particularly in resource-rich areas that the wealthy depend on for supplies. The recurrent "oil wars" are just the most obvious example. And the pollution and diseases spawned in poor countries are carried rapidly to the rich countries, one way or another, giving powerful nations even more incentives to intervene in poor regions.

American Unilateralism: Taxation Without Representation?

The classic question, given these interventions in developing countries, is whether the world is better off with just one major power (unipolar) or whether stability is easier to achieve in a multipolar world. This issue is epitomized by the explicit effort of the United States to manage the world unilaterally, as opposed to worldwide opposition, which calls for multilateral, multipolar management.

American hegemony is not as inevitable as capitalism or globalization, but American governments often behave as though it were. The United States was formed when colonists dumped British tea in the Boston Harbor, protesting the British government's taxation without representation. Yet American policy makers are surprised when they try to impose unilateral policies, then find that other countries do not go along when asked to contribute money and troops after the fact. An example of this is the protest of French and German governments by not supporting the United States after the U.S. government rejected the participation of United Nations in its policy making before and after the invasion of Iraq in 2003. American governmental efforts to dominate global management can often be characterized as a form of global taxation without representation.

This short-sighted perspective of self-righteous unilateralism in "preventive intervention by force" dominates not just American national security policy but money and trade policies, as well. For example, at the September 2003 meeting of the G-7 industrial states, the United States successfully pushed for the principle that all currencies should be "market-based," that is, reflecting "economic fundamentals." The United States is still the key reserve currency with huge advantages in terms of credit and credibility, skewing the outcomes of any such free market policy toward the American position. The American government policy was to stop countries such as China and Japan from intervening in their exchange markets in order to keep their currencies artificially low, making Chinese and Japanese export prices more competitive at the expense of U.S. exports. The international monetary system is not a level playing field. American policy makers often strive to preserve the status quo, whereas the Chinese, for example, pegged their currency to the dollar to help to keep their exports competitive and to tilt the status quo a bit in their favor.

The risk of a global crisis arises if U.S. government officials continue to overplay their hand in making unilateral decisions and policies. For example, the U.S. government sides with the Israeli government on virtually every vote in the United Nations, almost as though Israel were the fifty-first state. This, not surprisingly, alienates many countries in the world that cannot count on such preferential support. And the predictable American policy bias makes it almost impossible to create a balanced, permanent peace in the Middle East between the Palestinians and the Israelis (which would be in the long-term interest of both sides). Usually, U.S. government votes in the United Nations Security Council on the Israeli-Palestinian question reflect neither the majority preferences of Americans nor the majority preferences of people outside the United States. By becoming locked into the resulting anticipation that the overwhelming majority of the United Nations will vote against the American position, the U.S. government is tempted to circumvent the United Nations on other issues as well, relying on unilateral or bilateral solutions. A negative self-fulfilling prophecy has been created by the United States in the United Nations that serves *no one's* long-term interests for the sake of short-term, American domestic political considerations. Yet a radical change in this dynamic of alliances in the United Nations seems to be unlikely.

As the sole superpower in the world, it is in the interest of the United States to understate its power. Diplomacy, after all, is defined as letting others have your way. Imposing unilateral solutions by force or the threat of force consolidates global reactions against the American-dominated status quo, undermining American legitimacy as the world leader and lender of last resort. Unilateralism, although often tempting for a superpower, should be the exception to the rule; otherwise, international organizations such as the United Nations will become increasingly impotent, thrusting even more burdens and costs upon the United States. Accounting for nearly half of the world's military spending and as the richest economy in the world, the United States also has the greatest political and moral obligations toward less developed countries. Yet the accumulation of American power, technology, and wealth have exceeded the exercise of American government responsibility for the disadvantaged, both domestically and abroad. Explicit unilateralism merely brings this embarrassing gap more sharply into focus. If the United States continues to move from being a republic toward establishing itself as an empire (what psychologist Robert Lifton calls "the Superpower syndrome"), it risks overstretching its reach and inviting the inevitable decline that has been the fate of all empires in the past.

Proliferation of Nuclear, Chemical, and Biological Weapons

American superpower policy is guided by economist Charles Kindleberger's thesis that world stability *may* be better off with one sole superpower that keeps law and order and serves as the economic leader and "lender of last resort."[23] But *if* this superpower is not perceived as legitimate by most people on the earth, this constitutes a huge international crisis. This is why the United States has such a great stake in not overplaying its hand and in preserving respect for its ideals.

The United States must cultivate its "soft power" as much as its "hard power." Soft power is all about creating a social and political reality that everyone would want to join—not run away from. Soft power is what made students in the twentieth century do whatever they could to get into the United States to study, along with the illegal immigrants in desperately poor countries who risked their lives to get across the American border. The United States was "in"—economically, politically, and *culturally.* If you have enough soft power (pull, influence), you don't have to use as much hard power (force, weapons).

Soft power is Elvis Presley, Humphrey Bogart, the old "American dream," Silicon Valley, the Internet. Hard power is overwhelming superiority in nuclear weapons, 100% accurate missiles, impervious high-tech tanks. **If you have enough soft power, you don't have to use as much hard power.**

But why is U.S. soft power slipping so fast now? Why is the economic cost of maintaining American power so high? Was this caused by forces and events that the United States could not control (such as the September 11 attacks), or are the policies and behavior of the American government at fault (e.g., the marketing of U.S. policy or public relations)? Was it the inability to communicate sufficiently with other countries, giving them the sense of participation? Or was it the *loss of face* on the part of all those out-positioned by the United States in terms of economic, political, and technological predominance? Could soft power have been solidified just as hard power was in the reaction to the September 11 attacks, making it easier to use soft power rather than hard power? Or, given present trends, is it not more likely that the United States will use more hard power to make up for the loss of soft power?

If the United States has the dominant supply of nuclear, biological, and chemical weapons (*hard* hard power) and wants to persuade other countries *not* to develop these kinds of weapons, much less use them, how can this be done without building up soft power wherever possible? After all, such persuasion ultimately involves a swap of soft power for potential hard power.

Hard power is "in." American war strategy is to use lethal weapons in a way that minimizes U.S. casualties. Distance from the targets is the first step. Objects that appear as technological abstractions from the sky are easier to kill without a sense that they might be human. The technology of globalization has brought the accuracy of weapons efficiency to a level that increasingly distances the instigators of war from the victims of war (even from within a high-tech tank on the ground). Such warfare can lead to extreme reactions. Powerless groups are stimulated to use human beings as lethal weapons in suicide attacks to protest this kind of domination. The more hard power is used, the more it proliferates as the model for others to adopt. Conflict breeds conflict—more wars, increased terrorism, and violence will be the result. Nuclear weapons will spread to nations that do not yet possess them.

Winning hearts and minds of masses of people on the ground is soft power and is critical for legitimizing the use of hard power to back up law and order. To the extent the United States is perceived by global public opinion to bend over backward to help out and support less privileged countries economically and socially, soft power increases. If, on the other hand, soft power continues to decrease for the United States, superpower legitimacy will be undermined to that extent, and the world will become an increasingly unstable system.[24]

All the crises we have discussed point to a future of global disintegration. Neither the diffuse therapies initiated by international organizations (the World Bank, the IMF, the United Nations), the scattered efforts of nongovernmental organizations, nor the unilateral intervention in vital national security hot spots on the part of developed states are working to stabilize these crises. A new blueprint is required for a fresh start.

References

1. The Richest People in America," *Forbes*, October 6, 2003, pp. 136–270.

2. United Nations Population Division, 2003: *www.un.org/esa/population/unpop.*

3. William J. Baumol, *The Free-Market Innovation Machine* (Princeton, NJ: Princeton University Press, 2002).

4. Jeffrey Sachs, "Sachs on Development: Helping the World's Poor," *The Economist*, August 14, 1999, p.18.

5. UN Population Division Forecasts, 2003: Martin Wolf, "People, Plagues and Prosperity: Five Trends that Promise

to Transform the World's Population within 50 Years," *Financial Times*, February 27, 2003, p. 11.

6. Laura D'andrea Tyson, "For Developing Countries, Health Is Wealth," *Business Week*, January 14, 2002, p. 20.

7. Nicholas D. Kristof, "Killing Them Softly," *The New York Times*, September 20, 2003, Op-Ed.

8. International Labour Office, *Global Employment Trends* (Geneva: ILO, 2003), p. 1.

9. *The World in 2004* (London: *The Economist*, 2003), p. 28.

10. Anthony Winefield, "Unemployment, Underemployment, Occupational Stress and Psychological Well-Being," *Australian Journal of Management*, Vol. 27 (Sydney: 2002), pp. 137–148.

11. Pete Engario, Aaron Bernstein, and Manjeet Kripalani, "Is Your Job Next?" *Business Week*, February 3, 2003, pp. 50–60.

12. Steve Lohr, "Many New Causes for Old Problems of Jobs Lost Abroad," *The New York Times*, February 15, 2004.

13. "World Rankings: Education," *The Economist Pocket World in Figures* (London: Profile Books Ltd., 2002), p. 72.

14. Geoffrey E. Schneider, "Globalization and the Poorest of the Poor," *Journal of Economic Issues*, Vol. 37, No. 2, pp. 389–396.

15. Alexander Gerschenkron, *Economic Backwardness in Historical Development* (Cambridge, MA: The Belknap Press of Harvard University, 1962).

16. Michael Hardt and Antonio Negri, *Empire* (Cambridge, MA: Harvard University Press, 2000), pp. 306–307.

17. Walter Lippmann, *Public Philosophy* (Boston, MA: Little, Brown and Company, 1955). Also see R. Isaak, ed., *American Political Thinking: Readings from the Origins to the 21st Century* (Orlando, FL: Harcourt Brace, 1994).

18. *Bill Moyers, NOW*, Public Broadcasting Service, November 21, 2003.

19. Gregory A. Fossedal, *Direct Democracy in Switzerland* (New Brunswick, NJ: Transaction Publishers, 2002).

20. R. Isaak, *Green Logic: Ecopreneurship, Theory and Ethics* (West Hartford, CT: Kumarian Press, 1999; and Sheffield, UK: Greenleaf Publishers, 1998). Also see Malte Faber and Reiner Manstetten, *Mensch-Natur-Wissen: Grundlagen der Umweltbildung* (Göttingen: Vandenhoeck & Ruprecht, 2003).

21. Joel E. Cohen, *How Many People Can the Earth Support* (New York: W.W. Norton and Co., 1995), p. 352.

22. Colin Kahl, "Demographic Change, Natural Resources and Violence: The Current Debate," *Journal of International Affairs*, New York, Fall 2002, Vol. 56, No. 1, pp. 257–282.

23. Charles P. Kindleberger, "Hierarchy versus Inertial Cooperation," *International Organization* 40 (autumn 1986), p. 841.

24. Joseph Nye, "America's Soft Learning Curve," *The World in 2004*, pp. 31–32.

13 A Blueprint for Sharing Opportunity

No man becomes rich unless he enriches others.

—ANDREW CARNEGIE

To establish a sustainable basis for global growth and stability, the rich must target the poorest regions for high-tech development and access to education and markets. A reversal of the concentration of opportunity and investment in order to benefit the poor can be coordinated through a nongovernmental organization (NGO) for venture capital, avoiding diffusion in funding and circumventing corrupt governments and bureaucratic international organizations.

The Anglo-Saxon model that dominates globalization maximizes the *inequality* of opportunity in the name of economic growth and competitiveness. That is, what counts most is to lower the cost of what goes into products (including labor) and to increase their quality in order to produce and to market popular goods and services. The wealthy are moved by market incentives to act in such a way that it has the effect of creating an ever greater distance between themselves and the poor by concentrating opportunity and investment in "sure things"—that is, in places and companies returning the maximum short-term profit for the investor with least risk for the gains. Innovation is funded most where the record of past successes increases the chances for future returns. Globalization intensifies the "halo effect" of projecting positive results on existing winners, letting the losers shrivel up in the shadow countries on the periphery. Technology magnifies the "winner-take-all" accumulations of the most competitive companies and individuals.

The rich have a heavy impact on the poor in this process because if money, attention, and psychological support are directed toward one place, they do *not* go to another place. Or they go to neglected people, regions, or countries at exorbitant rates. The wealthy tend to invest in established, stable situations where the regulatory bodies are favorable to industry and short-term returns are the most secure. These usually are not poor regions or countries. Less developed regions or nations must therefore borrow from the rich at high interest rates and get heavily into debt. This leads to a capital flow from the poor—who can least afford it—to wealthy countries, international institutions, or commercial banks. This cycle is preprogrammed by free market capitalism, which rewards the corporate-regulated, most efficient, largest competitors who want to see this system kept, extended, and sped up. The poor contribute to the global economy by subsidizing the rich with their undervalued and underremunerated labor. It is in the *short-term* financial interest of the well-to-do that the poor do *not* become self-sufficient, continue to go into debt, and pay high interest rates. The International Monetary Fund (IMF) and World Bank allocate loans to developing countries in a way that puts them in a position of long-term dependence, keeping the control with the elites of these international institutions at the expense of increased self-sufficiency for their economically disadvantaged clients. Middle-class client countries have stopped borrowing from the World Bank loans because of unfavorable conditions. The World Bank has focused on the poor: It needs clients to justify its existence and, therefore, it needs to keep poor countries dependent on its services. Banks of all kinds live off of the spread between what they pay in interest for money coming in and the amount they can charge for the money lent out. The more dependent the client, the higher the risk, the higher the interest rate the client typically has to pay the bank, and the more indebted the client will become.

The acceleration due to globalization has increased the gap between the rich and poor, which, in turn, stimulates upheaval in the global economy. Slowing things down a bit might help the majority of cultures in the world adapt to these radical changes without losing their integrity. But such a slowdown alone would not be sufficient to stop the growth of the chasm between the rich and the poor, much less reverse it.

Managers of institutions dominated by wealthy countries are motivated to aid the poor in a way that maintains their dependence: Elites want to stay in control. Following the go-go late 1920s, it was not just altruism that led President Franklin D. Roosevelt to introduce the New Deal after the crash of the stock market—it was in his interest to buy the poor off with Social Security and public jobs in order to maintain his control of the political system and to avoid social and economic disintegration. Similarly, after the recession following the booming 1990s, the U.S. government elite is legislating to buy off the poor and unemployed in order to shore up their control. A case in point is the passage of the Medicare bill in 2003, which provides hypothetical discounts for prescription drugs to the elderly.

We need a blueprint that steers this fast-moving process of creative destruction toward sharing economic opportunity. Such a design must promise practical, sustainable solutions to crises such as those described in Chapter Twelve. It must establish conditions in which the poorest regions and countries *can* eventually become competitive in the global economy, if not self-sufficient. The following is an attempt to envision such a blueprint.

* * *

Keeping the Promise of Democratic Capitalism: Open Opportunity

The promise of the revolt of the rich and the ideology of liberal, democratic capitalism is that expanding free trade, free capital flows, and free markets will not only increase global prosperity and peace but will open opportunities everywhere. But, as we have seen, the liberation of the free market machine through globalization has resulted in concentrations of wealth, innovation, and opportunity in rich, developed areas or in newly industrializing nations that look like good bets for the future. The majority of countries in the past have been short-changed in this process. And the least developed countries have been left in the shadows of globalization.

Rates of poverty in Africa have increased in the past three decades. Today, more than 40% of the African population lives on less than a dollar a day. Two decades of so-called free-market reforms have not stopped the rise of poverty in Latin America. Poverty has become worse in the countries of the former Soviet Union after the 1989 fall of Communism than it was before. Most people in Russia are desperately poor; life expectancy has dropped; and oil, gas, and minerals remain the nation's only real resources. The political system is in bad shape. For example, the billionaire oligarch heading Yukos (the main Russian oil company), who became rich from the new deregulation and privatization wave, was jailed in a tax dispute and political conflict with the Russian government. Mikhail Khodorkovsky, Russia's richest man, threatened the power of President Vladimir Putin by establishing an independent, American-like corporate base that was too powerful. Despite such negative outcomes, the World Bank continues to peddle deregulation as a magic elixir for growth and prosperity.[1] The wave of globalization commencing with Margaret Thatcher's 1979 election and Ronald Reagan's 1980 election has made the poorest areas of the world worse off economically than they were before. The established have produced more poor while becoming much richer themselves.

Liberal democratic capitalism begins and ends with the freedom of the individual. Each individual should have the freedom to maximize his or her own interest, which will ultimately lead to productivity and economic growth for the whole community and the nation. The entrepreneur is the hero of this capitalist process of technological innovation and accumulation, forgetting history in order to create it. The entrepreneur works intensely to fulfill a dream, not worrying about who ends up paying the bills. As Harvard Professor Howard Stevenson puts it, entrepreneurship is a behavior or process by which individuals pursue opportunities without regard to the resources they currently control. He characterizes the entrepreneur as one who views risk differently: Let others take the risk while you take the reward.[2]

Each individual is a potential motor of economic growth, as long as the stifling regulations of the state and the unions can be cut back and state-run institutions can be privatized to free up competition. This theory has resulted in impressive results—more economic growth on a macro level and more potential individual freedom. But the very abstract, universal nature of the theory is indifferent to its specific social consequences. As long as economic growth is maximized globally, it does not matter which individuals or countries get the greatest opportunities to create businesses and wealth.

To survive in global competition, entrepreneurs tend to be indifferent "free-riders" when it comes to sources of capital or social and environmental implications of their behavior. **Success in entrepreneurial cultures tends to be correlated with the absence of social or ethical regulations—unless outside government intervention or corporate standards are imposed.**

Americans, with the most successful entrepreneurial culture in the world, wonder why there is no social "safety net" (e.g., adequate Social Security and health insurance) in the United States, as can be found in the social provisions for citizens of industrial democracies in continental Europe. The very competitive structure of the American system, where economic growth is the top priority, guarantees that the safety net will not be "safe." People should be motivated to work and to seek work. But if the safety net were safe, this would demotivate them and put more welfare burdens on the taxpayer. With an ironclad safety net, a culture of permanent dependence on the state would be fostered, and the nation as a whole would become less competitive.

The theory does work to create lower input costs (such as labor) for greater output—productivity leading to competitiveness. But if you happen to be poor, weak, old, ill, or disabled, this process is less rosy. It is hard to pull yourself up by your bootstraps if your boots don't have any straps (or you can't afford boots), if your résumé lacks educational credentials in a knowledge economy, if your bank won't lend you any money to start up a business, or if no insurance company will take you on because you are already too sick.

In the United States, there seems to be a tendency to forget the past and to focus on the present for the sake of the future. Similarly, to be an entrepreneur in our modern world, it is necessary to forget the past in order to create something new. This discounting of the past leads to high mobility but a loss of roots. In the United States, if individuals fail, they are given second and even third chances by society but may well leave homes, spouses, and children when they move on to the next opportunity. Social and community traditions suffer from this individual mobility. There is a downside for social stability when the art of the individual changing chameleon-like into something else overnight is rewarded in the economy. Ted Turner might be a great sailor, telecommunications entrepreneur, and the largest private landowner in the United States, but he leaves a swath of children, wives, and homes behind in his wake.

Liberal capitalist democracy encourages individuals to create their own worlds, regardless of where the resources come from or what the opportunity costs might be. In the United States, the minimum wage is set so low that workers earning the minimum often have to work up to 60 hours a week just to barely meet expenses, without taking health costs or health insurance into account. Today's criterion for "the poverty level" was established just after World War II, based on food costs that have not gone up as much as the costs of housing, health care, and university tuition, which have skyrocketed since that time. This inflation increasingly expands the number of "working poor" in the United States, as well as the level of average family debt. Pressures from even lower wages paid abroad (e.g., India and China), given open global competition, are apt to keep these minimum wages down. Ironically, the minimum wage jobs in the United States tend to be service jobs that cannot be globalized, and it is the higher paying jobs that go offshore. Meanwhile, American workers are apt to move wherever they can to find a living wage, leaving their roots behind.

To survive in this competitive global acceleration, entrepreneurs choose to maximize their free-rider options, looking for direct or indirect subsidies for their businesses. Because most business startups fail in the first five years, entrepreneurs will decide to reduce costs wherever they can and often free-ride on public services in order to realize their visions. This free-rider impulse must be converted into creative social entrepreneurship, or *ecopreneurship*, establishing government incentives for individuals to design "green" (environmentally sustainable) startup companies from the beginning.[3] The key is to build up social assets, in part by encouraging environmentally responsible processes to reduce costs for entrepreneurs through flexible regulations and tax discounts. Thus, economic growth can be transformed into sustainability, which is particularly critical in developing countries in which the natural environment often constitutes their main economic resource.

But even should the relative poor be funded to found green startups, this is not in itself going to reduce the increasing gap between the wealthy and the disadvantaged. The well-to-do must realize that it is in their interest to invest in the poor and to help them create sustainable communities. The wealthy will suffer if the global environment deteriorates, if terrorism becomes fashionable in regions that have not benefited from Western-oriented globalization, or if the well-off end up having to pay for the welfare costs of people who might otherwise have become capable of earning their own livelihoods, if given the chance.

Focusing on the rich initially when designing such a blueprint is purely a pragmatic strategy. As the famous American thief Willy Sutton answered when asked by a reporter why he robbed banks: "Because that's where the money is."

Why It Benefits the Richest of the Rich to Help the Poorest of the Poor

The super-rich have a problem: They want to preserve their wealth and its legitimacy in a way that leaves a positive legacy behind without wasting money on taxes and on unintended subsidies to corrupt governments. They are rightfully suspicious of handouts that get sunk in aid bureaucracies or are recycled to offshore bank accounts by government officials on the take. Not infrequently, they found their own philanthropic foundations (trying to find the best places where tax-deductible contributions to charity should be made—at least in the United States). But despite the good this philanthropy brings (consider the Rockefeller, Ford, and Carnegie foundations), the overall effect is not to make the poorest countries more self-sufficient nor to reduce the chasm between the wealthy and the disadvantaged. Rather, this philanthropy usually works like a Band-Aid on a gaping wound—like the generous donations of the Bill Gates Foundation to try to eliminate malaria in developing countries or the commitment by Ted Turner during the economic boom of the 1990s to give a billion dollars (his income for just one year at the time) to the United Nations. But short-term humanitarian aid and financing alone will not lead to the establishment of viable economic communities that can satisfy human needs in the long term. The motivation here is what the ancient Greeks called *areté*—general goodness or honor. And such noble behavior is, indeed, what will be required on a more massive scale to rescue the legitimacy of corporate leadership in the capitalist world in the eyes of public opinion.

Despite the nobility, there is a certain diffusion in these efforts that does not necessarily lead to long-term development. The funding is targeted at multiple objectives as the wealthy set up their own foundations—purposes largely uncoordinated with one another. One difficulty is that wealthy entrepreneurs whose drive for success was oriented toward power and control are apt to be reluctant to relinquish control over their own charities. But one transparent NGO could coordinate some of these efforts through a loosely structured committee. This NGO would still give full credit and publicity to the philanthropists involved, raise venture capital aimed at the same specific targets in the least developed countries, and thus build a sustainable legacy while avoiding the diffusion. Such a targeted effort could at least supplement existing programs and build sustainable communities with roots in specific places in poor regions.

Building High-Tech, Sustainable Communities

A *sustainable community* is one established to satisfy existing needs without depleting the resources required for future generations to satisfy their needs. To achieve such long-term sustainability, all countries will need to have access to the most modern and efficient technologies available. Given globalization, in order to be economically viable, even the smallest and poorest nation needs to be plugged in to the technology of the New Economy.[4] However, the least developed countries cannot afford to create high-tech centers on their own and require basic infrastructure (electricity, roads, potable water, sanitation), health care, and education before they can contemplate high-tech development. Yet without such a New Economy community, they will not have a chance to survive in the global economy. They risk becoming obsolete states. Targeted philanthropy can become the missing bridge between the overdeveloped and the underdeveloped regions of the world.

The objective should be for the richest individuals to coordinate their philanthropic efforts and investments in order to create sustainable, high-tech communities and learning centers in the poorest regions and nations. When doing so, the wealthy should:

1. Support the absolute poor.
2. Help create structures to enable those less poor to join the middle class.
3. Prepare emerging elites for global competition.

By not focusing on governments as donors or on governments as recipients of such targeted support, ultra-rich individuals would be less apt to be frustrated by state and international bureaucracy going in and would be more apt to circumvent the misdirection of funds by corrupt officials. The prerequisite would be adequate local government security to protect the chosen sites—no protection, no investment. If the government of a developing country or region turned down the offer to start up such a high-tech community, the NGO would simply go to other governments. Once successful in one place, the competition for such development would increase, and such targeted investment would be wooed by other needy regions. Initially, the first community established would have to overcome suspicions that the enterprise was a form of colonial corporatism. But if the organization was always open in its communications and diplomatically introduced, these fears could be overcome.

The wealthy investors would select the sites they deem most viable in terms of infrastructure and positive future socioeconomic impact in, perhaps, the poorest five countries of the world (then the next five, until the least developed 50 countries identified by the United Nations are included). The coordinating NGO would then target venture capital to develop high-tech businesses and educational facilities tailor-designed to "fit in" to the local culture and its comparative economic advantages. Thus, no two high-tech, sustainable communities would be the same, although they could be hooked up to learn and benefit from each other.

Within a specified time period, the business sector of the sustainable community would have to generate a mutually agreed-upon level of "profit" in order to receive new venture capital. Returns on investment would then be used to seed additional local initiatives or centers in the same country. A certain percentage of the profits would be reinvested in the community, not only to generate further returns but also to cover the infrastructure costs and to contribute to a social fund aimed at helping to lead local people out of "absolute poverty."

The aim is to create sustainable, profitable businesses that would serve as applied, high-tech learning centers for the native employees most likely to benefit from the training. Each center would have the obligation to contribute to one social or charitable cause for the absolute poor in the host country, based on maximum effectiveness for minimum cost.

The very existence of such high-tech education and business communities would serve to head off "brain drain" in the least developed countries and to train teachers and high-tech ecopreneurs for the future. The mere fact that super-rich individuals establish such communities would provide a "demonstration effect" and show that there are wealthy individuals who care and who want to make a difference. This is especially vital in an era of dehumanizing globalization that threatens to overwhelm the integrity, dignity, and full human development of individuals. German philosopher Rüdiger Safranski pondered the question, How much globalization can one human being take?[5] Or, recast for our theme: Without projecting a "halo" of positive expectation on worthy individuals, how are they supposed to become models of full human development? Should poverty automatically exclude human beings from the educational and financial support required for such development? What is to become of the multitudes of young, curious, capable, and poor in the least developed countries? Young people in such environments are apt to suffer from a projection of negative expectations on them by neglect or by a lack of attention, care, or investment.

What will make this investment worthwhile? By replicating a sustainable "Silicon Valley" in a disadvantaged region, one has the chance to set a good example and model of human achievement. Even a partial success in this direction—such as that of Bangalore's formidable achievements in software in India—can inspire millions of people with hope and pride in what their own people can accomplish in this globalized world of hypereconomic competition. It would attract money where it is most needed. Human dignity, ambition, and creativity can arise from masses who have been trampled down and under by circumstances into which they were born beyond their control. The new sector of the sustainable community would aim to train the relatively poor in order to bring them into middle-class professions. Simultaneously, a seedbed for ecopreneurs and high-tech innovators would be created to lead the community in establishing a competitive niche. As Albert Schweitzer once said, setting an example is not just a factor that leads to influence—it is the only factor.

Ten Steps for Replicating Sustainable Silicon Valleys

In an ongoing study of what characteristics of Silicon Valley would need to be present to replicate such high-tech community development in other cultures, 10 preliminary steps can be identified.[6]

1. Create an ecosystem of synergistic, high-tech learning and innovation that attracts and keeps the best minds in the country—a magnet of "soft power."

2. Cultivate an intellectual center that draws the smartest students seeking competitiveness at the highest level in innovative applied fields, as well as in basic scientific fields.

3. Nurture an entrepreneurial culture that inspires people to bypass obstacles and traditional ways of doing things and absorbs new talent, encouraging radical innovation and providing extraordinary material rewards for extraordinary achievement.

4. Select an attractive location that is not so beautiful as to undermine the work ethic. Invest money back into the local school system and community infrastructure and avoid exporting talent to wealthier regions.

5. Provide targeted financial support for cutting-edge research with flexible boundaries and the continuous expectation of new grants or investments.

6. Found an industrial park within walking or biking distance of the intellectual center with constant interchange of personnel and a dynamic atmosphere that attracts private venture capital.

7. Support the development of a stable political economic system. Complement this objective by emphasizing those elements in the local cultural tradition that are most apt to encourage tinkering with new technology. This can lead to new discoveries and innovations.

8. Position the sustainable community to catch new waves of technological development early as a "first mover" in a specific niche before the practical applications have become clear to others and the price has been bid up by competitors and the market.

9. Stimulate an egalitarian youth culture where bureaucracy, titles, and secrecy are understated, along with hierarchy in the workplace. Encourage networking, trust, and commitment to teams as well as to excellence and cutting-edge innovation based on learning from foreign models.

10. Manage the transportation infrastructure, pollution, and environment to make the community a model of sustainable development. Maintain the attractiveness of what will become an increasingly dense location, not only for the best and the brightest but for their families, as well. The design of the center should be "green" from the outset and kept that way.[7]

* * *

Attracting Venture Capital: A Transparent NGO with a Nonbusiness Service Division

To avoid the criticisms of the IMF and World Bank for being indifferent to building self-sufficient democracies, the NGO for establishing sustainable, innovative communities must be transparent and include a nonbusiness, service-sector division. Although it should have a right to keep information concerning its core businesses secret in a hypercompetitive world economy, the NGO's personnel policies and salary scales must be made public. The required social capital and trust needed for innovative networking will be enhanced by this transparency. And the NGO must have an educational and service arm to help the least developed countries in the most cost-effective way. This "educational window" should help the NGO to gain legitimacy in the local community and to avoid the conflict of interest and corruption charges made against multinational companies and international organizations. The NGO should be perceived as a means of developing self-sufficiency for the host country, rather than being perceived as an instrument of the multinational corporate power structure[8]. Without building up regional legitimacy as it evolves, an effort to replicate a sustainable Silicon Valley is unlikely to survive. Ideally, the NGO should serve as a model for other similar developments later on. As such, the more transparent its operations, the greater its attractiveness as a model, and the more easily it will be accepted in the local culture. Its educational division should focus on an effort to help alleviate the overwhelming pressures that will be put on the services of the city near the sustainable community as people from the rural areas continue to move there, seeking opportunities.

The NGO's service sector should operate as an "opportunity multiplier" for the poor. To be acceptable to the local culture and its regional and national government authorities, every effort should be made in both the NGO's business core and service division to use local staff, local suppliers, and local designers to create a stakeholder commitment on the part of the community. Sustainable green designs should be established from the outset in an ongoing collective learning process in order to preserve the integrity of the local environment and to help monitor clean water, clean air, and clean energy use. **The main agenda of the NGO should be to empower local people to become active agents working toward sustainable self-sufficiency in a high-tech globalized economy.**

This effort will push the limits in the least developed countries. But the very challenge of such an attempt will be proof that the richest and most educated people in the world have full confidence that eventually the natives of these nations can join as equal partners. The NGO does have a precedent that might provide a guideline—the nine "digital villages" set up in South Africa as of 1997 by Microsoft with local and other American partners. These "villages" aim to provide communities with technology access and training in information technology and management and to facilitate the employability of community members. The design of the NGO can be targeted as well for poor rural areas of developed countries, using "village ventures"(local venture capital firms) in the United States as an inspiration.

The structures of the NGO should be designed to change working behavior and to stimulate people to go beyond the traditional way of doing things. Initiating a positive collective learning process may permit the disadvantaged population to become more self-sufficient through sustainable, competitive work. Human beings do not buy into just a blueprint. Anthropologist Gregory Bateson noted that in social manipulation, the tools are people who learn and acquire habits more subtle and intricate than the tricks the blueprinter would teach them.[9] People assess the expectations, incentives, and role models behind the blueprint to see what the "real rules" are.

The Western cultural tradition has both advantages and disadvantages when it comes to creating structures that lead to desired kinds of entrepreneurial behavior. The drawbacks have to do with people believing too much in the structures themselves that have been set up in an organization, the concrete things—as though structures could do the job alone. Too often, the assumption is that if the correct structures are in place (for example, work assignments), the desired behaviors will automatically follow if people are just left free to try to figure things out on their own—the laissez-faire assumption.

But most poor people in developing regions do not have the luxury of a second chance if they don't perform well the first time. If they are fired, they have few if any resources or assets to fall back on. They must be provided with trainers, mentors, and a systematic learning framework that is set up from the outset so that they can succeed right from the start.

Once individuals have learned the basics of a field, they should be provided with enough opportunities to freely test their skills on their own. Freedom implies going beyond structure and behavioral guidelines in order to take innovative, entrepreneurial risks *after* the basics have been mastered: This is the essence of educating for self-sufficiency. The freedom to fail must be built into the collective learning process in a way that will not risk the basic necessities of life in a poor community. A minimal safety net must be provided while individuals are in NGO educational training. As has been demonstrated in developed countries, if a minimal family health insurance program is established by the government, individuals are much more apt to take time out for further education or for attempting to set up small businesses of their own.

* * *

Resistance to Free Market Ideology Due to the Democratic Deficit

The free market ideology that dominates globalization is that empirically based, material economic growth is the highest priority in life because it will produce individual freedom. The values are innovation, entrepreneurship, corporate competitiveness, technological speed, wealth, power, and cosmopolitanism. There is no time left to focus on the people or nations left behind—for developing the least developed. The knowledge economy empowers elites who must make fast, specialized decisions to maintain their own competitiveness and status.

Social protest movements proliferate against the democratic deficit of this elitism at the meetings of the elites of the World Trade Organization (WTO), the IMF, the World Bank, and even the European Union (EU). Protest comes in attacks by journalists against elite conflicts of interest in the public and corporate sectors. Too much of the decision making is perceived to be too narrow and closed at the top, with no effort to solicit the voices of the overwhelming majority citizens below. Some who have found existing jobs and wages to be unsatisfactory have given them up altogether in order to become full-time professional protestors against globalization wherever it might manifest itself. This social resistance may make the launching of pilot communities in the developing countries more difficult, due to a fear that these efforts might just be another extension of corporate domination. This is why the NGO must be careful to plan and to build trust with its potential stakeholders as it is created.

The Interface with Governments and International Organizations

Resistance to the proposed NGO can be expected from existing governments and international organizations, as well. Governments in the least developed countries may fear that they will be undermined by a neocolonial Trojan horse of Western corporate values. Therefore, in asking for their support and protection, it is vital to target areas where these governments can be of assistance without the NGO losing the autonomy critical to the success of establishing a sustainable, high-tech community. Developed governments that want to control developing countries through their foreign aid or private investment may also feel miffed.

The NGO would have to create something on the order of a foreign policy to keep its autonomy while avoiding antagonistic relations. Finally, international organizations, such as the IMF, WTO, and World Bank, might resent a new, development-enhancing actor on their turf. Alliances would have to be formed with these international organizations, based on clear principles that would preserve the NGO's autonomy while soliciting help in infrastructure development, basic health care, and other joint initiatives.

One such principle might be to suggest to the WTO, for example, that tariffs on goods and services should be set in developed and developing countries, based on the following:

- Adopting a minimum wage that is a "living wage"
- Establishing minimal family health care coverage
- Establishing minimal standards of environmental protection to assure sustainability

Tariffs should be high against countries without these specified minimum conditions and lowered gradually as the countries adopt such minimal standards.

Having only one foreign policy tenet such as this might clearly differentiate the NGO from other international actors. Advocating such a principle would also help the NGO to gain the support and legitimacy among the low-income, working poor in both developed and developing countries needed for its activities in their neighborhoods.

Karl Marx and the structuralist economist Raul Prebisch were correct in observing that there is a radical tilt of the world capitalist system toward the rich and developed at the expense of the poor and the exploited. But capitalism and globalization appear to be inevitable. We must stretch our imaginations and cultivate new models. Sustainable, high-tech centers in the poorest countries and regions could help to balance the existing concentration of opportunities of the advantaged (in the corporate world, for example). New initiatives for the least advantaged could also help to stabilize a world political economy threatened with chaos. More evenly distributed, increased global economic growth should reduce the intensity of resentment people feel about social and economic differences. Such coordinated economic development would test economist Benjamin Friedman's thesis that economic growth can lead to openness of opportunity, democracy, tolerance, mobility, and fairness across groups and individuals, increasing per capita income.[10]

Just as the Federal Reserve and other central banks act counter-cyclically to stabilize the money supply, so must rich individuals act counter-cyclically to head off global disintegration stemming from the inability of the free markets to distribute opportunities fairly. A concentrated shift to develop sustainable centers of synergy and innovation in the least developed countries would be a significant first step. Equally important would be to multiply opportunities for the disadvantaged *within* industrialized societies. Each of the private schools or quality schools in wealthy real estate areas could adopt one of the schools in a poor area to ease the national budget pressures and to raise the consciousness of advantaged pupils to the need for civic involvement.

Governments may help out with this blueprint for sharing opportunity, but their budget constraints and political perspectives may prevent it. The World Bank and the United Nations may provide some aid, but this may be tied to conditions that make it difficult for the NGO to succeed. A small group of wealthy philanthropists donating venture capital to an NGO that aims to create high-tech, sustainable education centers and businesses in the poorest regions of the world—this just might work. Multinational corporations might ultimately perceive such sustainable high-tech centers as good investments for global market share. The centers should be established to provide *long-term* investment returns to investors and tax write-offs in their home countries without becoming mere instruments of foreign, corporate, or state powers. The objectives are:

- To raise the standard of living
- To develop a sustainable community with disposable income
- To make time to facilitate market growth
- To reduce social instability

Leaders in these disadvantaged regions must learn to manage their economy in a way that brings stable returns to foreign and local investors who employ the local people. For the natives, it is a process of opportunities for collective learning without losing cultural integrity.[11] For the wealthy, who might otherwise continue to distance themselves economically from the poor, it is a question of legitimacy, of honor and of stabilizing a world that has treated them very well. We live in a global economy that cries out for models of moral behavior and sustainable economic development that bring self-respect to both those who give and those who receive.

References

1. See Michael Schroeder and Terence Roth, "Heavy Regulation Seen as an Obstacle," *Wall Street Journal*, October 7, 2003, p.2.

2. H. H. Stevenson, M. J. Roberts, and H. J. Grousbeck, *New Business Ventures and the Entrepreneur* (Homewood, IL: Irwin, 1989), and John Kao, *Entrepreneurship, Creativity and Organization* (Englewood Cliffs, NJ: Prentice Hall, 1989), p. 168.

3. R. Isaak, *Green Logic: Ecopreneurship, Theory and Ethics* (West Hartford, CT: Kumarian Press, 1999 and Sheffield, UK: Greenleaf , 1998) and "The Making of the Ecopreneur," *Greener Management International:The Journal of Corporate Environmental Strategy and Practice* , no. 38 , Summer 2002, pp. 81-91.

4. R. Isaak, "The Digital Divide," in Gabriele Suder, ed., *Terrorism and the International Business Environment: The Security-Business Nexus* (London: Edgar Elgar, 2004), Chapter 6.

5. Rüdiger Safranski, *Wieviel Globalisierung veträgt der Mensch?* (Vienna: Carl Hanser Verlag, 2003).

6. R. Isaak, "Prerequisites for Replicating Silicon Valley in Other Cultures: Some Hypotheses," a paper presented at the New England Business Administration Association, May 30–31, 2002 at Southern Connecticut State University, New Haven, Connecticut.

7. R. Isaak, "Entrepreneurship, Creativity and Ecodesign," Chapter One in *Green Logic*, and Charles O. Holliday, Stephan Schmidheiny, and Philip Watts, *Walking the Talk: The Business Case for Sustainable Development* (Sheffield, U.K.: Greenleaf Publishing and San Francisco: Berrett-Koehler Publishers, 2002)

8. Keith Henderson, "Alternative Service Delivery in Developing Countries: NGOs and Other Non-Profits in Urban

Areas," *Public Organization Review: A Global Journal*, Vol. 2 (The Netherlands: Kluwer Academic Publishers, 2002) pp. 99–116.

9. Gregory Bateson, "Social Planning and the Concept of Deutero-Learning," *Steps to an Ecology of Mind*, (New York: Balentine Books, 1972), pp. 159–176.

10. Benjamin Friedman, "The Moral Consequences of Economic Growth," 3rd Annual Henry George Lecture, Pace University, New York, April 3, 2003.

11. R. Isaak, "Collective Learning and the Maintenance Model," in *Managing World Economic Change: International Political Economy*, 3rd edition (Upper Saddle River, NJ: Prentice Hall, 2000), pp. 17–22.

Acknowledgments

This is one of those rare books that initially seemed almost to write itself. The world fell out onto its pages, and I just happened to be present to write it down. But then a number of people facilitated the process of improving the manuscript from its rough first version to the finished product who deserve a word of thanks. Conversations with former Ambassador Jorge Pinto of Mexico, now a colleague at Pace University, were invaluable in strengthening my focus on opportunity and in alerting me to the importance of transparency in the Nongovernmental Organization solution I end up advocating. Another Mexican, Virginia Sanchez, provided an example of helping to organize such self-reliance on the part of those who are disadvantaged in the globalization process. Suren Kaushik was my host in Malsisar in India, where he founded a college for women as a shining example of what can be done; his invaluable comments on the manuscript as a colleague at Pace reflect much more than his specialization in finance. Thanks also to Shabrir Chema of the United Nations, whose experience at the UNDP informed his helpful comments on the ideas in last chapter.

Other Pace colleagues have also provided stimulation and useful criticism and encouragement: Joe Pastore, mentor and friend, who went through the manuscript with thoughtful comments; Farouk Harmozi, who gave me an economist's slant from the public sector; Larry Bridwell, the friend who plugs me in to cutting-edge trends;

Roger Salerno, whose sociological sensitivity kept me grounded; Arthur Centonze, a dean who has consistently been supportive of my work however odd the venue and Joseph Morreale, a provost who actually finds time between administrative duties to interact intellectually with faculty and raise important questions. This book is dedicated to the Pace University community since it provides a seedbed for intellectual entrepreneurship in a familial context of social and environmental responsibility.

My brother, Professor James Isaak of the Southern New Hampshire University, gave me his usual sharp, analytical overview and a number of specific suggestions. Russ Hall and Tim Moore (my dynamic editor and sounding board at Financial Times/Prentice Hall) were constantly helpful and responsive, not to mention the two reviewers they tapped. Morgen Witzel and Bob Slater, Kerry Reardon, and Marti Jones were excellent at improving the manuscript through production and copyediting. Thanks, too, to Carol Lallier for a transparent index.

Marie Loprieno and Lucille Kenny helped with the word processing, along with Gail Weldon. Michele Lang and her staff at the Pace Library provided great assistance, surpassed only by the tireless efforts of my research assistant, Stoyan Panayotov, who made me aware of more things than I had time to digest.

My encouraging wife, Gudrun, carefully went through the text for order and style, and tolerated my chaos during the writing process. My children, Andrew (who made suggestions throughout the manuscript) and Sonya, were constant supportive inspirations. A book of this kind is a social product, an intense conversation about the state of the world, and a pointer to an uncertain future in which we all become either part of the problem or part of the solution.

Index

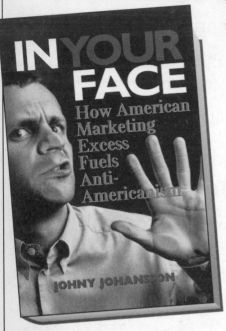